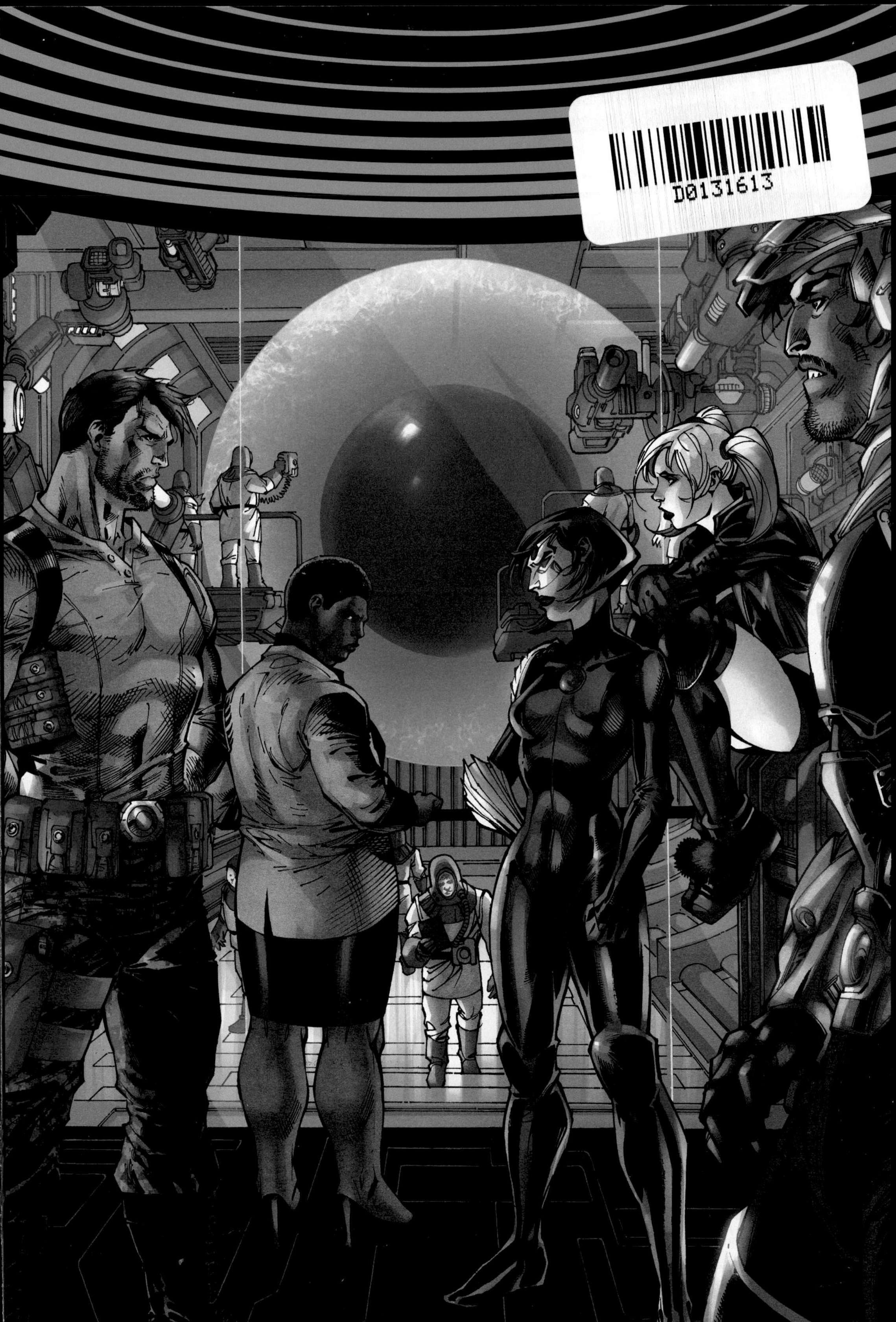

SUICIDE SQUAD

VOL.2 GOING SANE

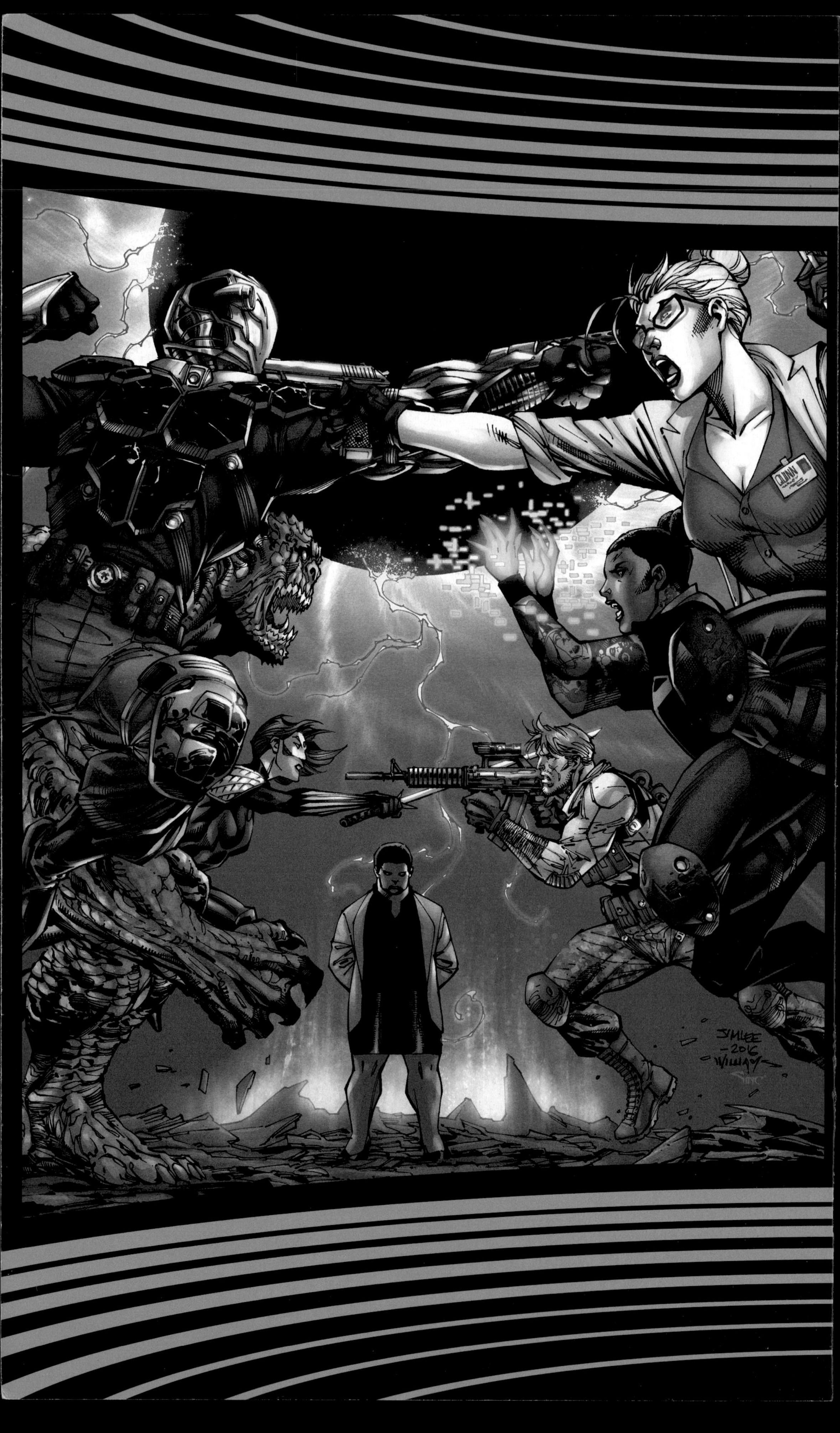

SUICIDE SQUAD
VOL.2 GOING SANE

ROB WILLIAMS
writer

JIM LEE ＊ **STEPHEN BYRNE** ＊ **CARLOS D'ANDA**
CHRISTIAN WARD ＊ **GIUSEPPE CAMUNCOLI**
FRANCESCO MATTINA ＊ **SEAN "CHEEKS" GALLOWAY**
SCOTT WILLIAMS ＊ **JONATHAN GLAPION**
SANDRA HOPE ＊ **MATT BANNING** ＊ **RICHARD FRIEND**
artists

ALEX SINCLAIR ＊ **STEPHEN BYRNE** ＊ **GABE ELTAEB**
JEREMIAH SKIPPER ＊ **CHRISTIAN WARD**
HI-FI ＊ **SEAN "CHEEKS" GALLOWAY**
colorists

PAT BROSSEAU ＊ **ROB LEIGH** ＊ **JOSH REED**
DAVE SHARPE ＊ **TRAVIS LANHAM**
letterers

JIM LEE, SCOTT WILLIAMS & ALEX SINCLAIR
collection cover art and original series covers

SUPERMAN created by **JERRY SIEGEL** and **JOE SHUSTER**
By special arrangement with the Jerry Siegel family.
HARLEY QUINN created by **PAUL DINI** and **BRUCE TIMM**.

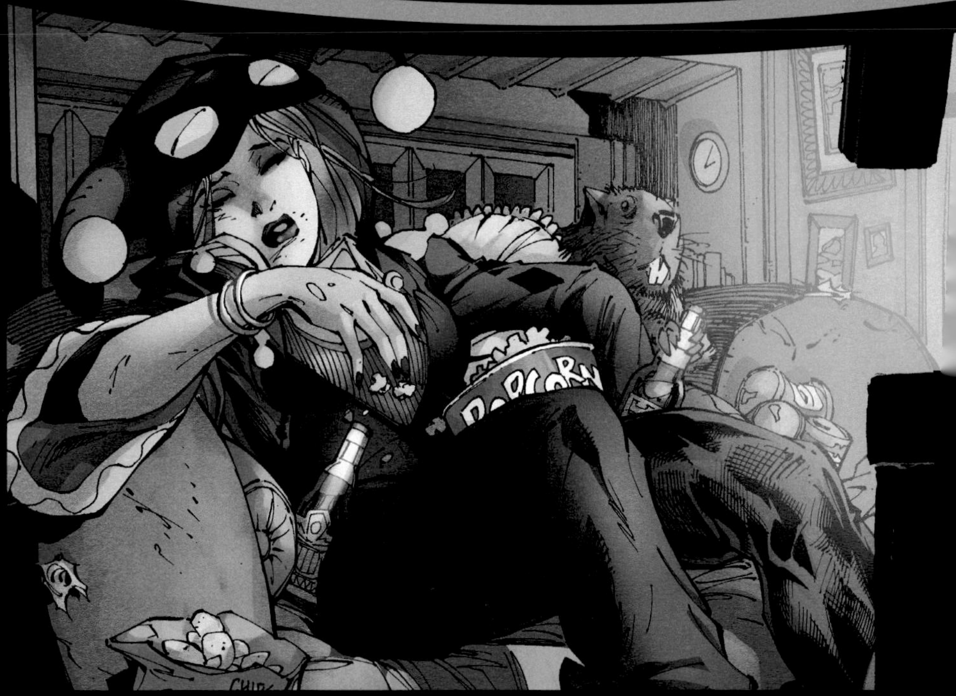
POPCORN
CHIPS

ANDY KHOURI Editor - Original Series * **HARVEY RICHARDS** Associate Editor - Original Series
JEB WOODARD Group Editor - Collected Editions * **SCOTT NYBAKKEN** Editor - Collected Edition
STEVE COOK Design Director - Books * **MONIQUE GRUSPE** Publication Design

BOB HARRAS Senior VP - Editor-in-Chief, DC Comics

DIANE NELSON President * **DAN DiDIO** Publisher * **JIM LEE** Publisher * **GEOFF JOHNS** President & Chief Creative O
AMIT DESAI Executive VP - Business & Marketing Strategy, Direct to Consumer & Global Franchise Manageme
SAM ADES Senior VP - Direct to Consumer * **BOBBIE CHASE** VP - Talent Development
MARK CHIARELLO Senior VP - Art, Design & Collected Editions * **JOHN CUNNINGHAM** Senior VP - Sales & Trade Ma
ANNE DePIES Senior VP - Business Strategy, Finance & Administration * **DON FALLETTI** VP - Manufacturing Oper
LAWRENCE GANEM VP - Editorial Administration & Talent Relations * **ALISON GILL** Senior VP - Manufacturing & Op
HANK KANALZ Senior VP - Editorial Strategy & Administration * **JAY KOGAN** VP - Legal Affairs
THOMAS LOFTUS VP - Business Affairs * **JACK MAHAN** VP - Business Affairs
NICK J. NAPOLITANO VP - Manufacturing Administration * **EDDIE SCANNELL** VP - Consumer Marketing
COURTNEY SIMMONS Senior VP - Publicity & Communications
JIM (SKI) SOKOLOWSKI VP - Comic Book Specialty Sales & Trade Marketing
NANCY SPEARS VP - Mass, Book, Digital Sales & Trade Marketing

SUICIDE SQUAD VOL. 2: GOING SANE

DC Comics, 2900 West Alameda Ave., Burbank, CA 91505
Printed by LSC Communications, Salem, VA, USA. 5/5/17. First Printing.
ISBN: 978-1-4012-7097-1

Library of Congress Cataloging-in-Publication Data is available.

PEFC Certified
Printed on paper from sustainably managed forests, controlled sources
PEFC
PEFC/29-31-337
www.pefc.org

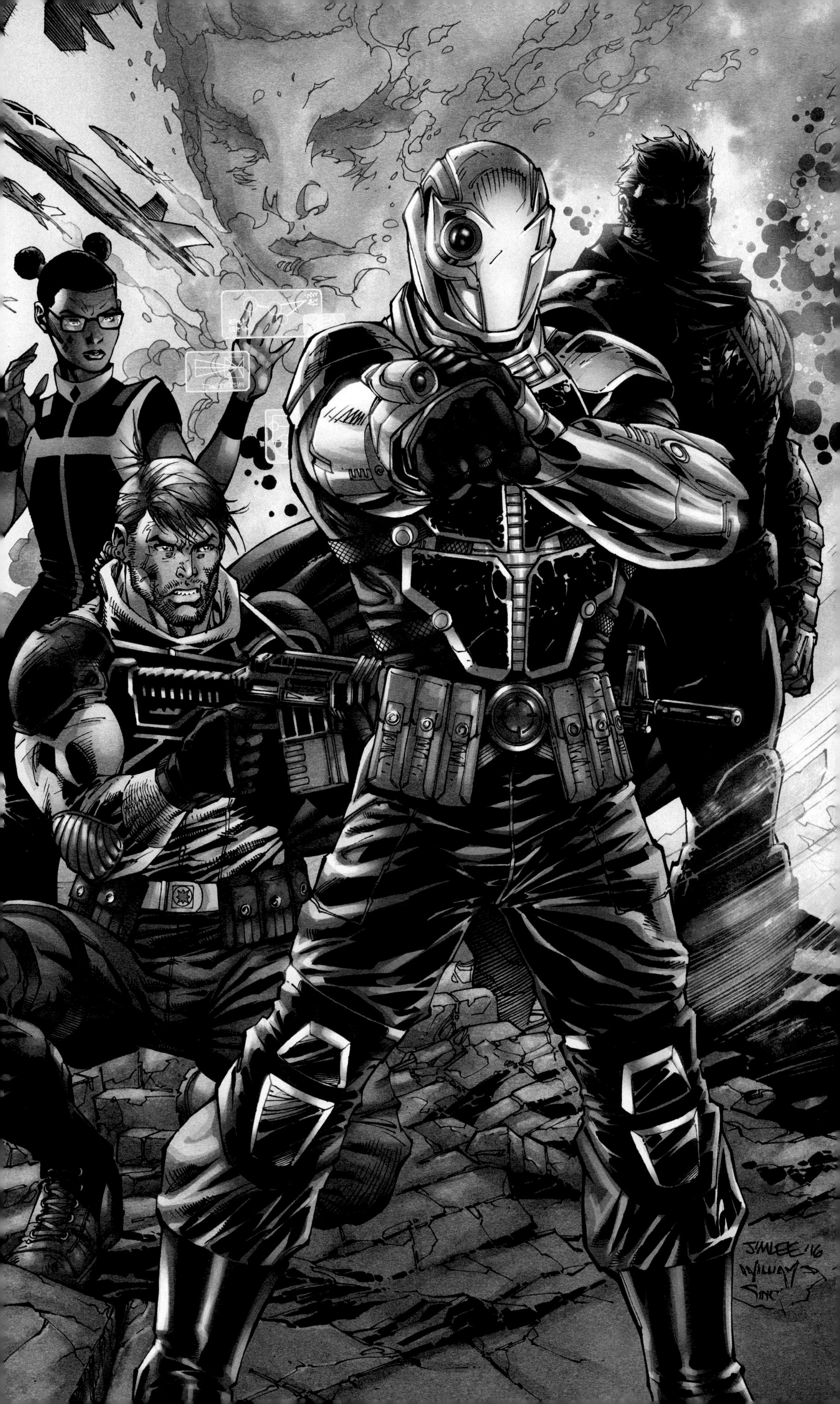
JIMLEE '16

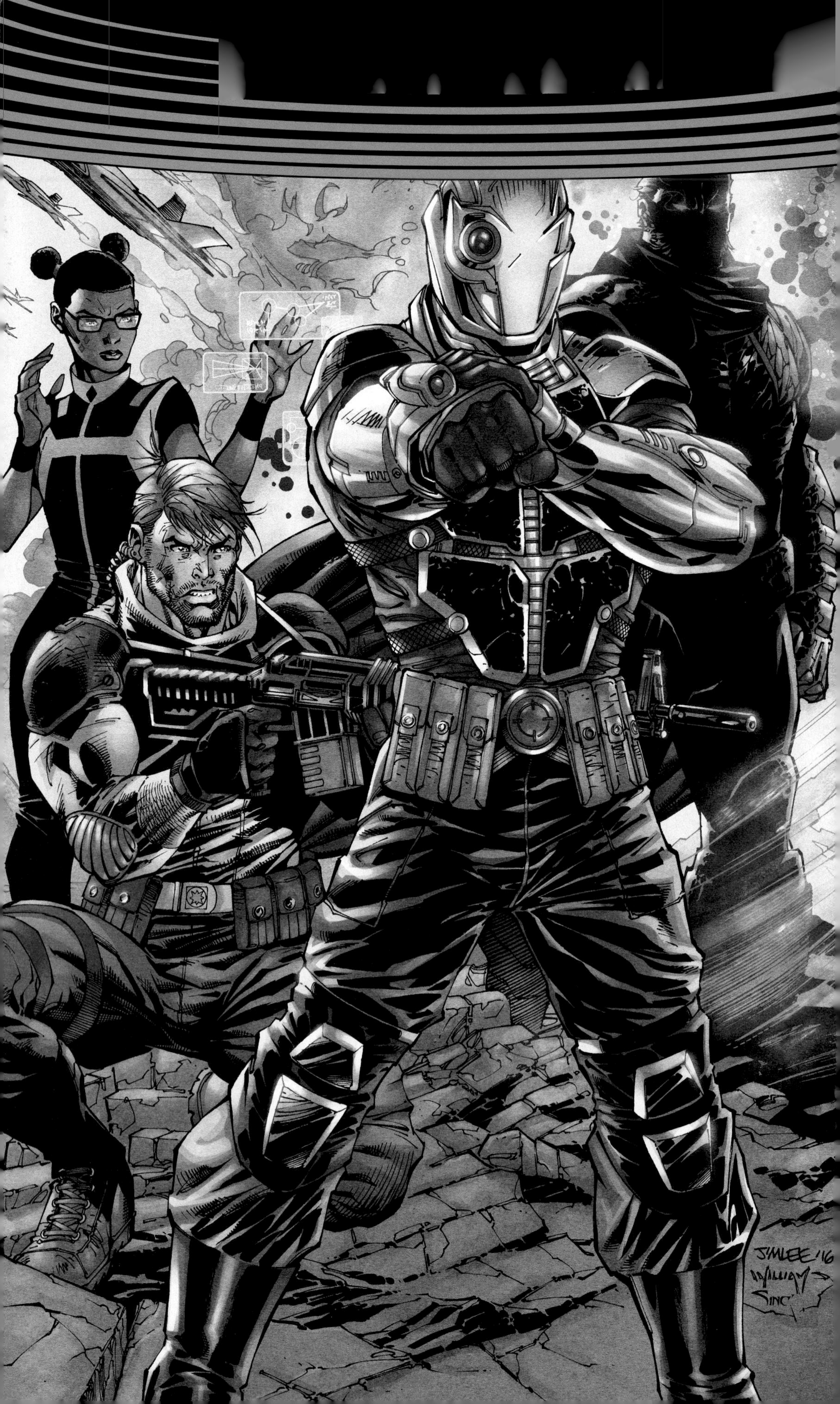
JIM LEE '16
WILLIAMS
SINC

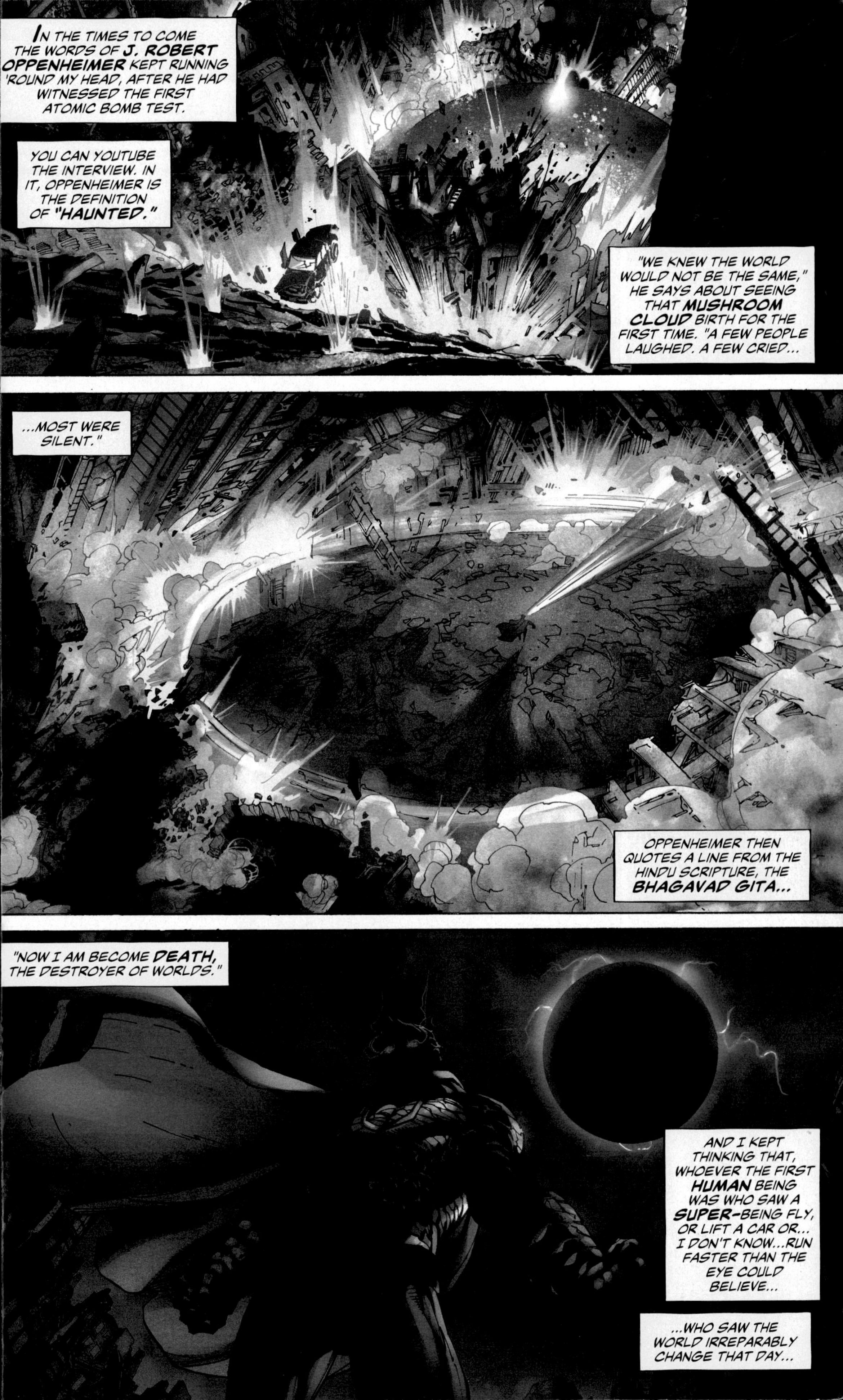
IN THE TIMES TO COME THE WORDS OF J. ROBERT OPPENHEIMER KEPT RUNNING 'ROUND MY HEAD, AFTER HE HAD WITNESSED THE FIRST ATOMIC BOMB TEST.
YOU CAN YOUTUBE THE INTERVIEW. IN IT, OPPENHEIMER IS THE DEFINITION OF "HAUNTED."
"WE KNEW THE WORLD WOULD NOT BE THE SAME," HE SAYS ABOUT SEEING THAT MUSHROOM CLOUD BIRTH FOR THE FIRST TIME. "A FEW PEOPLE LAUGHED. A FEW CRIED...
...MOST WERE SILENT."
OPPENHEIMER THEN QUOTES A LINE FROM THE HINDU SCRIPTURE, THE BHAGAVAD GITA...
"NOW I AM BECOME DEATH, THE DESTROYER OF WORLDS."
AND I KEPT THINKING THAT, WHOEVER THE FIRST HUMAN BEING WAS WHO SAW A SUPER-BEING FLY, OR LIFT A CAR OR... I DON'T KNOW...RUN FASTER THAN THE EYE COULD BELIEVE...
...WHO SAW THE WORLD IRREPARABLY CHANGE THAT DAY...

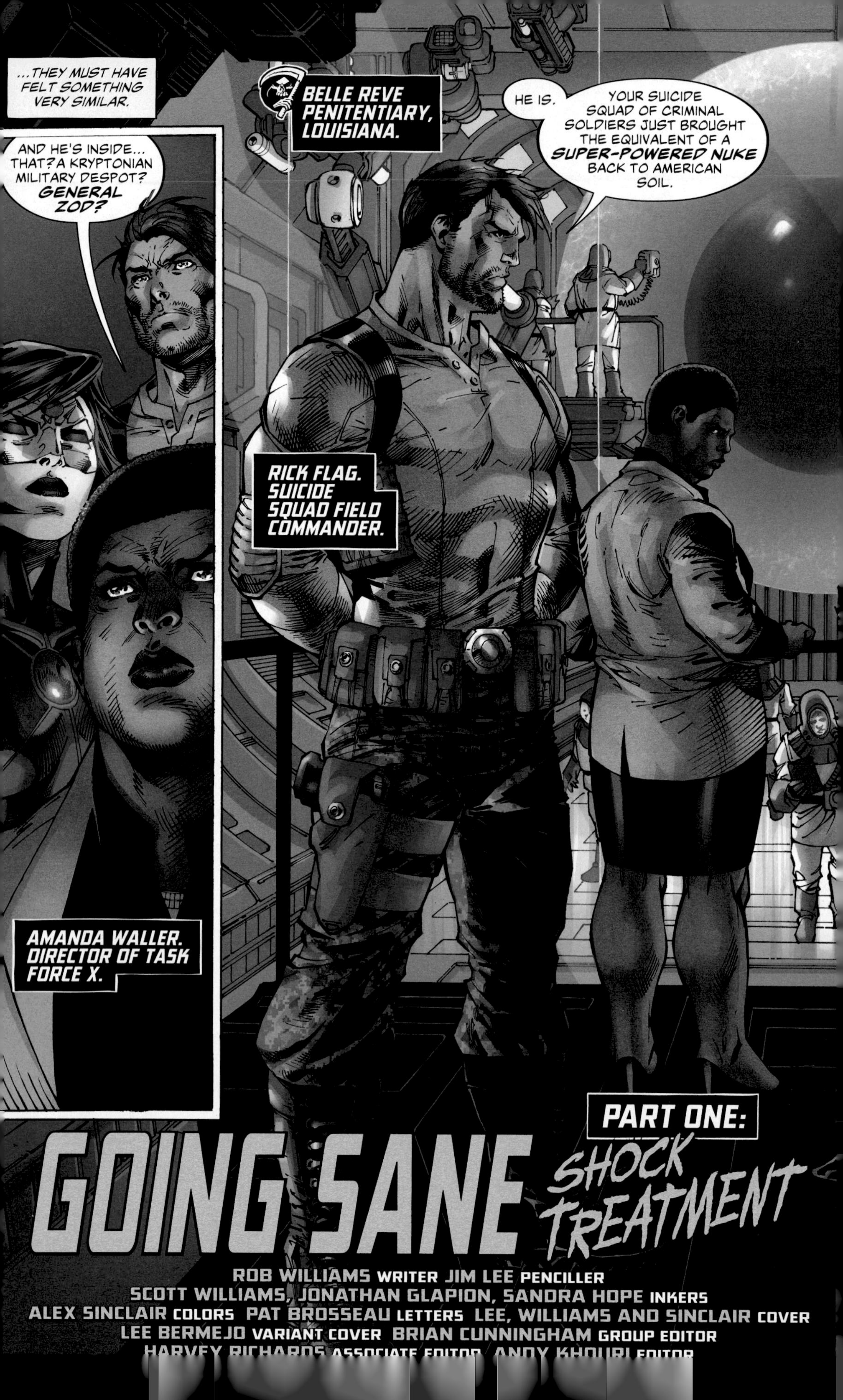

...THEY MUST HAVE FELT SOMETHING VERY SIMILAR.
BELLE REVE PENITENTIARY, LOUISIANA.
AND HE'S INSIDE... THAT? A KRYPTONIAN MILITARY DESPOT? GENERAL ZOD?
HE IS.
YOUR SUICIDE SQUAD OF CRIMINAL SOLDIERS JUST BROUGHT THE EQUIVALENT OF A SUPER-POWERED NUKE BACK TO AMERICAN SOIL.
RICK FLAG. SUICIDE SQUAD FIELD COMMANDER.
AMANDA WALLER. DIRECTOR OF TASK FORCE X.
PART ONE:
GOING SANE
SHOCK TREATMENT
ROB WILLIAMS WRITER JIM LEE PENCILLER
SCOTT WILLIAMS, JONATHAN GLAPION, SANDRA HOPE INKERS
ALEX SINCLAIR COLORS PAT BROSSEAU LETTERS LEE, WILLIAMS AND SINCLAIR COVER
LEE BERMEJO VARIANT COVER BRIAN CUNNINGHAM GROUP EDITOR
HARVEY RICHARDS ASSOCIATE EDITOR ANDY KHOURI EDITOR

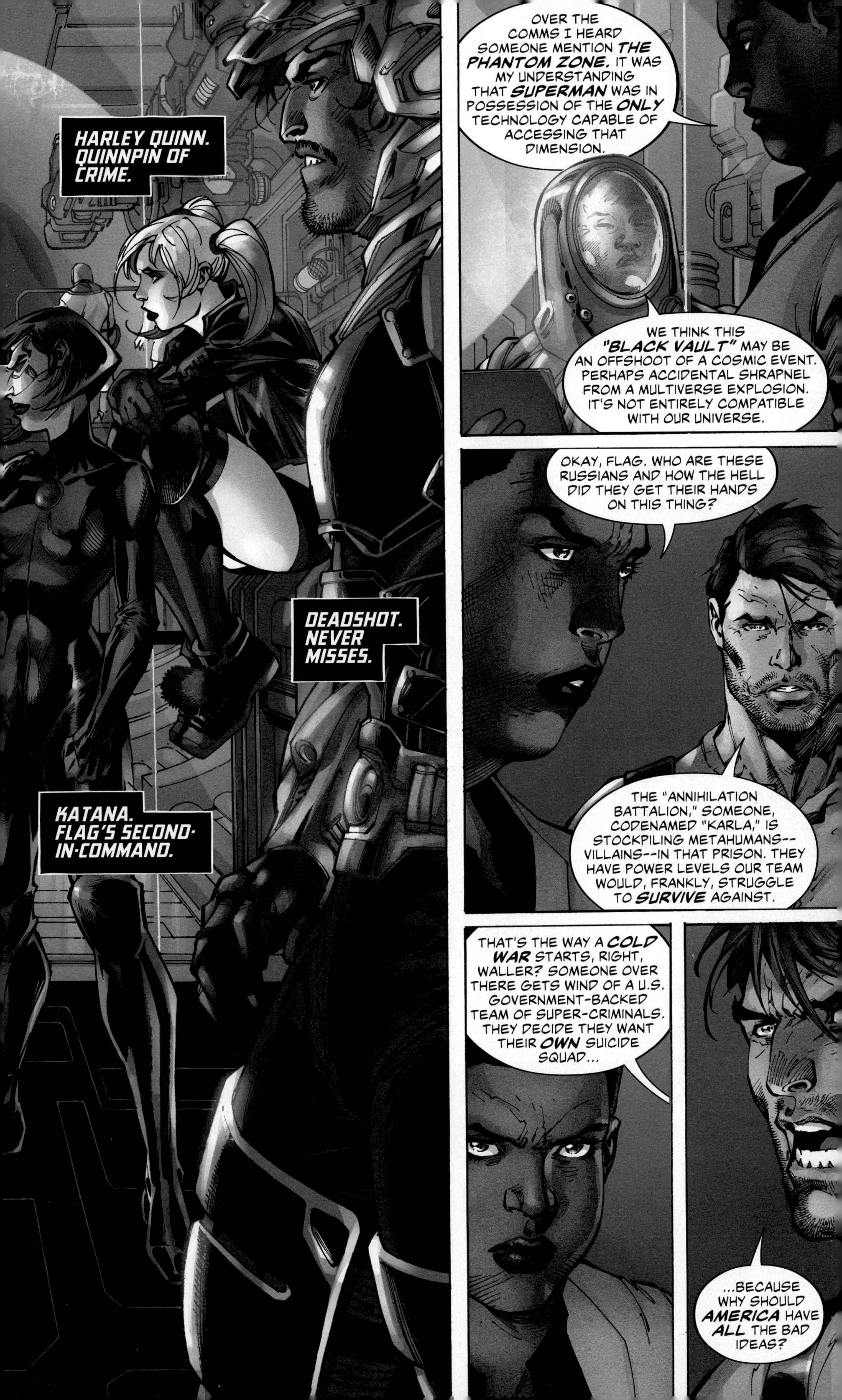

HARLEY QUINN. QUINNPIN OF CRIME.
DEADSHOT. NEVER MISSES.
KATANA. FLAG'S SECOND-IN-COMMAND.
OVER THE COMMS I HEARD SOMEONE MENTION THE PHANTOM ZONE. IT WAS MY UNDERSTANDING THAT SUPERMAN WAS IN POSSESSION OF THE ONLY TECHNOLOGY CAPABLE OF ACCESSING THAT DIMENSION.
WE THINK THIS "BLACK VAULT" MAY BE AN OFFSHOOT OF A COSMIC EVENT. PERHAPS ACCIDENTAL SHRAPNEL FROM A MULTIVERSE EXPLOSION. IT'S NOT ENTIRELY COMPATIBLE WITH OUR UNIVERSE.
OKAY, FLAG. WHO ARE THESE RUSSIANS AND HOW THE HELL DID THEY GET THEIR HANDS ON THIS THING?
THE "ANNIHILATION BATTALION," SOMEONE, CODENAMED "KARLA," IS STOCKPILING METAHUMANS--VILLAINS--IN THAT PRISON. THEY HAVE POWER LEVELS OUR TEAM WOULD, FRANKLY, STRUGGLE TO SURVIVE AGAINST.
THAT'S THE WAY A COLD WAR STARTS, RIGHT, WALLER? SOMEONE OVER THERE GETS WIND OF A U.S. GOVERNMENT-BACKED TEAM OF SUPER-CRIMINALS. THEY DECIDE THEY WANT THEIR OWN SUICIDE SQUAD...
...BECAUSE WHY SHOULD AMERICA HAVE ALL THE BAD IDEAS?

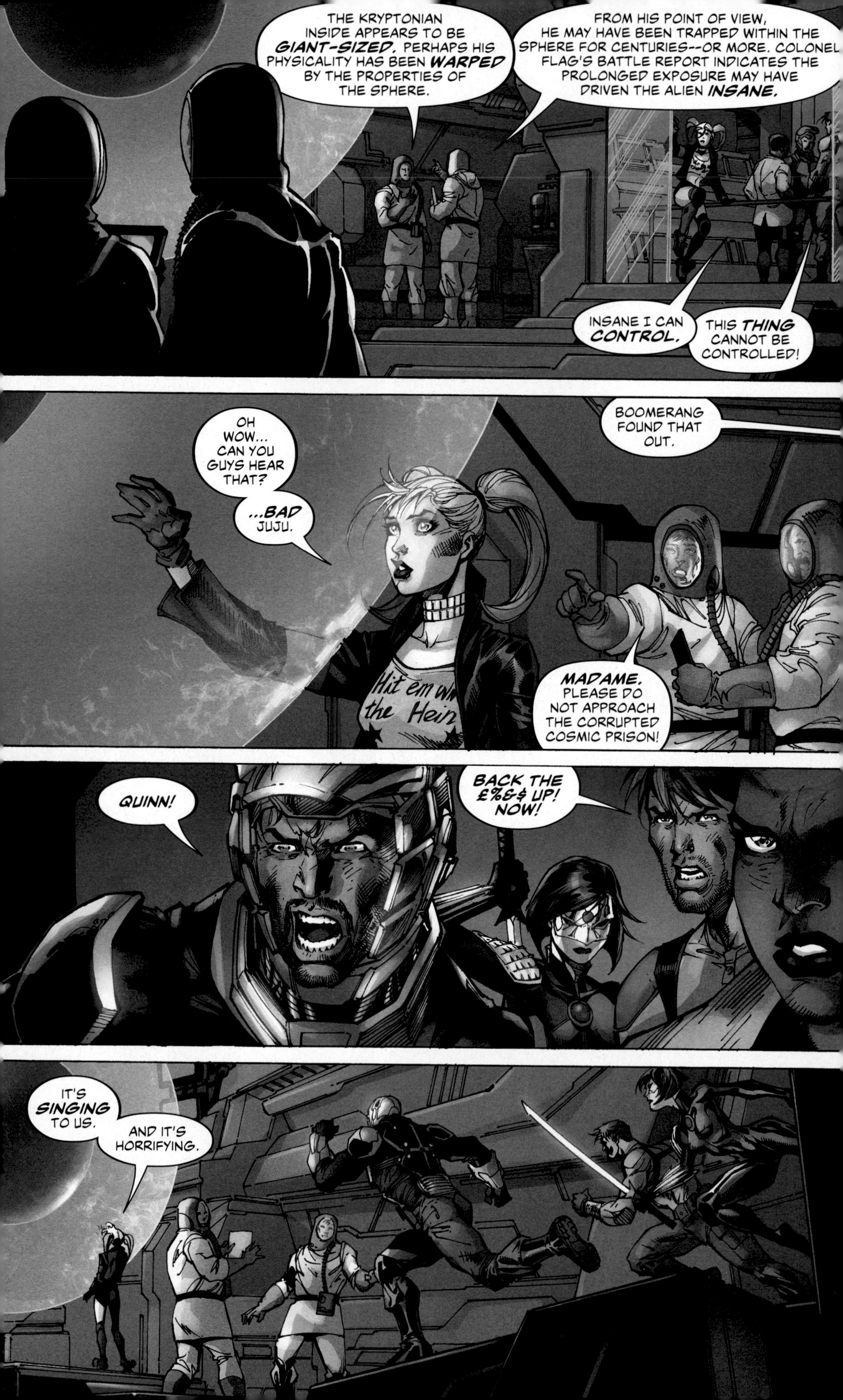
THE KRYPTONIAN INSIDE APPEARS TO BE GIANT-SIZED. PERHAPS HIS PHYSICALITY HAS BEEN WARPED BY THE PROPERTIES OF THE SPHERE.
FROM HIS POINT OF VIEW, HE MAY HAVE BEEN TRAPPED WITHIN THE SPHERE FOR CENTURIES--OR MORE. COLONEL FLAG'S BATTLE REPORT INDICATES THE PROLONGED EXPOSURE MAY HAVE DRIVEN THE ALIEN INSANE.
INSANE I CAN CONTROL.
THIS THING CANNOT BE CONTROLLED!
BOOMERANG FOUND THAT OUT.
OH WOW... CAN YOU GUYS HEAR THAT?
...BAD JUJU.
MADAME. PLEASE DO NOT APPROACH THE CORRUPTED COSMIC PRISON!
QUINN!
BACK THE £%&$ UP! NOW!
IT'S SINGING TO US.
AND IT'S HORRIFYING.

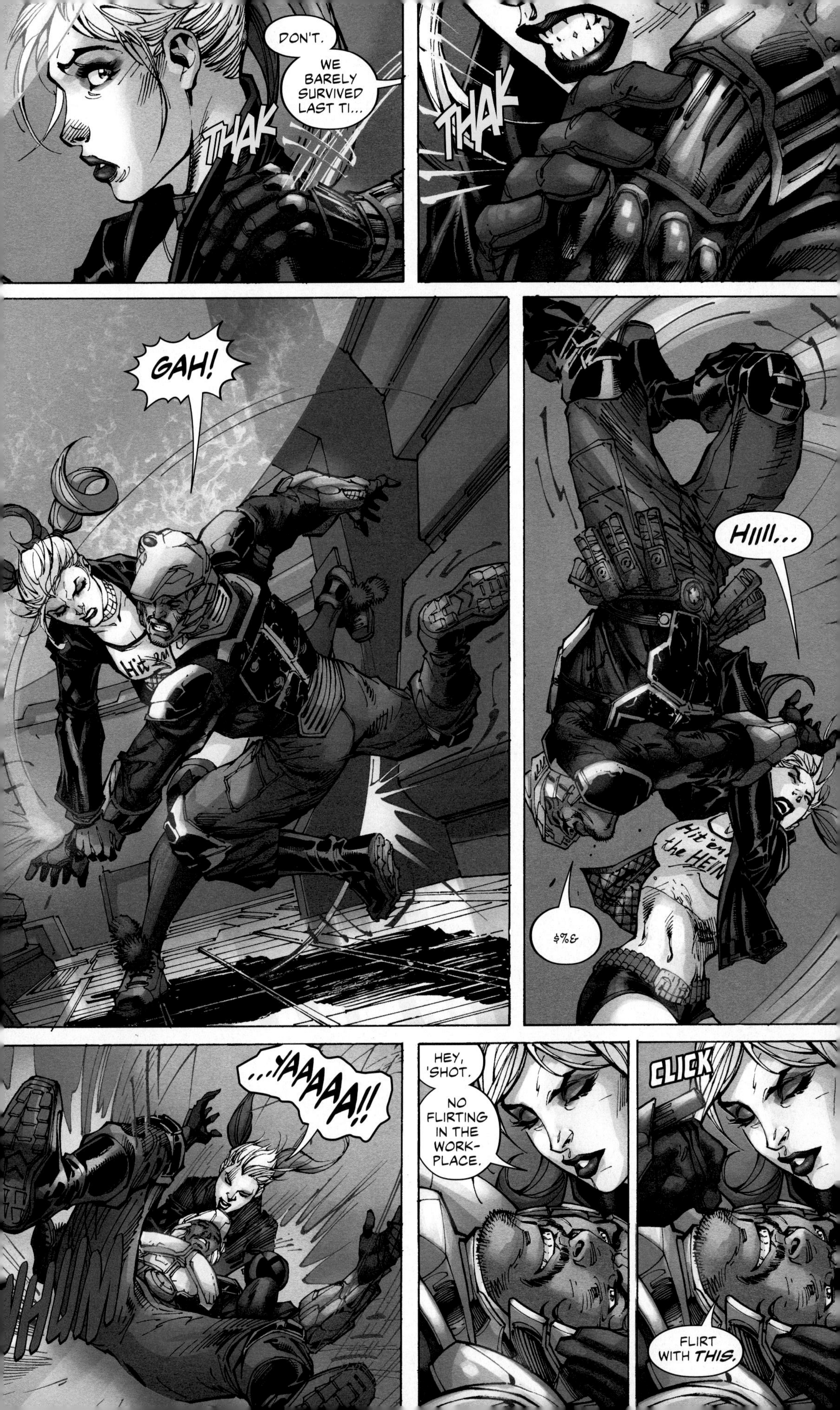

DON'T.
WE BARELY SURVIVED LAST TI...
THAK
THAK
GAH!
HIIII...
$%&
...YAAAAA!!
HEY, 'SHOT.
NO FLIRTING IN THE WORK-PLACE.
CLICK
FLIRT WITH THIS.

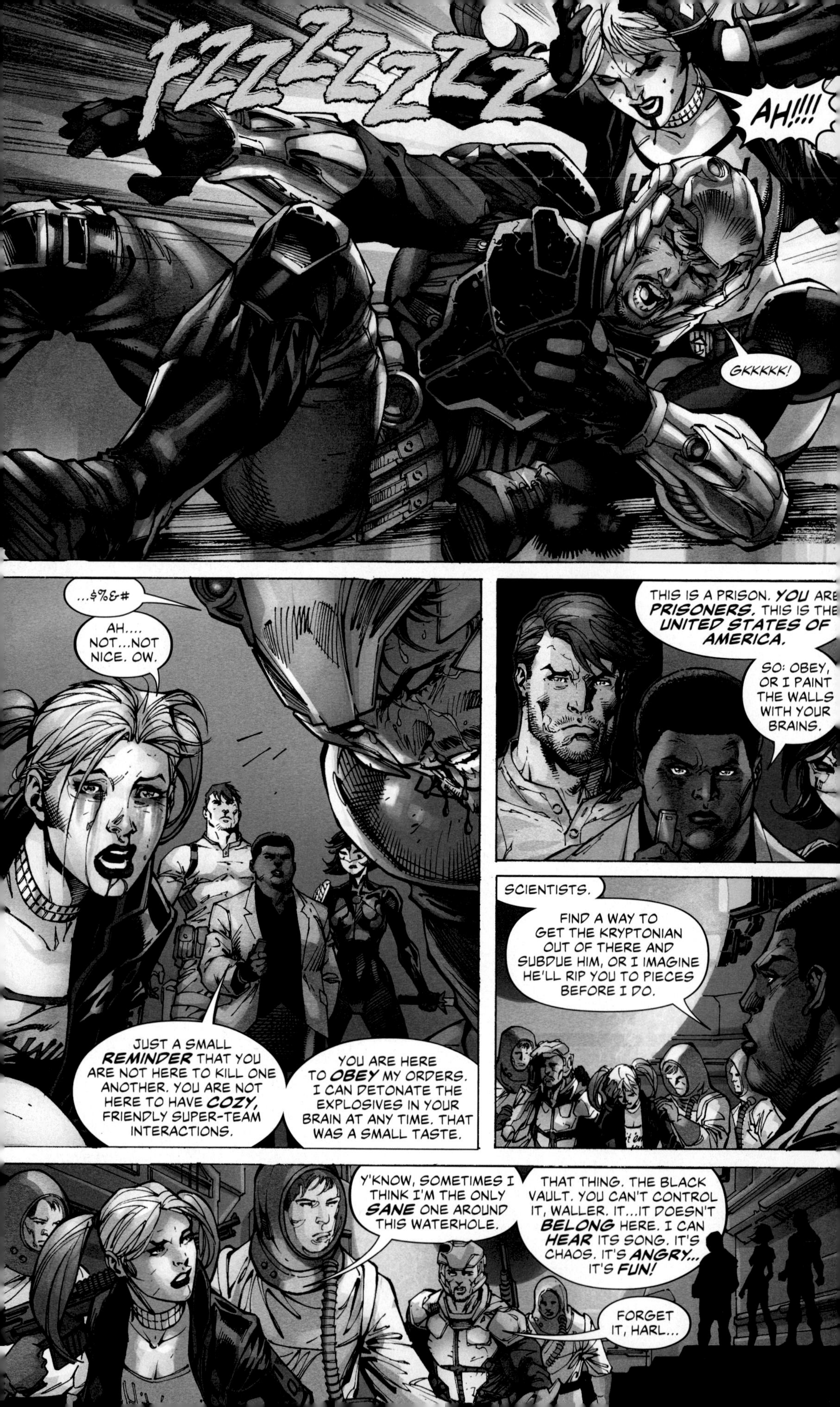
FZZZZZZZZ
AH!!!!
GKKKKK!
...$%&#
AH.... NOT...NOT NICE. OW.
THIS IS A PRISON. YOU ARE PRISONERS. THIS IS THE UNITED STATES OF AMERICA.
SO: OBEY, OR I PAINT THE WALLS WITH YOUR BRAINS.
SCIENTISTS.
FIND A WAY TO GET THE KRYPTONIAN OUT OF THERE AND SUBDUE HIM, OR I IMAGINE HE'LL RIP YOU TO PIECES BEFORE I DO.
JUST A SMALL REMINDER THAT YOU ARE NOT HERE TO KILL ONE ANOTHER. YOU ARE NOT HERE TO HAVE COZY, FRIENDLY SUPER-TEAM INTERACTIONS.
YOU ARE HERE TO OBEY MY ORDERS. I CAN DETONATE THE EXPLOSIVES IN YOUR BRAIN AT ANY TIME. THAT WAS A SMALL TASTE.
Y'KNOW, SOMETIMES I THINK I'M THE ONLY SANE ONE AROUND THIS WATERHOLE.
THAT THING. THE BLACK VAULT. YOU CAN'T CONTROL IT, WALLER. IT...IT DOESN'T BELONG HERE. I CAN HEAR ITS SONG. IT'S CHAOS. IT'S ANGRY... IT'S FUN!
FORGET IT, HARL...

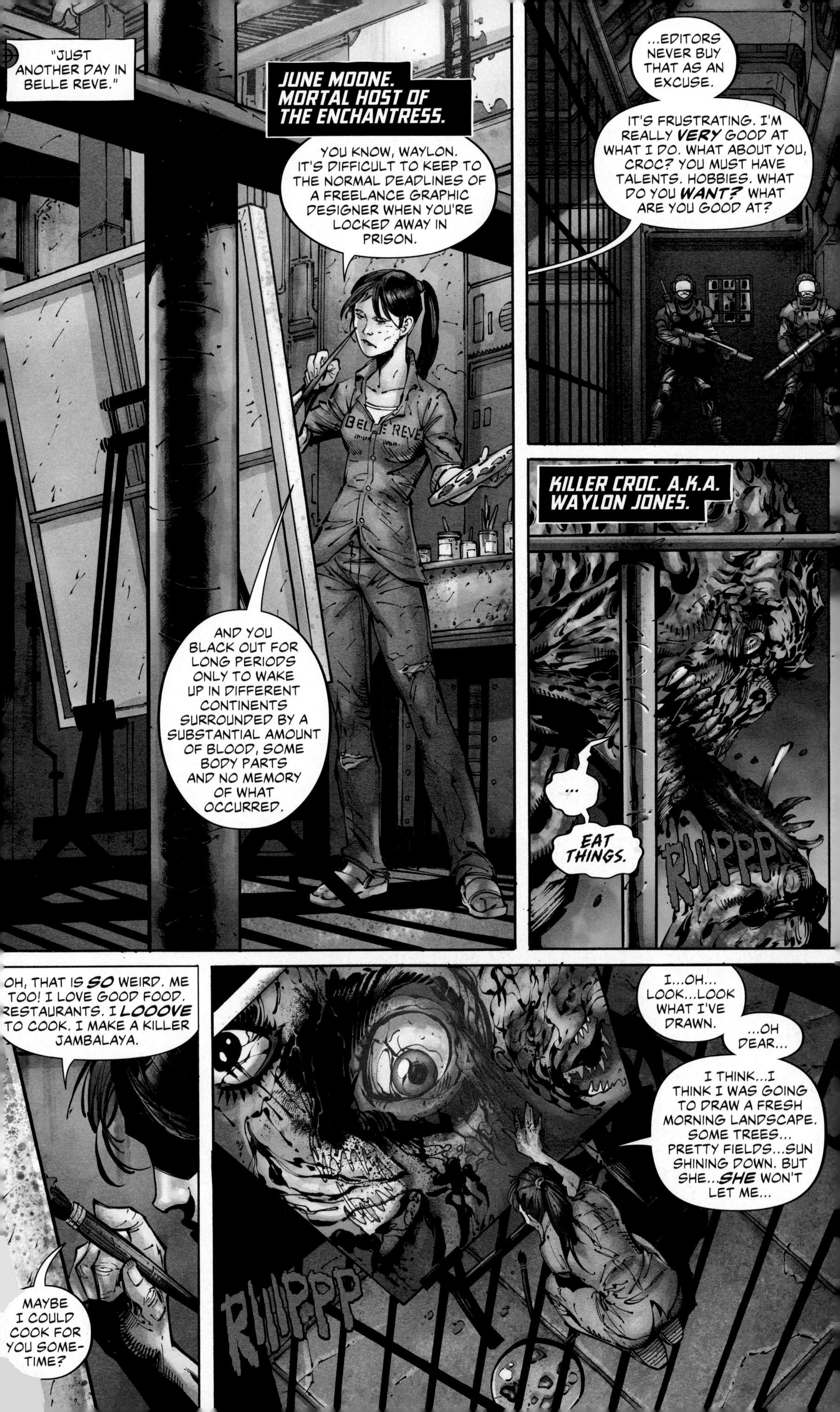
"JUST ANOTHER DAY IN BELLE REVE."
JUNE MOONE. MORTAL HOST OF THE ENCHANTRESS.
YOU KNOW, WAYLON. IT'S DIFFICULT TO KEEP TO THE NORMAL DEADLINES OF A FREELANCE GRAPHIC DESIGNER WHEN YOU'RE LOCKED AWAY IN PRISON.
AND YOU BLACK OUT FOR LONG PERIODS ONLY TO WAKE UP IN DIFFERENT CONTINENTS SURROUNDED BY A SUBSTANTIAL AMOUNT OF BLOOD, SOME BODY PARTS AND NO MEMORY OF WHAT OCCURRED.
BELLE REVE
...EDITORS NEVER BUY THAT AS AN EXCUSE.
IT'S FRUSTRATING. I'M REALLY VERY GOOD AT WHAT I DO. WHAT ABOUT YOU, CROC? YOU MUST HAVE TALENTS. HOBBIES. WHAT DO YOU WANT? WHAT ARE YOU GOOD AT?
KILLER CROC. A.K.A. WAYLON JONES.
...
EAT THINGS.
RIIPPP
OH, THAT IS SO WEIRD. ME TOO! I LOVE GOOD FOOD. RESTAURANTS. I LOOOVE TO COOK. I MAKE A KILLER JAMBALAYA.
MAYBE I COULD COOK FOR YOU SOME-TIME?
RIIPPP
I...OH... LOOK...LOOK WHAT I'VE DRAWN.
...OH DEAR...
I THINK...I THINK I WAS GOING TO DRAW A FRESH MORNING LANDSCAPE. SOME TREES... PRETTY FIELDS...SUN SHINING DOWN. BUT SHE...SHE WON'T LET ME...

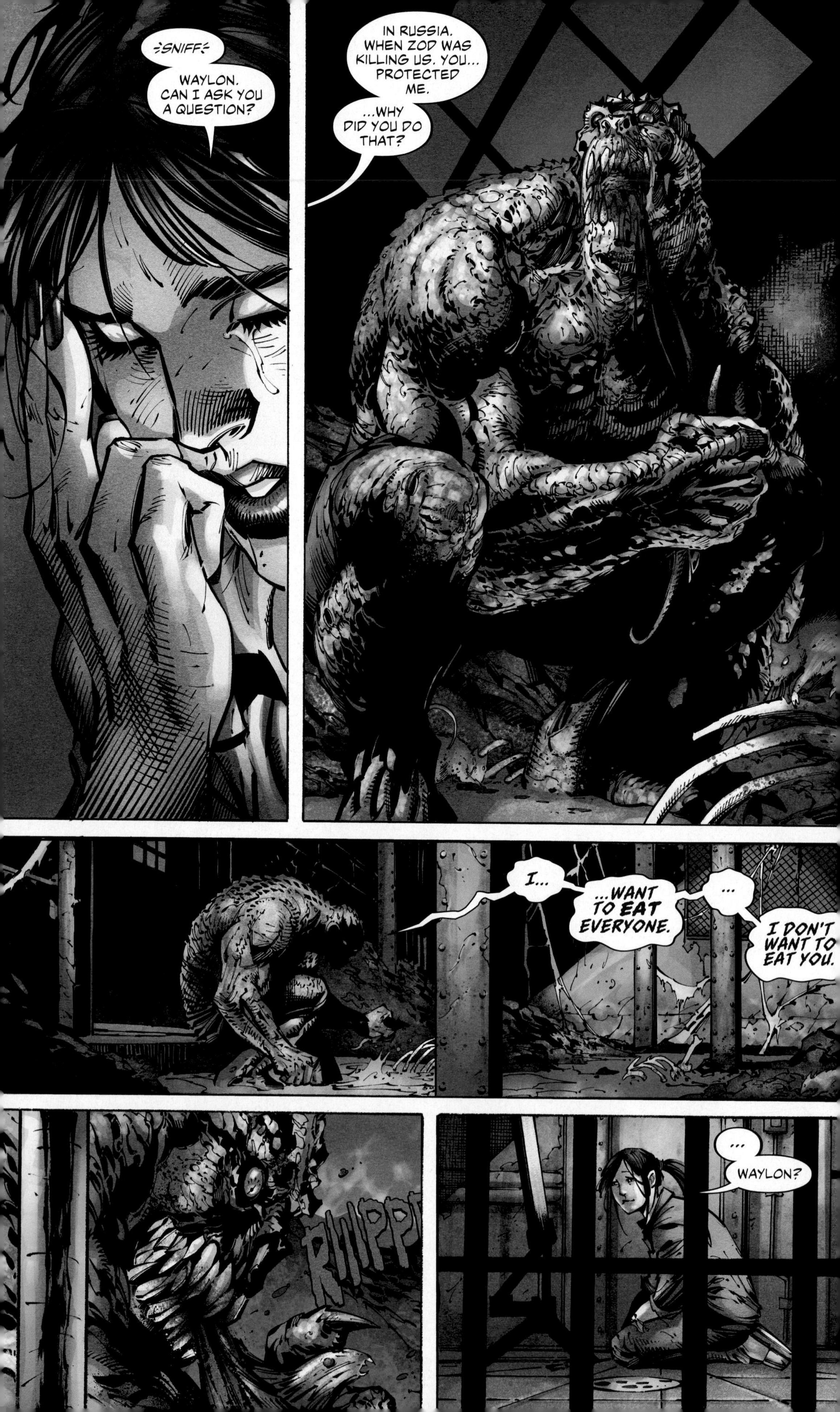

-SNIFF-
WAYLON. CAN I ASK YOU A QUESTION?
IN RUSSIA. WHEN ZOD WAS KILLING US. YOU... PROTECTED ME.
...WHY DID YOU DO THAT?
I...
...WANT TO EAT EVERYONE.
...
I DON'T WANT TO EAT YOU.
RIIPP
...
WAYLON?

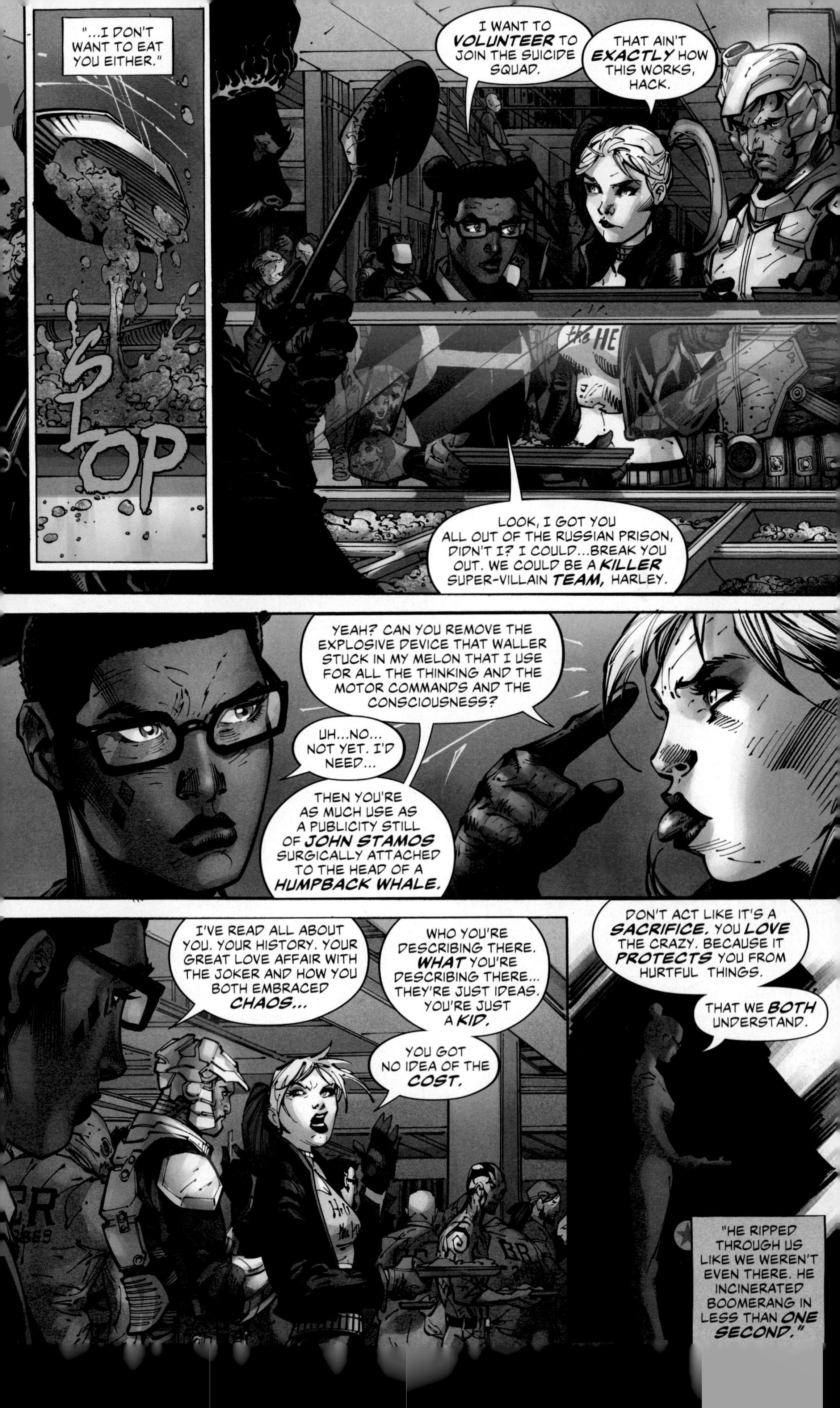

"...I DON'T WANT TO EAT YOU EITHER."
SLOP
I WANT TO VOLUNTEER TO JOIN THE SUICIDE SQUAD.
THAT AIN'T EXACTLY HOW THIS WORKS, HACK.
LOOK, I GOT YOU ALL OUT OF THE RUSSIAN PRISON, DIDN'T I? I COULD...BREAK YOU OUT. WE COULD BE A KILLER SUPER-VILLAIN TEAM, HARLEY.
YEAH? CAN YOU REMOVE THE EXPLOSIVE DEVICE THAT WALLER STUCK IN MY MELON THAT I USE FOR ALL THE THINKING AND THE MOTOR COMMANDS AND THE CONSCIOUSNESS?
UH...NO... NOT YET. I'D NEED...
THEN YOU'RE AS MUCH USE AS A PUBLICITY STILL OF JOHN STAMOS SURGICALLY ATTACHED TO THE HEAD OF A HUMPBACK WHALE.
I'VE READ ALL ABOUT YOU. YOUR HISTORY. YOUR GREAT LOVE AFFAIR WITH THE JOKER AND HOW YOU BOTH EMBRACED CHAOS...
WHO YOU'RE DESCRIBING THERE. WHAT YOU'RE DESCRIBING THERE... THEY'RE JUST IDEAS. YOU'RE JUST A KID.
YOU GOT NO IDEA OF THE COST.
DON'T ACT LIKE IT'S A SACRIFICE. YOU LOVE THE CRAZY. BECAUSE IT PROTECTS YOU FROM HURTFUL THINGS.
THAT WE BOTH UNDERSTAND.
"HE RIPPED THROUGH US LIKE WE WEREN'T EVEN THERE. HE INCINERATED BOOMERANG IN LESS THAN ONE SECOND."

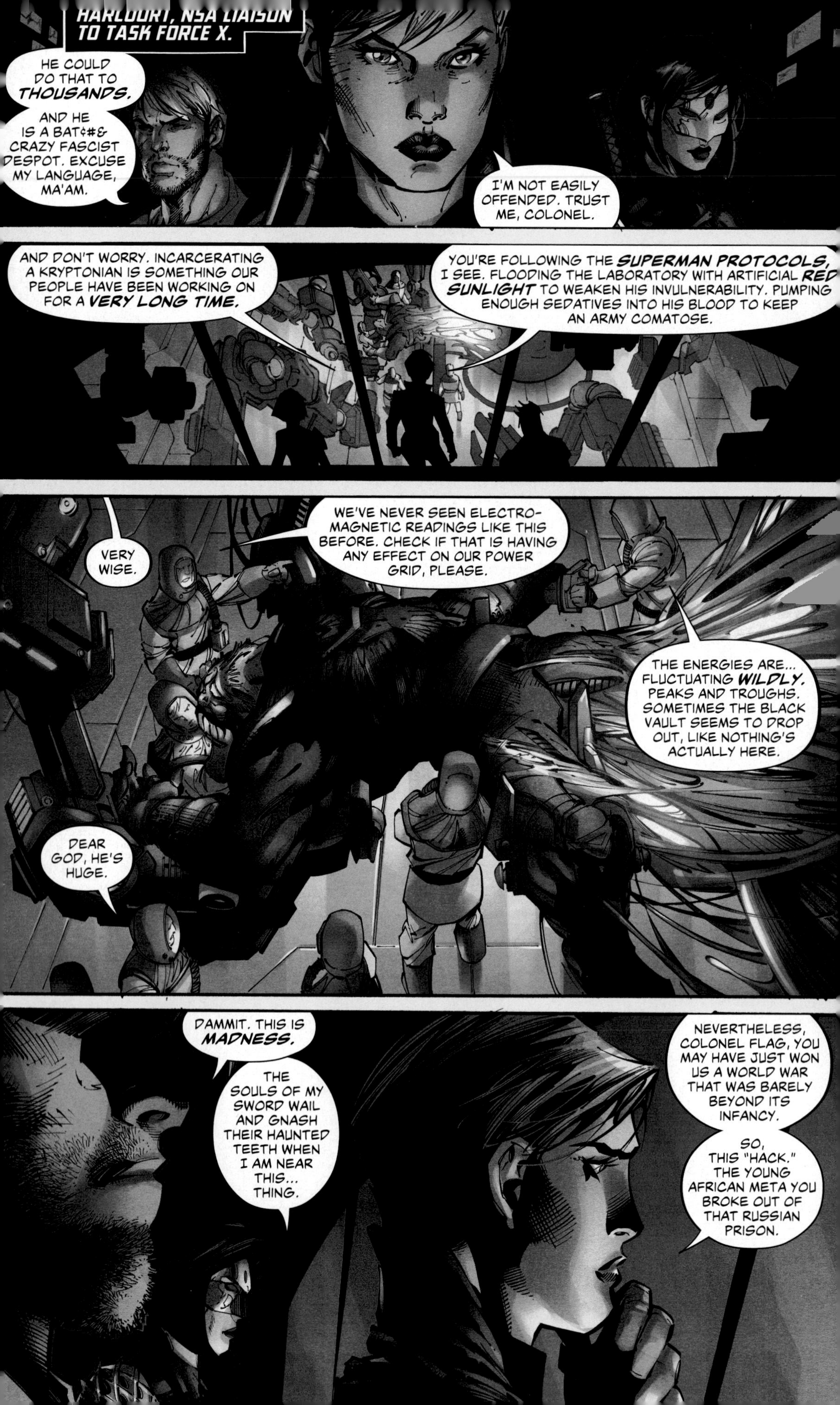
HARCOURT, NSA LIAISON TO TASK FORCE X.
HE COULD DO THAT TO THOUSANDS.
AND HE IS A BAT¢#& CRAZY FASCIST DESPOT. EXCUSE MY LANGUAGE, MA'AM.
I'M NOT EASILY OFFENDED. TRUST ME, COLONEL.
AND DON'T WORRY. INCARCERATING A KRYPTONIAN IS SOMETHING OUR PEOPLE HAVE BEEN WORKING ON FOR A VERY LONG TIME.
YOU'RE FOLLOWING THE SUPERMAN PROTOCOLS, I SEE. FLOODING THE LABORATORY WITH ARTIFICIAL RED SUNLIGHT TO WEAKEN HIS INVULNERABILITY. PUMPING ENOUGH SEDATIVES INTO HIS BLOOD TO KEEP AN ARMY COMATOSE.
VERY WISE.
WE'VE NEVER SEEN ELECTRO-MAGNETIC READINGS LIKE THIS BEFORE. CHECK IF THAT IS HAVING ANY EFFECT ON OUR POWER GRID, PLEASE.
THE ENERGIES ARE... FLUCTUATING WILDLY. PEAKS AND TROUGHS. SOMETIMES THE BLACK VAULT SEEMS TO DROP OUT, LIKE NOTHING'S ACTUALLY HERE.
DEAR GOD, HE'S HUGE.
DAMMIT. THIS IS MADNESS.
THE SOULS OF MY SWORD WAIL AND GNASH THEIR HAUNTED TEETH WHEN I AM NEAR THIS... THING.
NEVERTHELESS, COLONEL FLAG, YOU MAY HAVE JUST WON US A WORLD WAR THAT WAS BARELY BEYOND ITS INFANCY.
SO, THIS "HACK." THE YOUNG AFRICAN META YOU BROKE OUT OF THAT RUSSIAN PRISON.

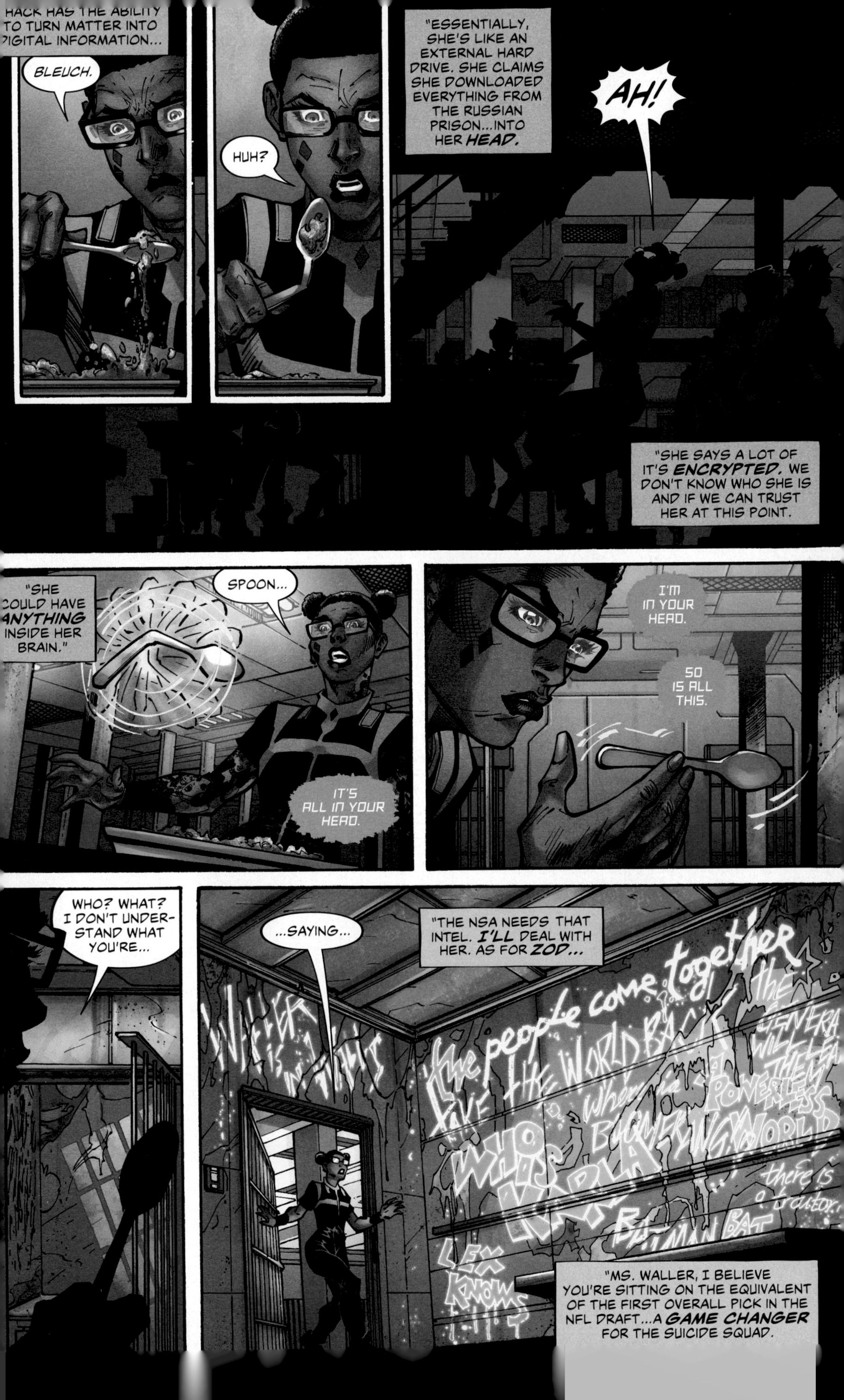
HACK HAS THE ABILITY TO TURN MATTER INTO DIGITAL INFORMATION...
BLEUCH.
HUH?
"ESSENTIALLY, SHE'S LIKE AN EXTERNAL HARD DRIVE. SHE CLAIMS SHE DOWNLOADED EVERYTHING FROM THE RUSSIAN PRISON...INTO HER HEAD.
AH!
"SHE SAYS A LOT OF IT'S ENCRYPTED. WE DON'T KNOW WHO SHE IS AND IF WE CAN TRUST HER AT THIS POINT.
"SHE COULD HAVE ANYTHING INSIDE HER BRAIN."
SPOON...
IT'S ALL IN YOUR HEAD.
I'M IN YOUR HEAD.
SO IS ALL THIS.
WHO? WHAT? I DON'T UNDERSTAND WHAT YOU'RE...
...SAYING...
"THE NSA NEEDS THAT INTEL. I'LL DEAL WITH HER. AS FOR ZOD...
the people come together
POWERLESS
there is a traitor
LEX KNOWS
"MS. WALLER, I BELIEVE YOU'RE SITTING ON THE EQUIVALENT OF THE FIRST OVERALL PICK IN THE NFL DRAFT...A GAME CHANGER FOR THE SUICIDE SQUAD.

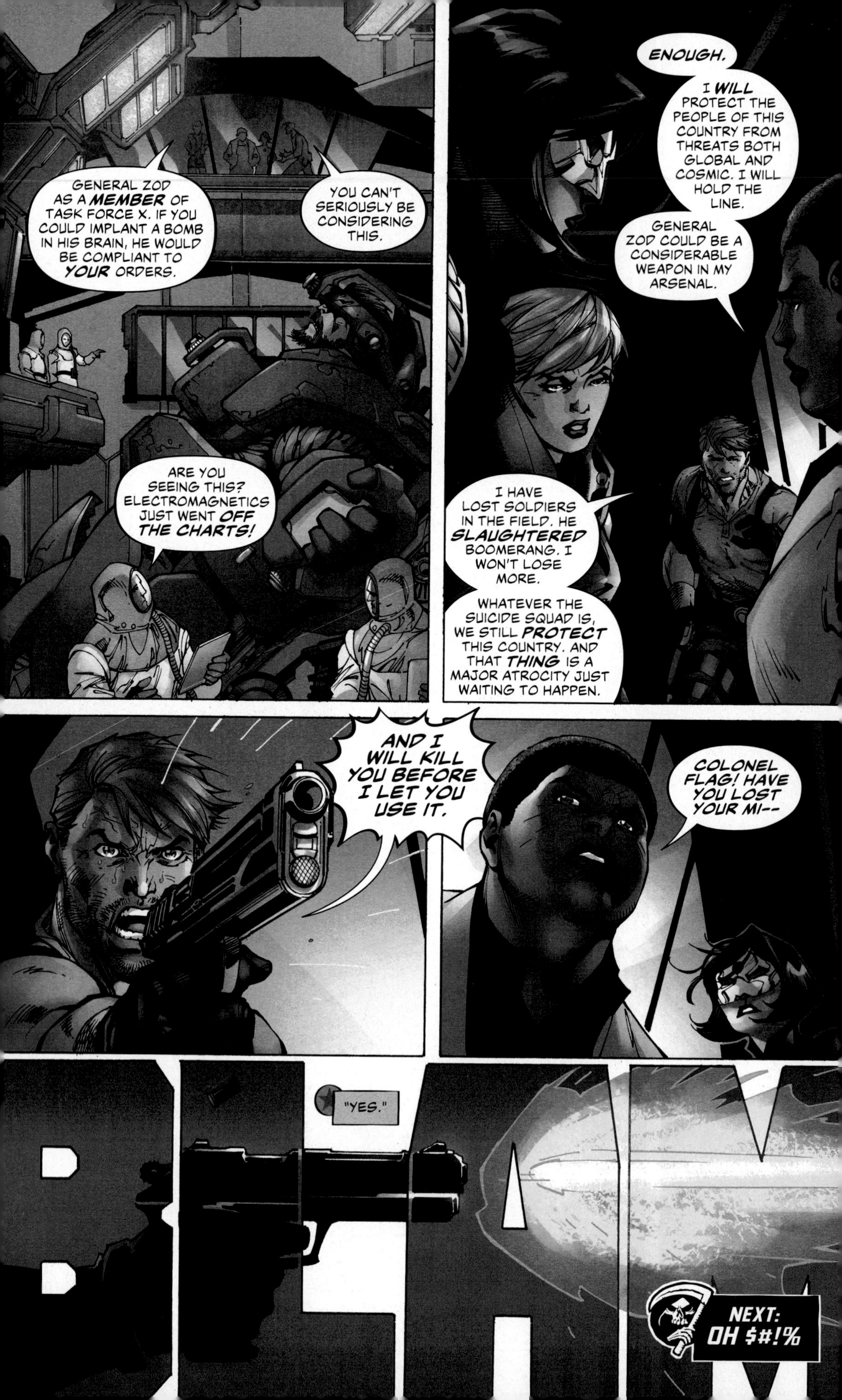
GENERAL ZOD AS A MEMBER OF TASK FORCE X. IF YOU COULD IMPLANT A BOMB IN HIS BRAIN, HE WOULD BE COMPLIANT TO YOUR ORDERS.
YOU CAN'T SERIOUSLY BE CONSIDERING THIS.
ARE YOU SEEING THIS? ELECTROMAGNETICS JUST WENT OFF THE CHARTS!
ENOUGH.
I WILL PROTECT THE PEOPLE OF THIS COUNTRY FROM THREATS BOTH GLOBAL AND COSMIC. I WILL HOLD THE LINE.
GENERAL ZOD COULD BE A CONSIDERABLE WEAPON IN MY ARSENAL.
I HAVE LOST SOLDIERS IN THE FIELD. HE SLAUGHTERED BOOMERANG. I WON'T LOSE MORE.
WHATEVER THE SUICIDE SQUAD IS, WE STILL PROTECT THIS COUNTRY. AND THAT THING IS A MAJOR ATROCITY JUST WAITING TO HAPPEN.
AND I WILL KILL YOU BEFORE I LET YOU USE IT.
COLONEL FLAG! HAVE YOU LOST YOUR MI--
"YES."
NEXT: OH $#!%

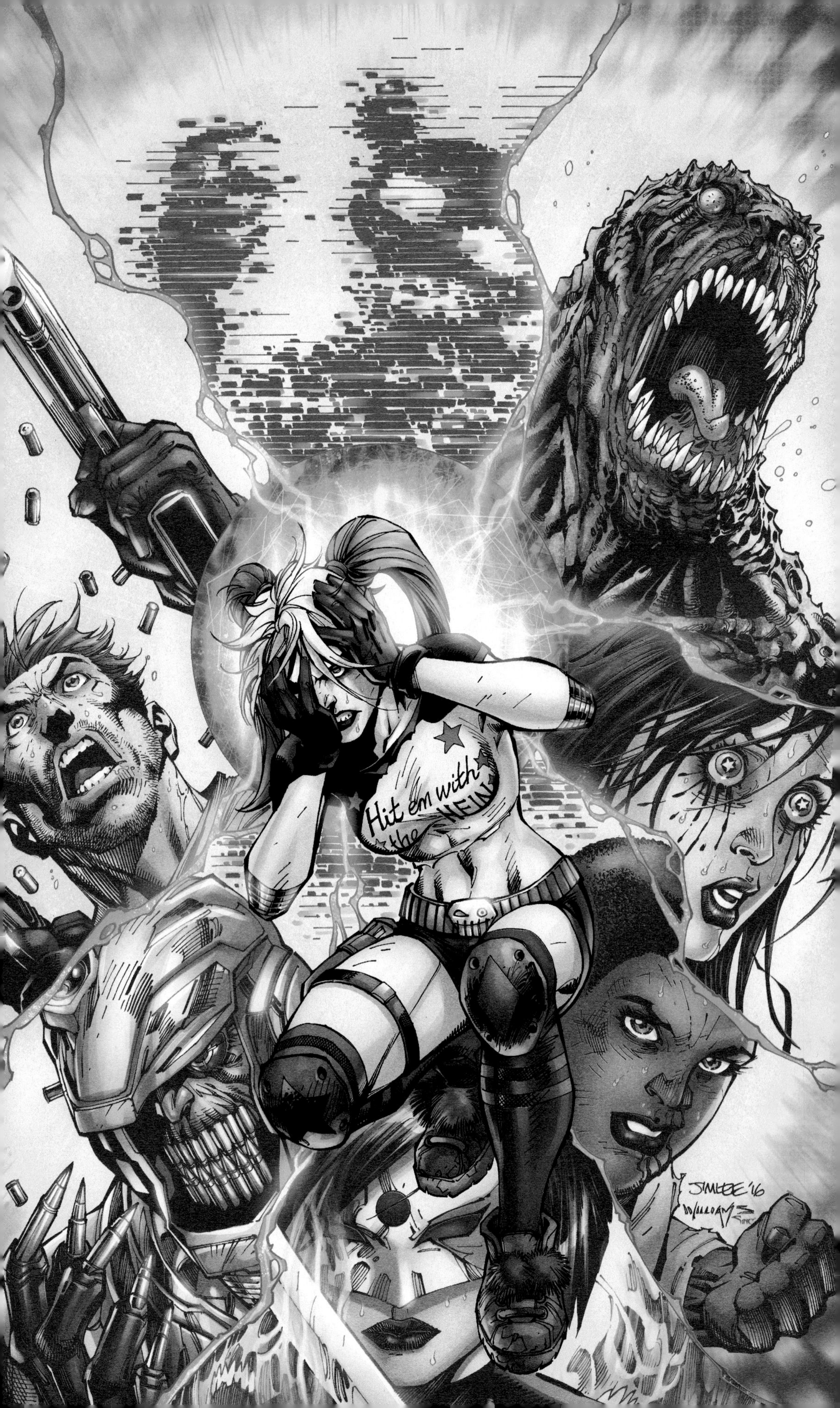
Hit em with
the
JIMLEE '16

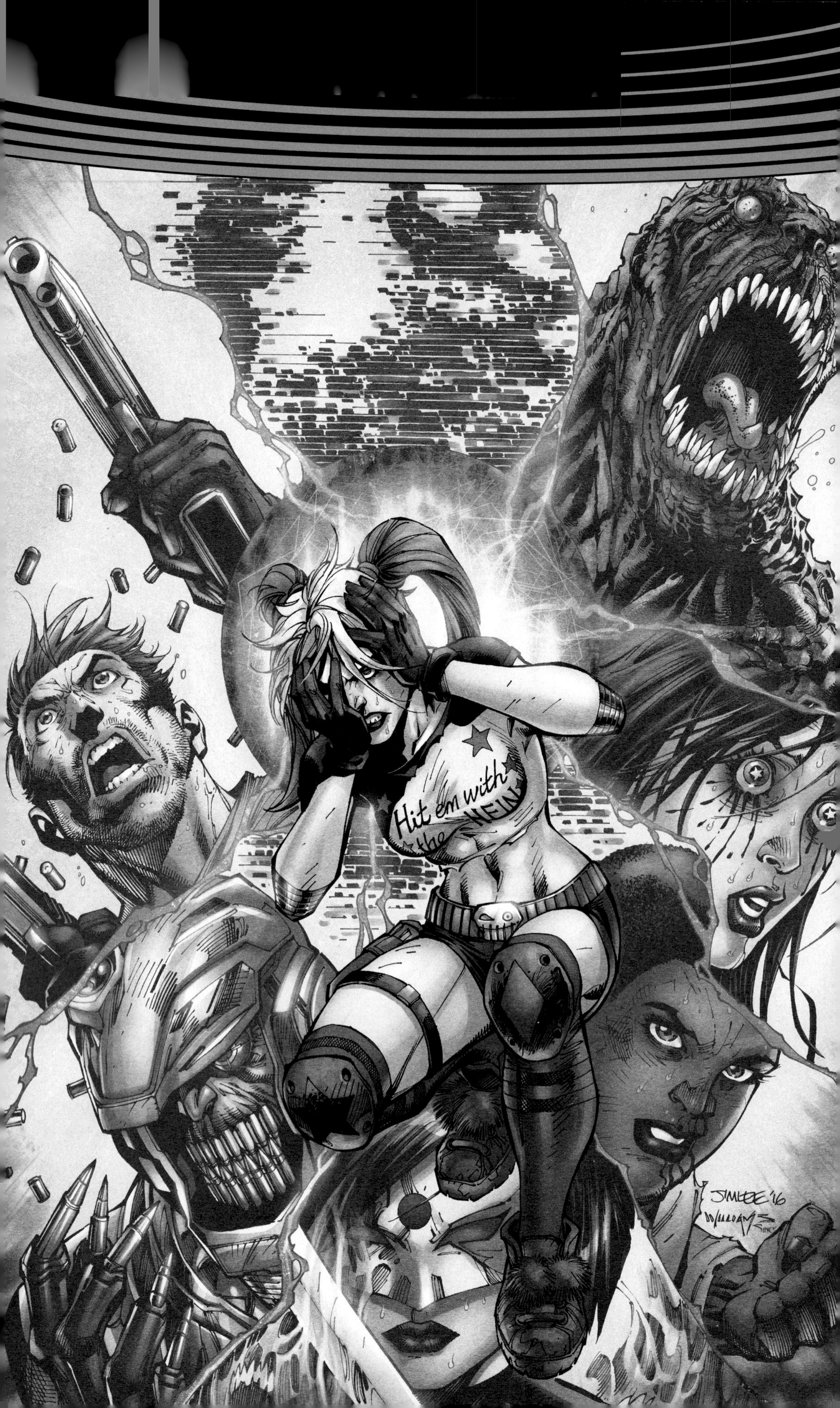
Hit em with the
JIMLEE '16

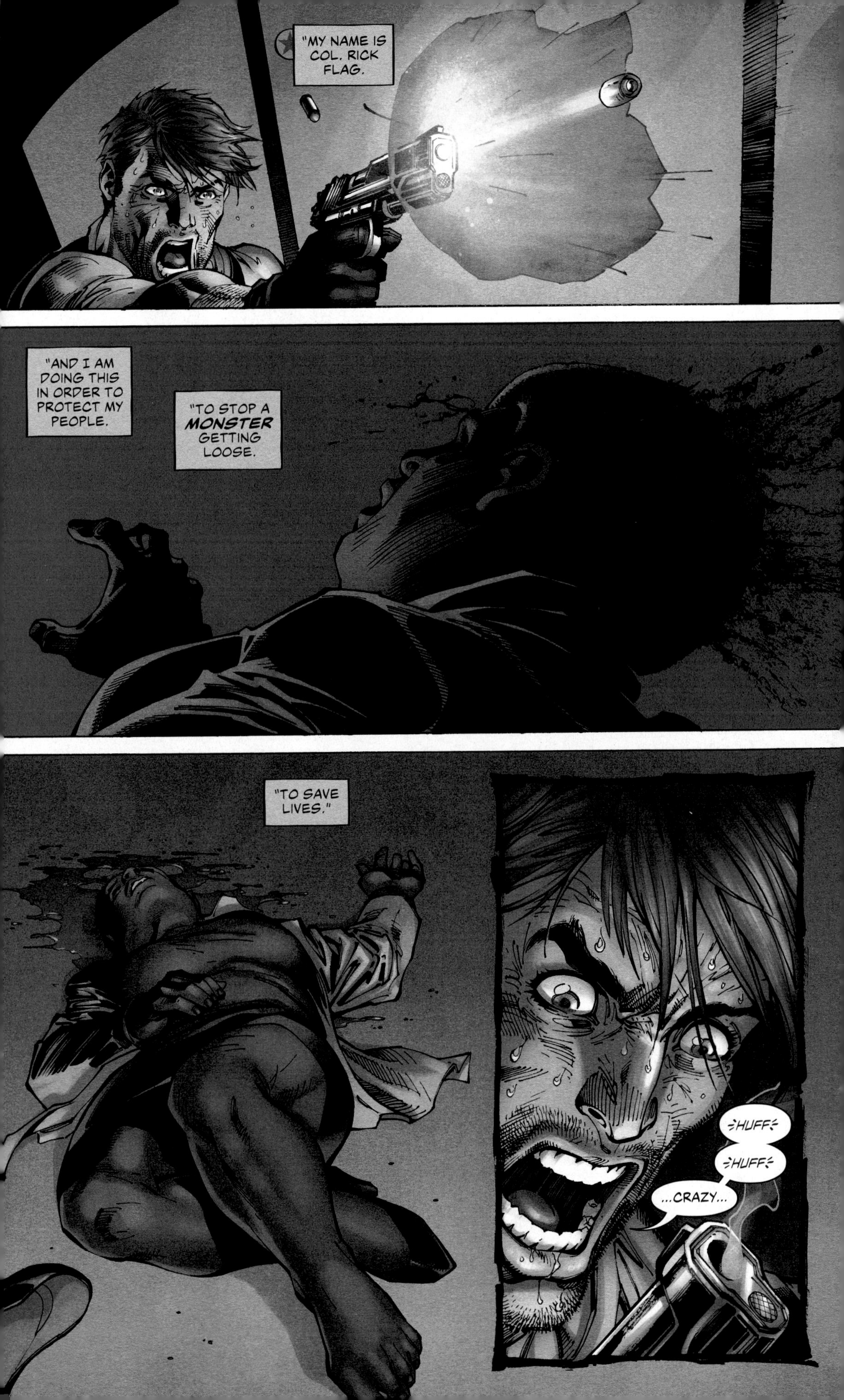
"MY NAME IS COL. RICK FLAG.
"AND I AM DOING THIS IN ORDER TO PROTECT MY PEOPLE.
"TO STOP A MONSTER GETTING LOOSE.
"TO SAVE LIVES."
HUFF
HUFF
...CRAZY...

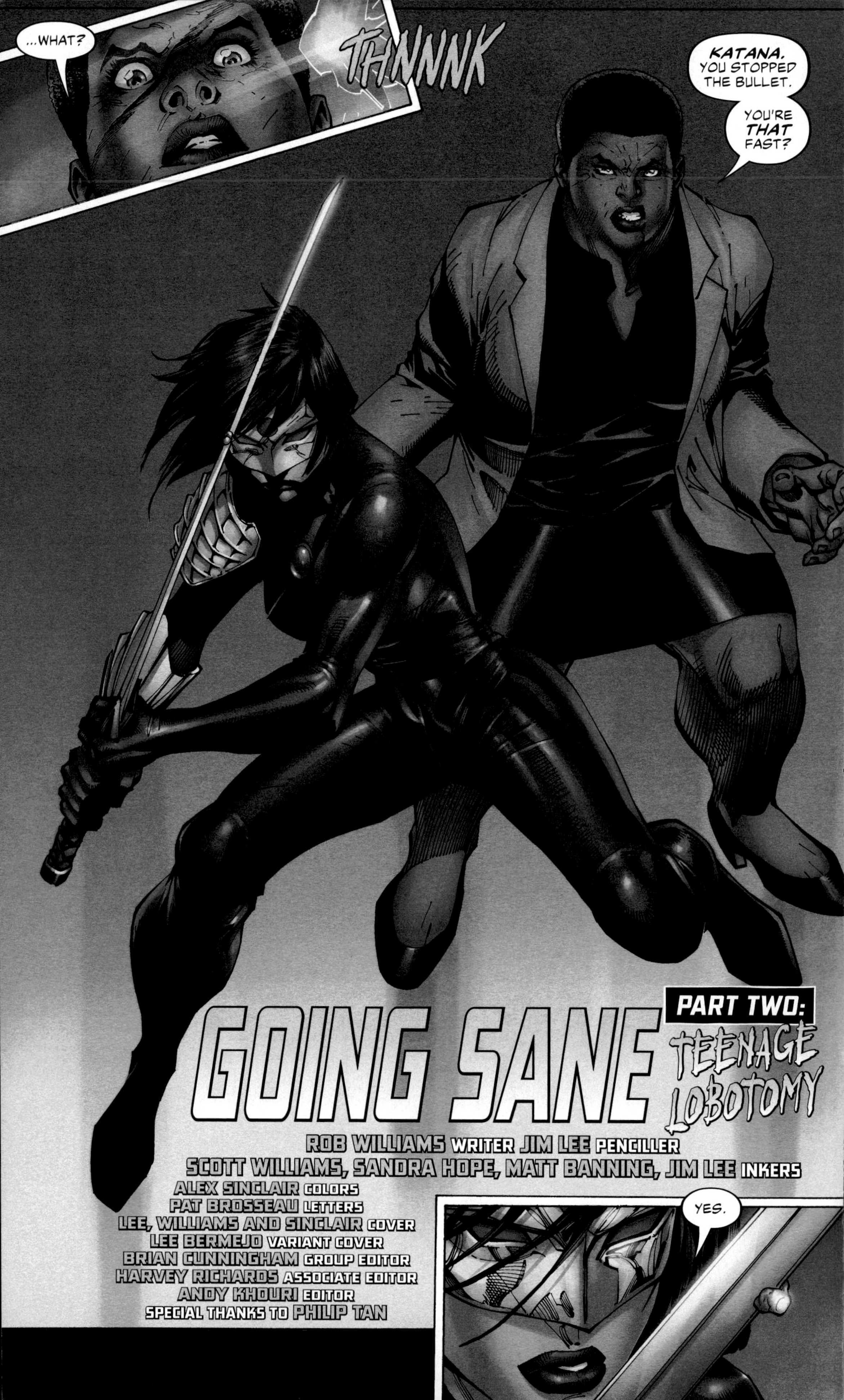
...WHAT?
THNNNK
KATANA. YOU STOPPED THE BULLET.
YOU'RE THAT FAST?
GOING SANE
PART TWO: TEENAGE LOBOTOMY
ROB WILLIAMS WRITER JIM LEE PENCILLER
SCOTT WILLIAMS, SANDRA HOPE, MATT BANNING, JIM LEE INKERS
ALEX SINCLAIR COLORS
PAT BROSSEAU LETTERS
LEE, WILLIAMS AND SINCLAIR COVER
LEE BERMEJO VARIANT COVER
BRIAN CUNNINGHAM GROUP EDITOR
HARVEY RICHARDS ASSOCIATE EDITOR
ANDY KHOURI EDITOR
SPECIAL THANKS TO PHILIP TAN
YES.

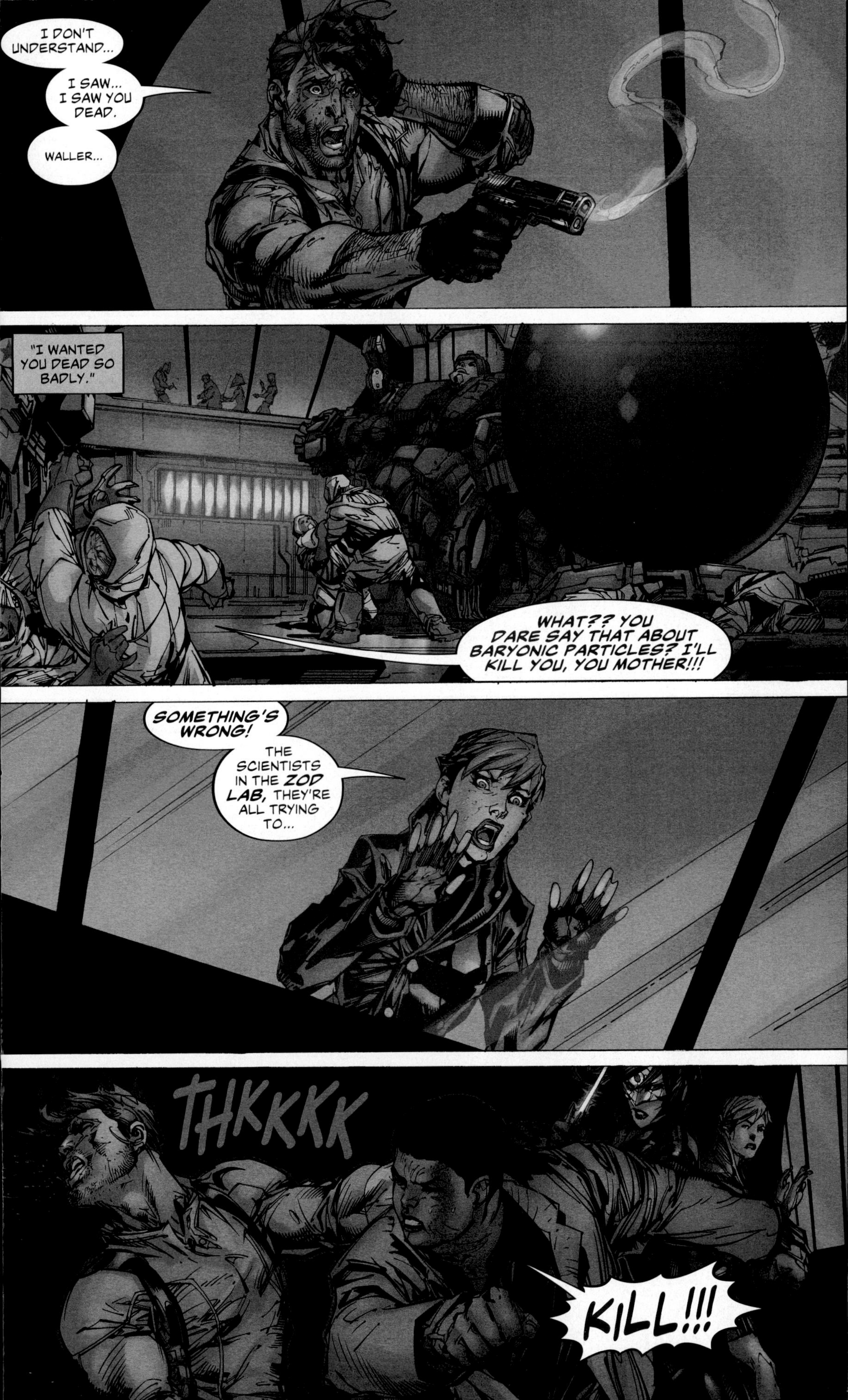
I DON'T UNDERSTAND...
I SAW... I SAW YOU DEAD.
WALLER...
"I WANTED YOU DEAD SO BADLY."
WHAT?? YOU DARE SAY THAT ABOUT BARYONIC PARTICLES? I'LL KILL YOU, YOU MOTHER!!!
SOMETHING'S WRONG!
THE SCIENTISTS IN THE ZOD LAB, THEY'RE ALL TRYING TO...
THKKKK
KILL!!!

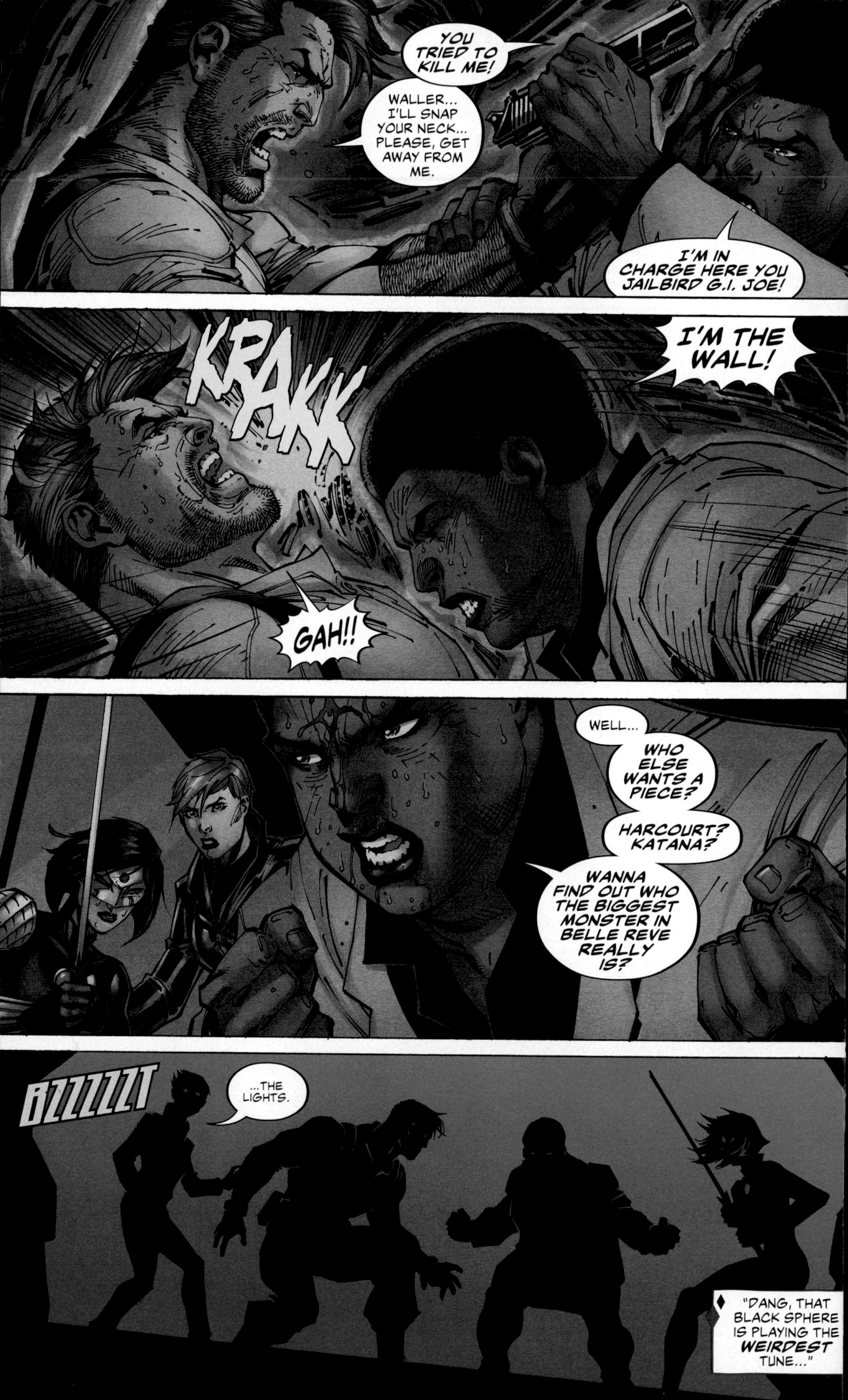
YOU TRIED TO KILL ME!
WALLER... I'LL SNAP YOUR NECK... PLEASE, GET AWAY FROM ME.
I'M IN CHARGE HERE YOU JAILBIRD G.I. JOE!
KRAKK
I'M THE WALL!
GAH!!
WELL...
WHO ELSE WANTS A PIECE?
HARCOURT? KATANA?
WANNA FIND OUT WHO THE BIGGEST MONSTER IN BELLE REVE REALLY IS?
BZZZZZT
...THE LIGHTS.
"DANG, THAT BLACK SPHERE IS PLAYING THE WEIRDEST TUNE..."

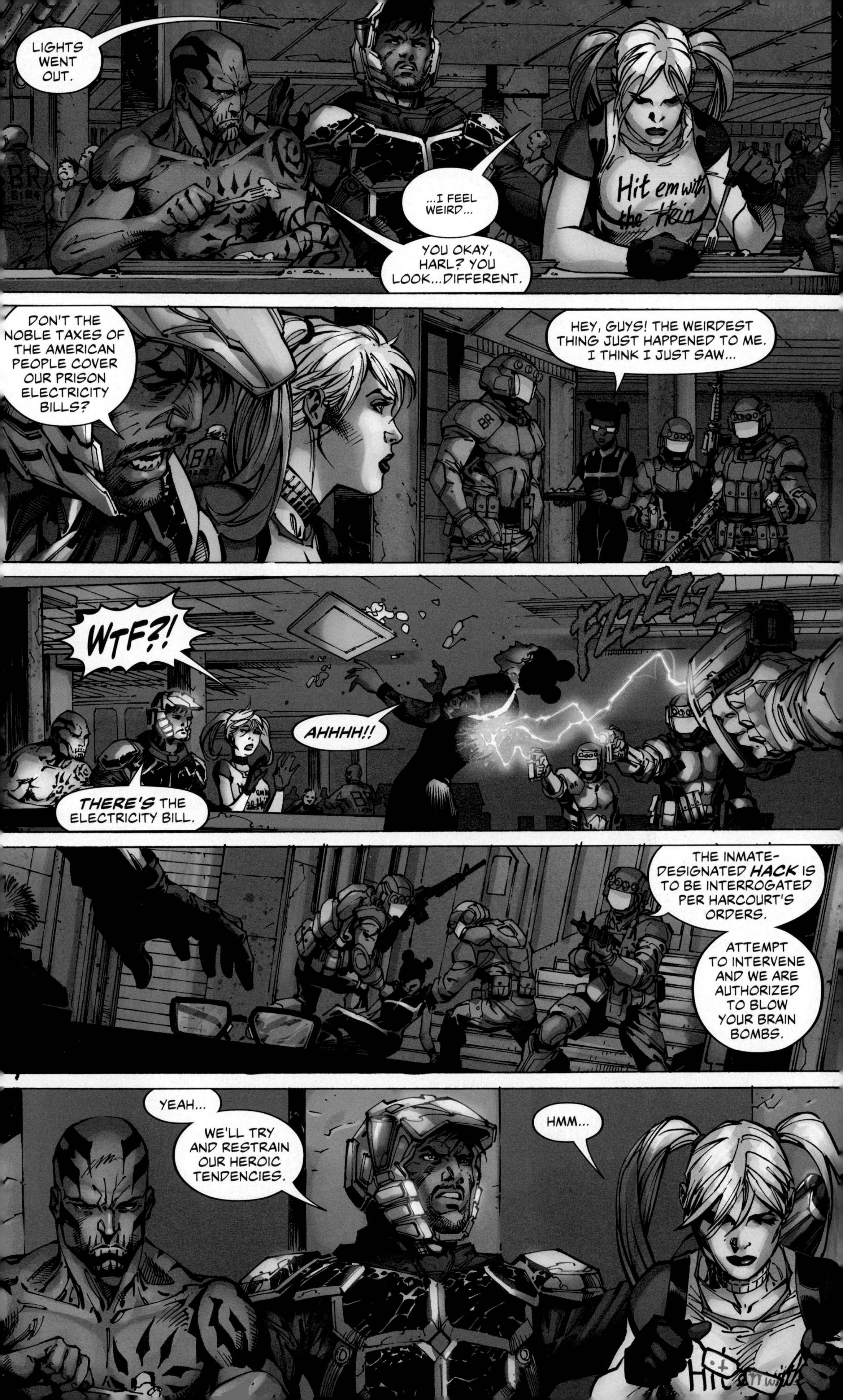
LIGHTS WENT OUT.
...I FEEL WEIRD...
YOU OKAY, HARL? YOU LOOK...DIFFERENT.
DON'T THE NOBLE TAXES OF THE AMERICAN PEOPLE COVER OUR PRISON ELECTRICITY BILLS?
HEY, GUYS! THE WEIRDEST THING JUST HAPPENED TO ME. I THINK I JUST SAW...
WTF?!
FZZZZZ
AHHHH!!
THERE'S THE ELECTRICITY BILL.
THE INMATE-DESIGNATED HACK IS TO BE INTERROGATED PER HARCOURT'S ORDERS.
ATTEMPT TO INTERVENE AND WE ARE AUTHORIZED TO BLOW YOUR BRAIN BOMBS.
YEAH...
WE'LL TRY AND RESTRAIN OUR HEROIC TENDENCIES.
HMM...

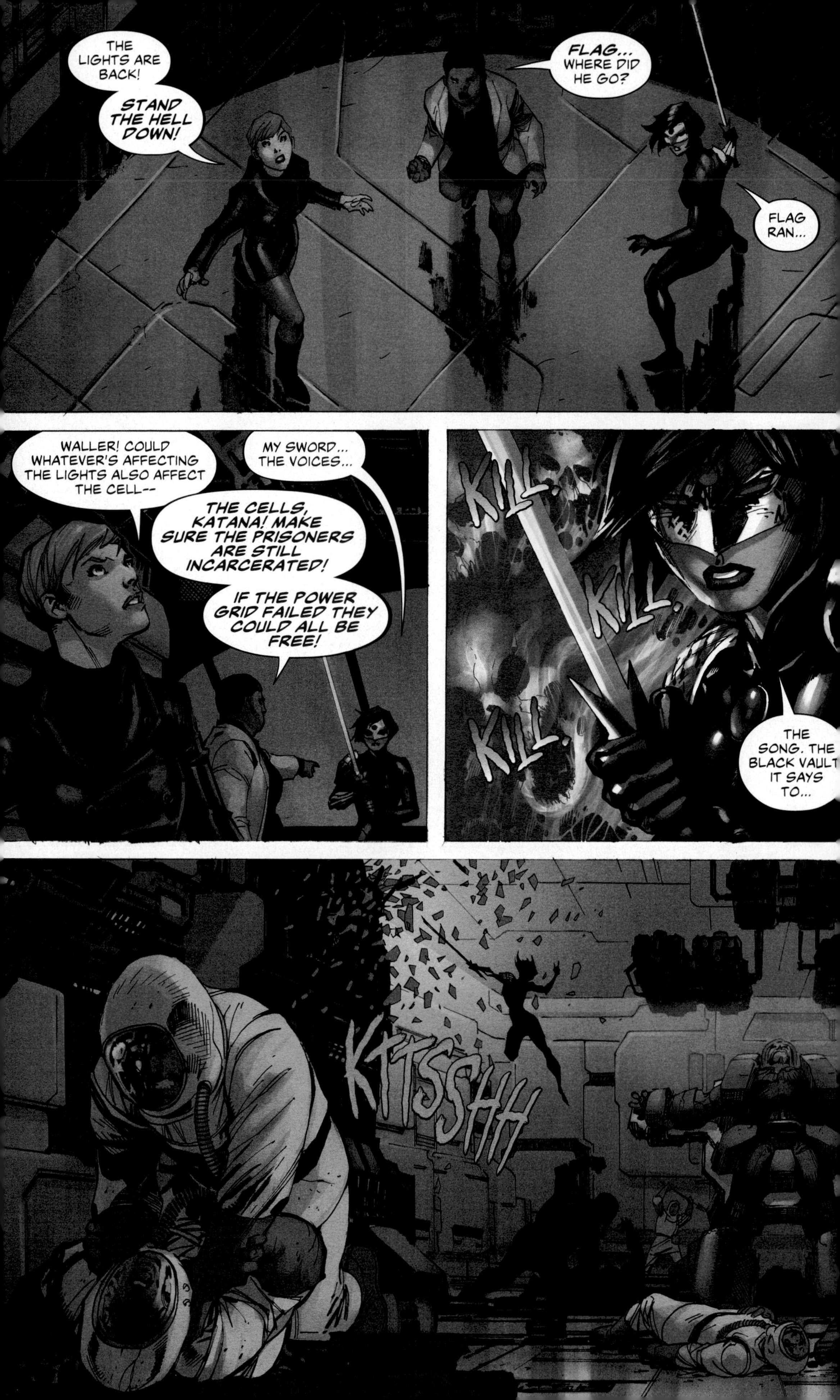
THE LIGHTS ARE BACK!
STAND THE HELL DOWN!
FLAG... WHERE DID HE GO?
FLAG RAN...
WALLER! COULD WHATEVER'S AFFECTING THE LIGHTS ALSO AFFECT THE CELL--
MY SWORD... THE VOICES...
THE CELLS, KATANA! MAKE SURE THE PRISONERS ARE STILL INCARCERATED!
IF THE POWER GRID FAILED THEY COULD ALL BE FREE!
KILL.
KILL.
KILL.
THE SONG. THE BLACK VAULT IT SAYS TO...
KTTSSHH

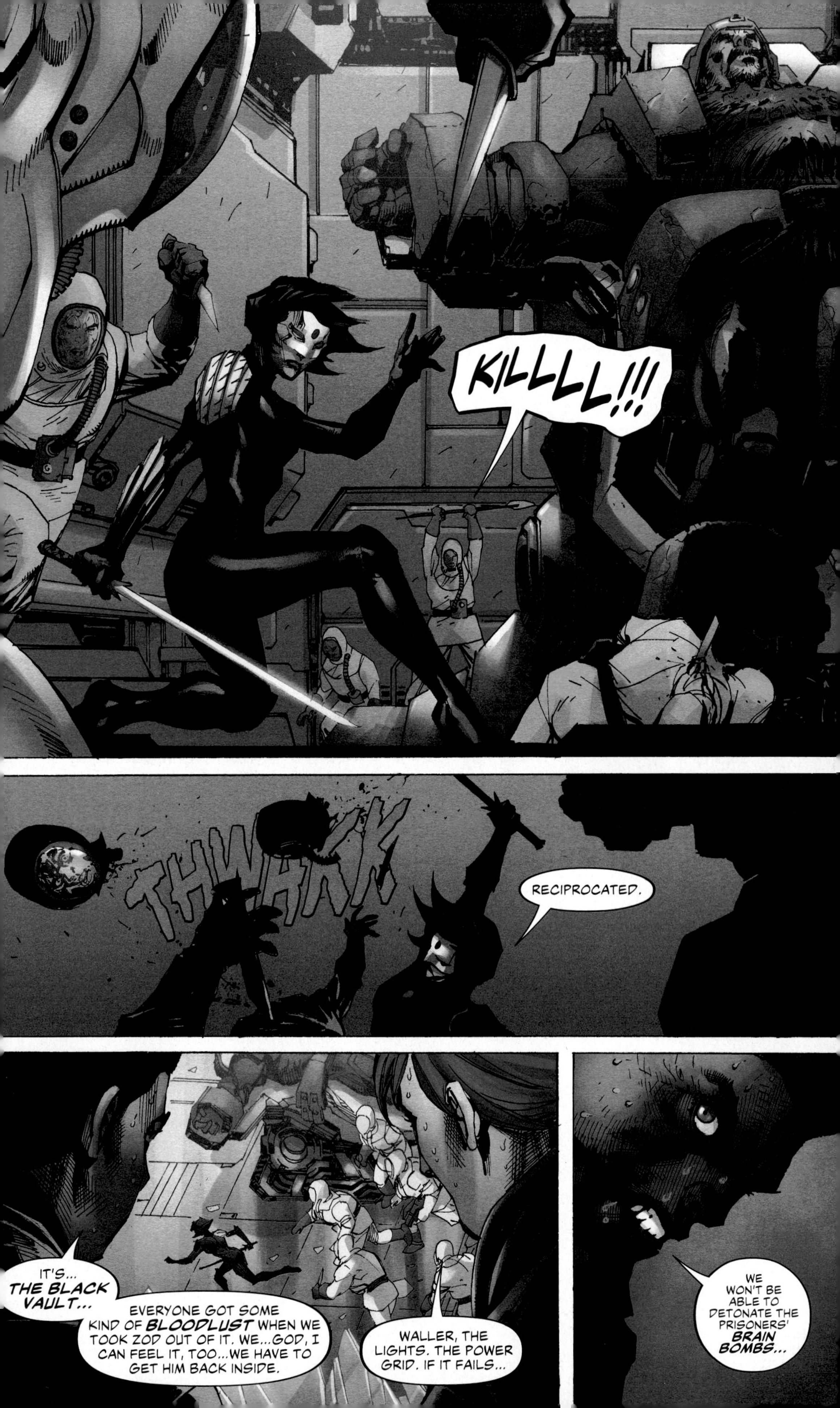
KILLLL!!!
THWAK
RECIPROCATED.
IT'S... THE BLACK VAULT...
EVERYONE GOT SOME KIND OF BLOODLUST WHEN WE TOOK ZOD OUT OF IT. WE...GOD, I CAN FEEL IT, TOO...WE HAVE TO GET HIM BACK INSIDE.
WALLER, THE LIGHTS. THE POWER GRID. IF IT FAILS...
WE WON'T BE ABLE TO DETONATE THE PRISONERS' BRAIN BOMBS...

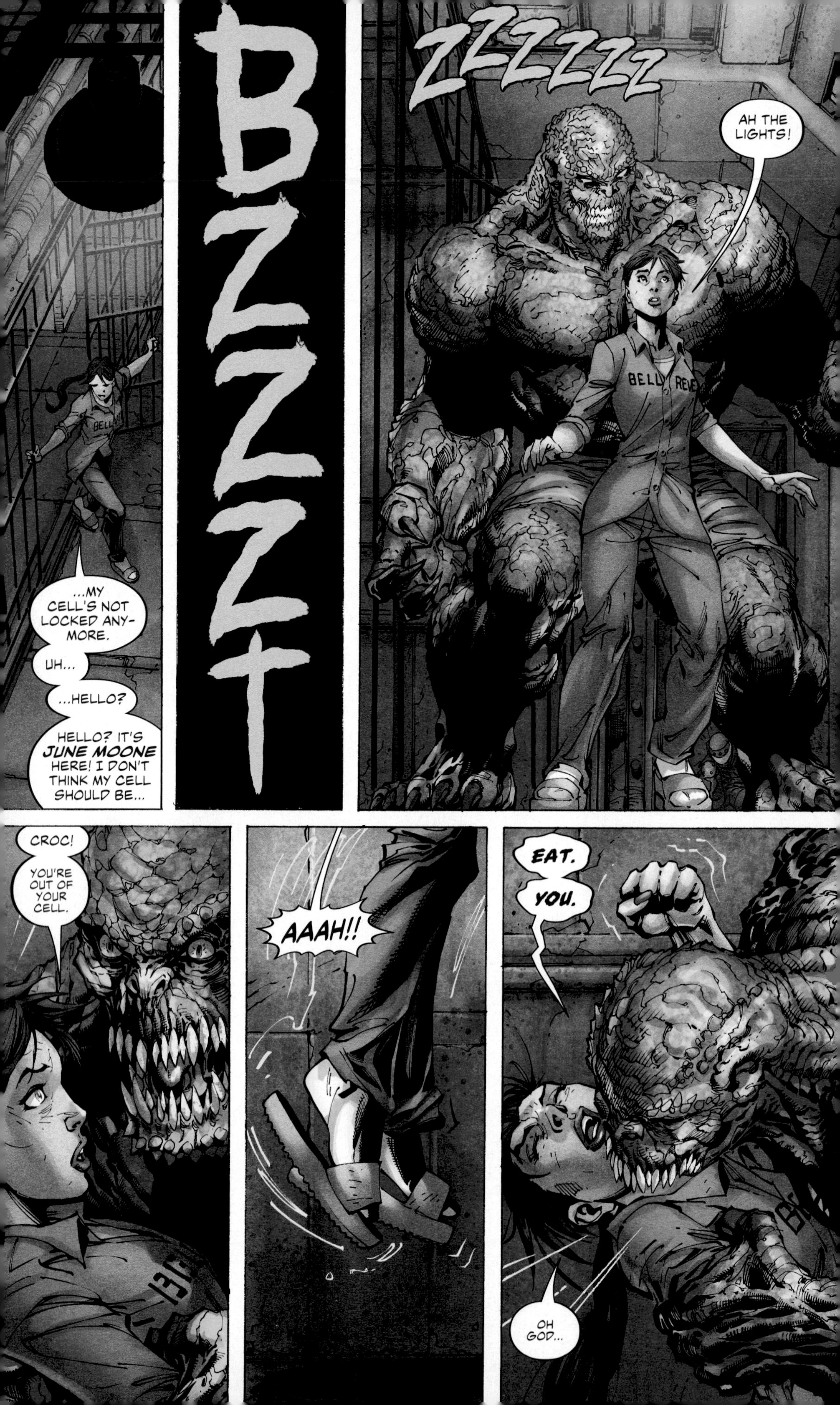
...MY CELL'S NOT LOCKED ANY-MORE.
UH...
...HELLO?
HELLO? IT'S JUNE MOONE HERE! I DON'T THINK MY CELL SHOULD BE...
BZZZZT
ZZZZZZZ
AH THE LIGHTS!
BELLE REVE
CROC!
YOU'RE OUT OF YOUR CELL.
AAAH!!
EAT.
YOU.
OH GOD...

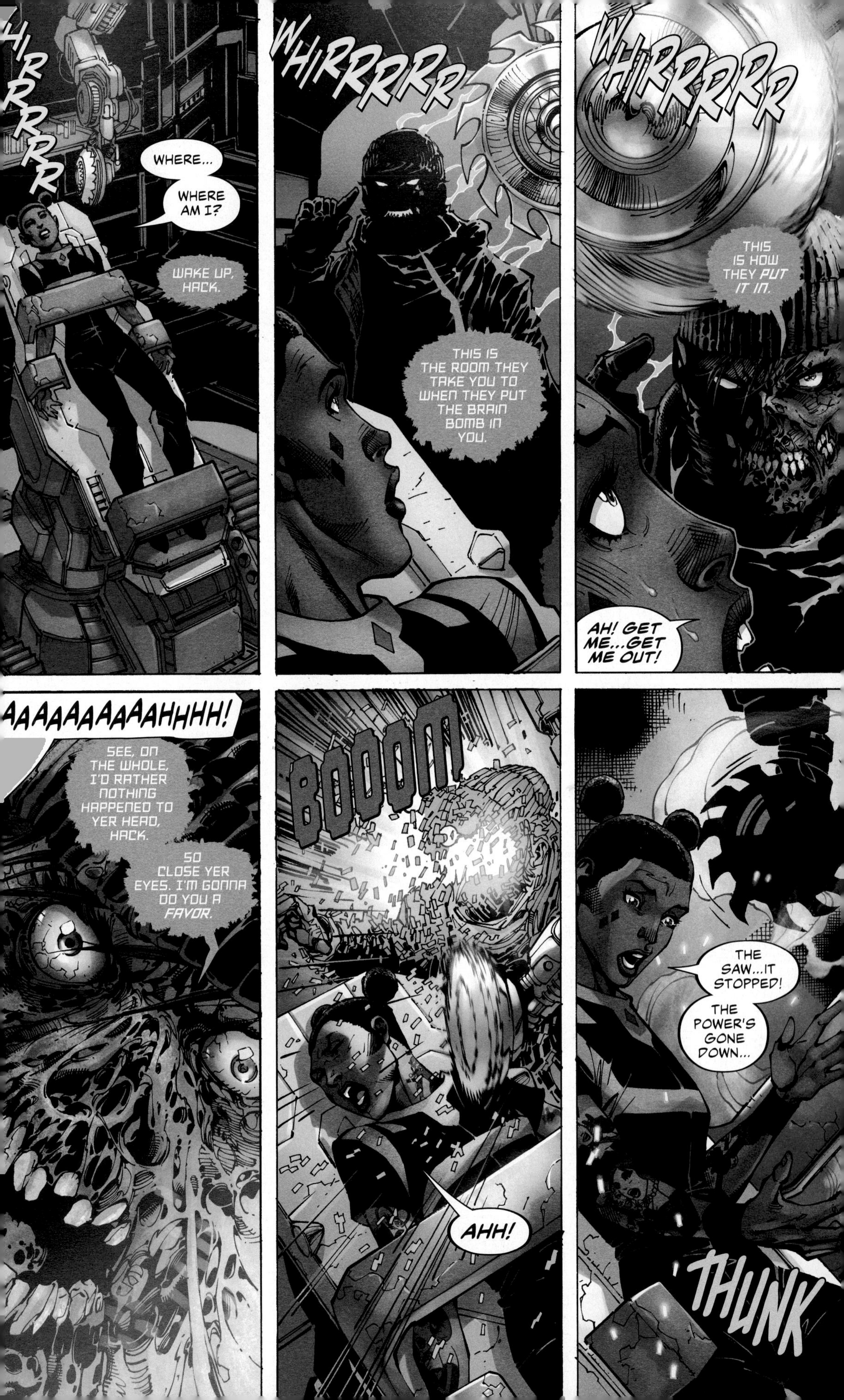
WHIRRRRR
WHERE...
WHERE AM I?
WAKE UP, HACK.
WHIRRRRRR
THIS IS THE ROOM THEY TAKE YOU TO WHEN THEY PUT THE BRAIN BOMB IN YOU.
WHIRRRRRR
THIS IS HOW THEY *PUT IT IN.*
AH! GET ME...GET ME OUT!
AAAAAAAAAAHHHH!
SEE, ON THE WHOLE, I'D RATHER NOTHING HAPPENED TO YER HEAD, HACK.
SO CLOSE YER EYES. I'M GONNA DO YOU A *FAVOR.*
BOOOM
AHH!
THE SAW...IT STOPPED!
THE POWER'S GONE DOWN...
THUNK

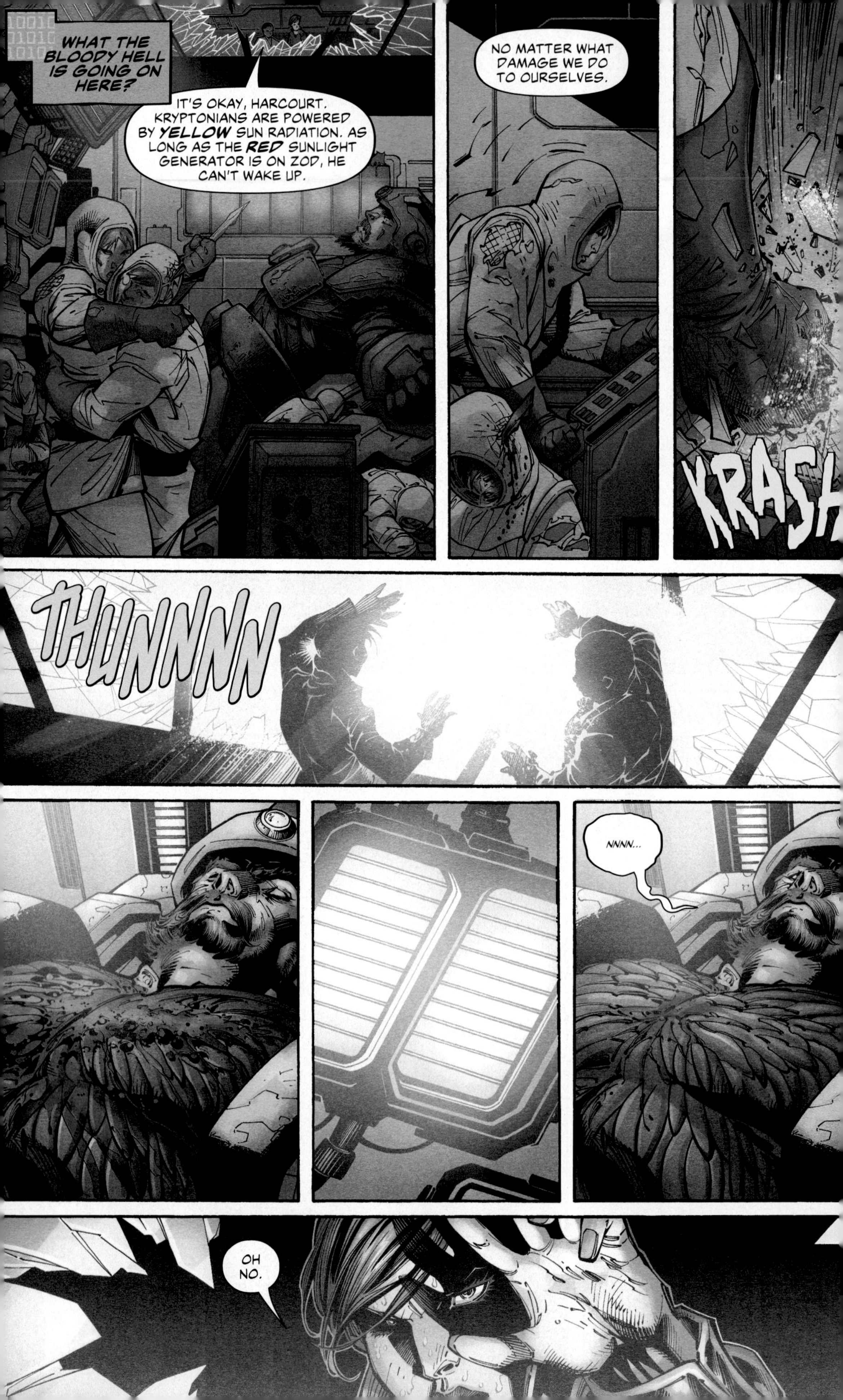

WHAT THE BLOODY HELL IS GOING ON HERE?
IT'S OKAY, HARCOURT. KRYPTONIANS ARE POWERED BY YELLOW SUN RADIATION. AS LONG AS THE RED SUNLIGHT GENERATOR IS ON ZOD, HE CAN'T WAKE UP.
NO MATTER WHAT DAMAGE WE DO TO OURSELVES.
KRASH
THUNNNNN
NNNN...
OH NO.

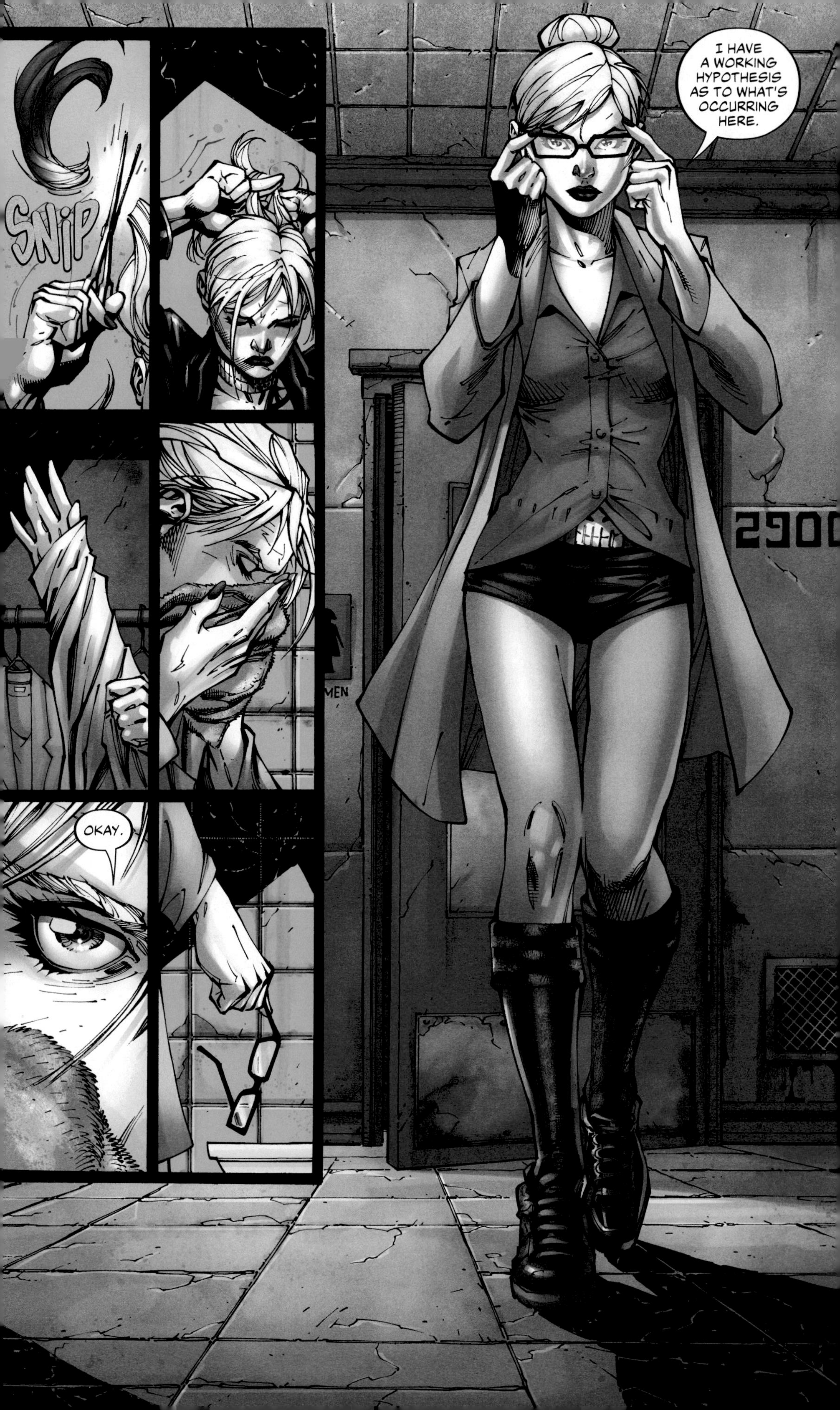
SNIP
OKAY.
I HAVE A WORKING HYPOTHESIS AS TO WHAT'S OCCURRING HERE.
2900
MEN

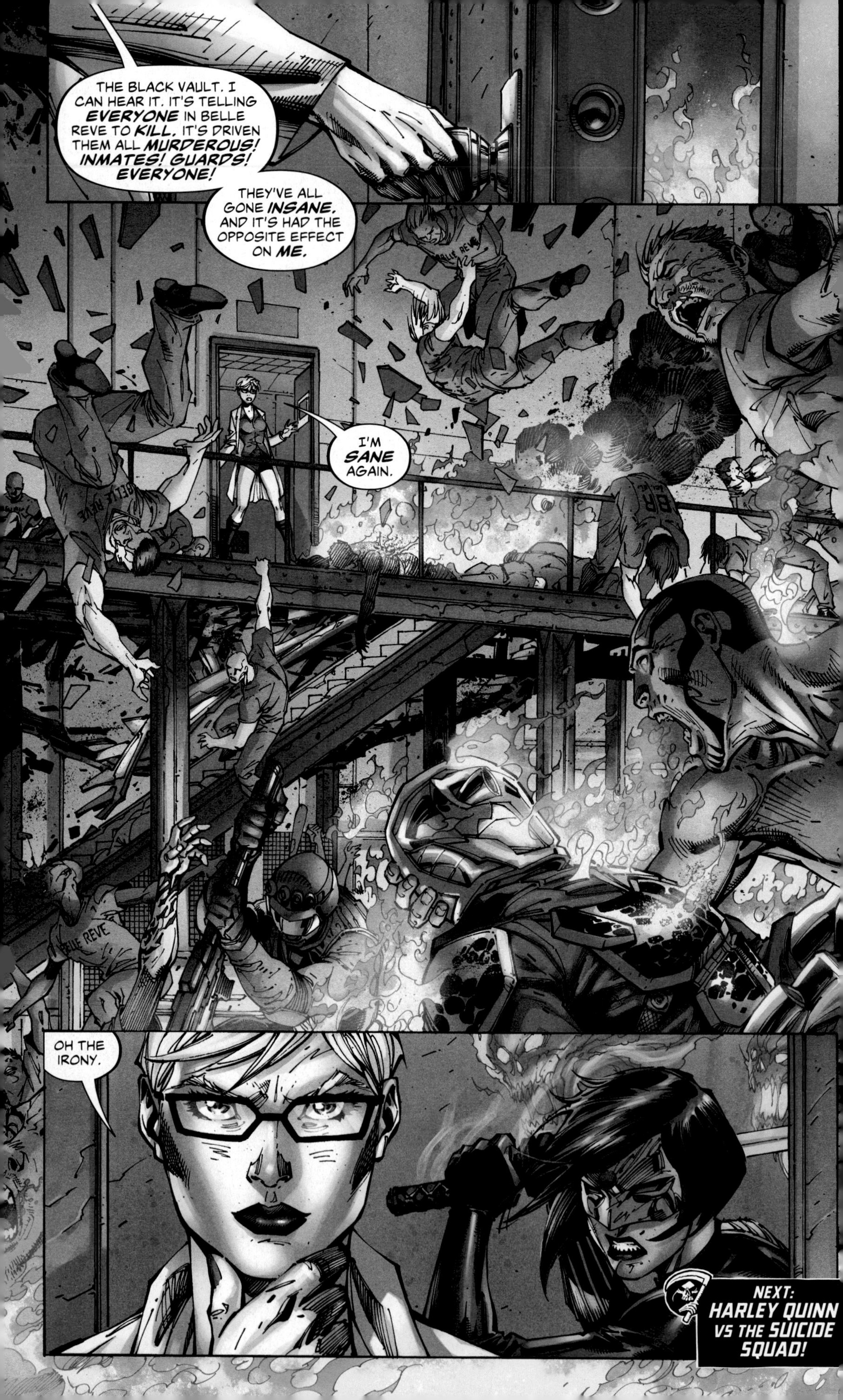
THE BLACK VAULT. I CAN HEAR IT. IT'S TELLING **EVERYONE** IN BELLE REVE TO **KILL.** IT'S DRIVEN THEM ALL **MURDEROUS! INMATES! GUARDS! EVERYONE!**
THEY'VE ALL GONE **INSANE.** AND IT'S HAD THE OPPOSITE EFFECT ON **ME.**
I'M **SANE** AGAIN.
OH THE IRONY.
NEXT: HARLEY QUINN VS THE SUICIDE SQUAD!

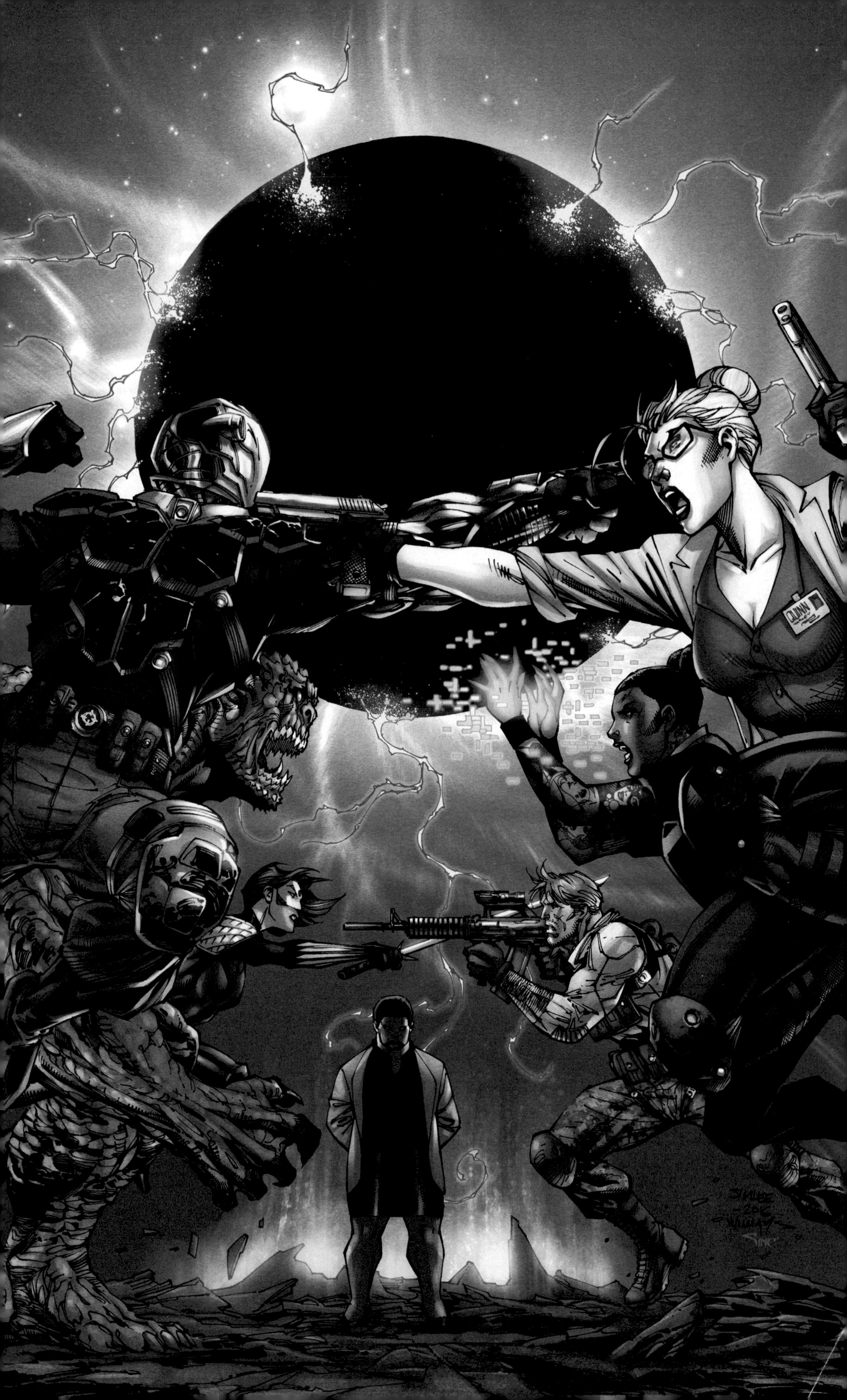
QUINN

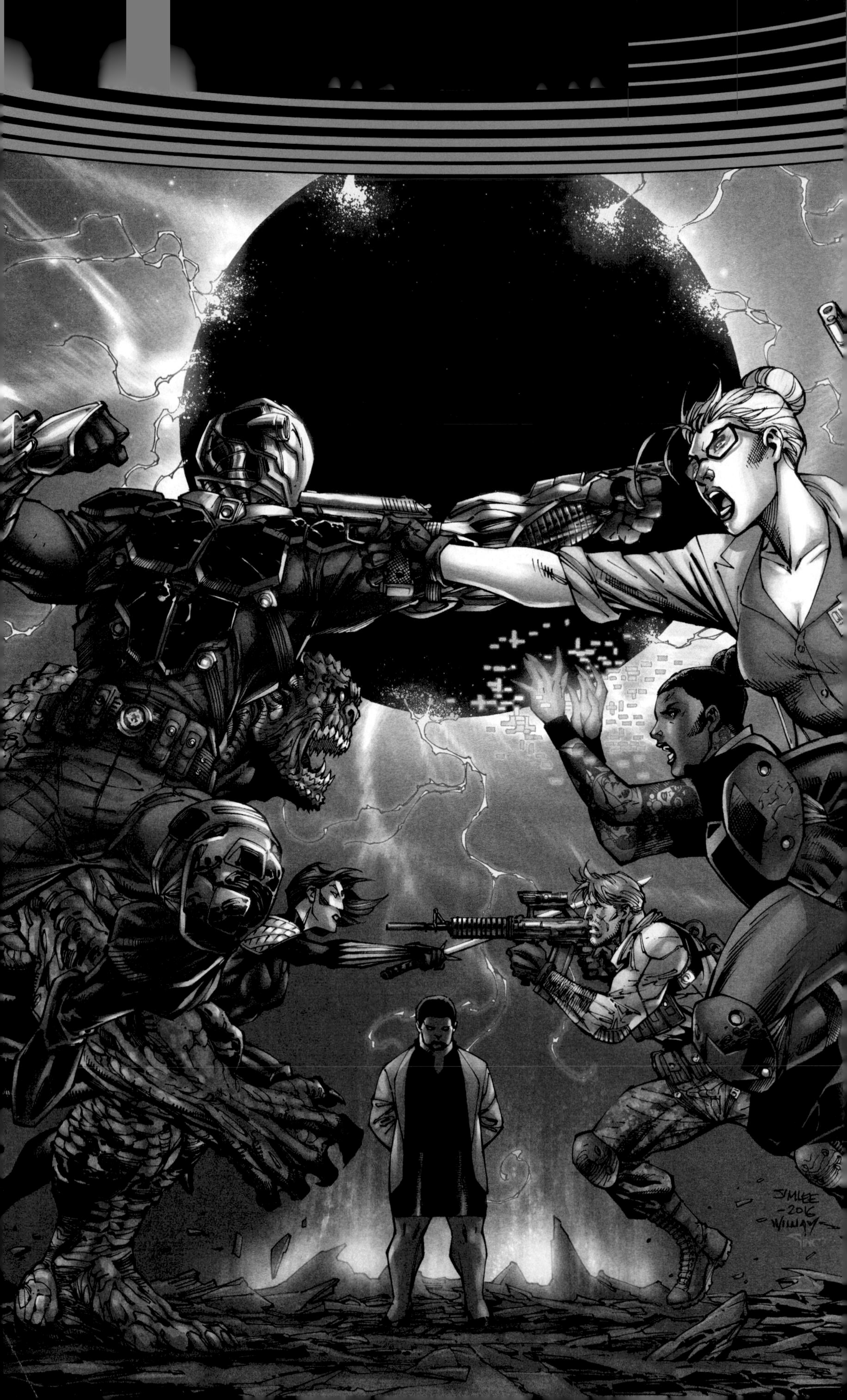

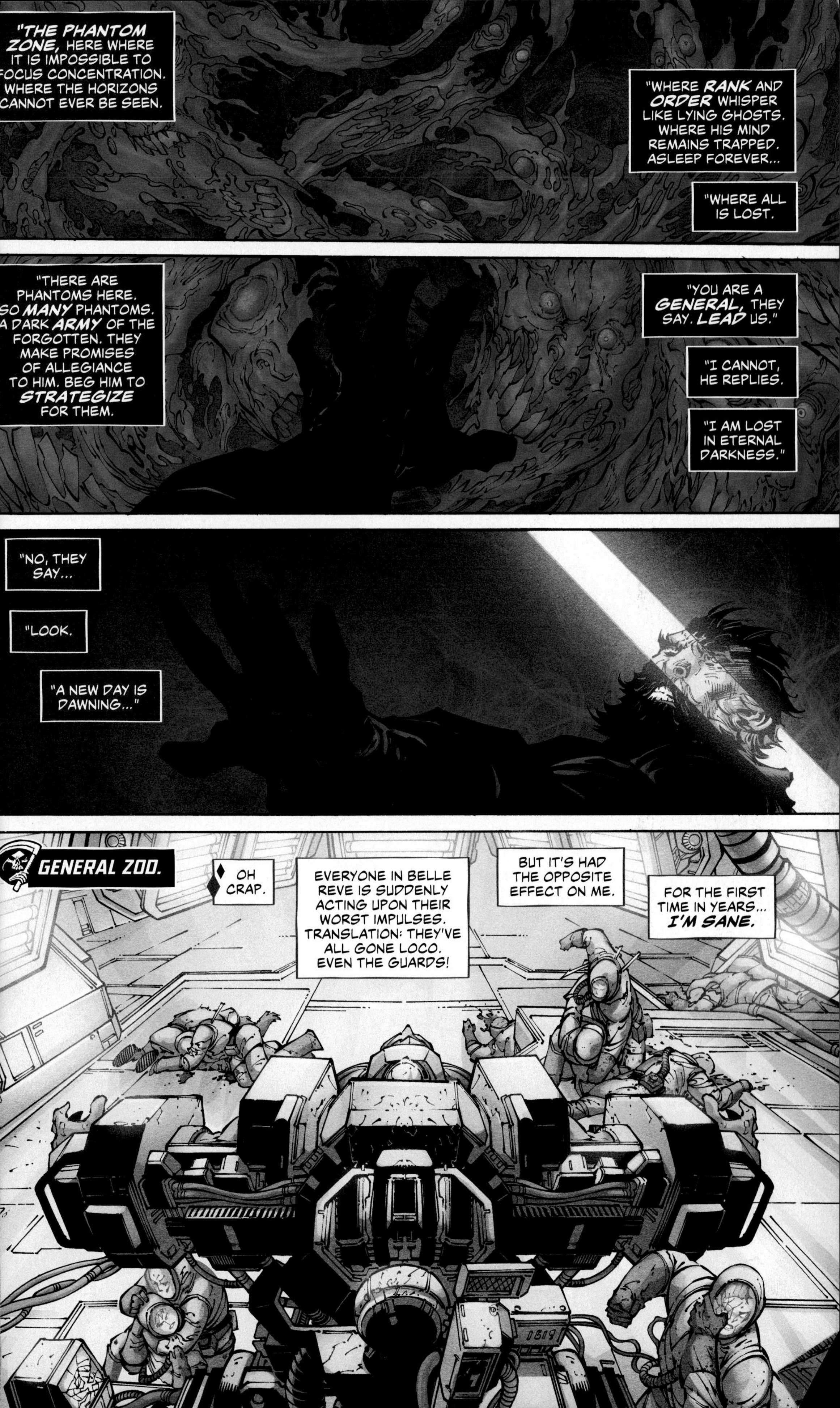

"THE PHANTOM ZONE, HERE WHERE IT IS IMPOSSIBLE TO FOCUS CONCENTRATION. WHERE THE HORIZONS CANNOT EVER BE SEEN.
"WHERE RANK AND ORDER WHISPER LIKE LYING GHOSTS. WHERE HIS MIND REMAINS TRAPPED. ASLEEP FOREVER...
"WHERE ALL IS LOST.
"THERE ARE PHANTOMS HERE. SO MANY PHANTOMS. A DARK ARMY OF THE FORGOTTEN. THEY MAKE PROMISES OF ALLEGIANCE TO HIM. BEG HIM TO STRATEGIZE FOR THEM.
"YOU ARE A GENERAL, THEY SAY. LEAD US."
"I CANNOT, HE REPLIES.
"I AM LOST IN ETERNAL DARKNESS."
"NO, THEY SAY...
"LOOK.
"A NEW DAY IS DAWNING..."
GENERAL ZOD.
OH CRAP.
EVERYONE IN BELLE REVE IS SUDDENLY ACTING UPON THEIR WORST IMPULSES. TRANSLATION: THEY'VE ALL GONE LOCO. EVEN THE GUARDS!
BUT IT'S HAD THE OPPOSITE EFFECT ON ME.
FOR THE FIRST TIME IN YEARS... I'M SANE.

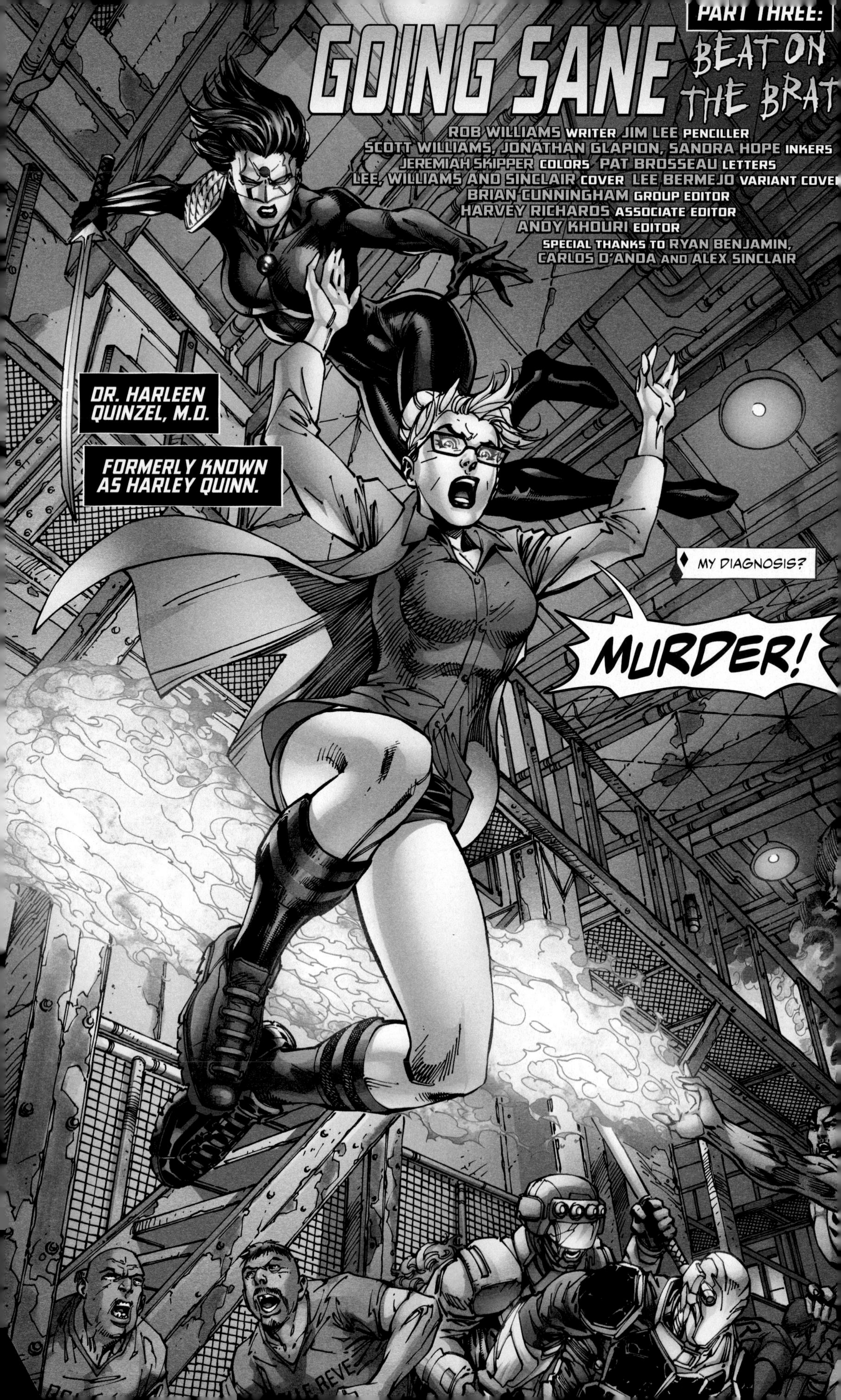
PART THREE:
GOING SANE
BEAT ON THE BRAT
ROB WILLIAMS WRITER JIM LEE PENCILLER
SCOTT WILLIAMS, JONATHAN GLAPION, SANDRA HOPE INKERS
JEREMIAH SKIPPER COLORS PAT BROSSEAU LETTERS
LEE, WILLIAMS AND SINCLAIR COVER LEE BERMEJO VARIANT COVE
BRIAN CUNNINGHAM GROUP EDITOR
HARVEY RICHARDS ASSOCIATE EDITOR
ANDY KHOURI EDITOR
SPECIAL THANKS TO RYAN BENJAMIN, CARLOS D'ANDA AND ALEX SINCLAIR
DR. HARLEEN QUINZEL, M.D.
FORMERLY KNOWN AS HARLEY QUINN.
MY DIAGNOSIS?
MURDER!

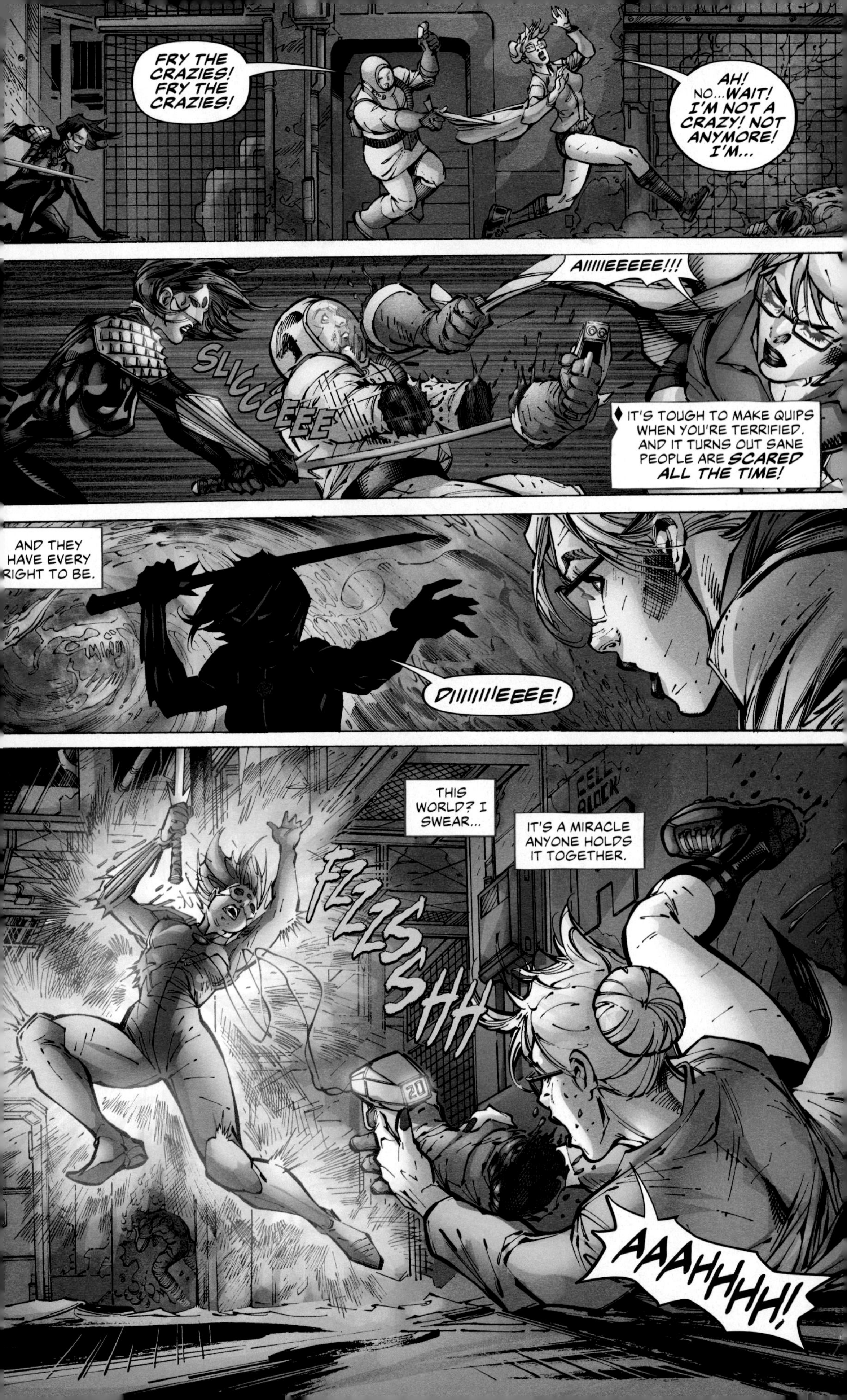
FRY THE CRAZIES! FRY THE CRAZIES!
AH! NO...WAIT! I'M NOT A CRAZY! NOT ANYMORE! I'M...
AIIIIEEEEE!!!
SLICCCEEEE
IT'S TOUGH TO MAKE QUIPS WHEN YOU'RE TERRIFIED. AND IT TURNS OUT SANE PEOPLE ARE SCARED ALL THE TIME!
AND THEY HAVE EVERY RIGHT TO BE.
DIIIIIIIEEEE!
THIS WORLD? I SWEAR...
IT'S A MIRACLE ANYONE HOLDS IT TOGETHER.
FZZZSSHH
AAAHHHH!

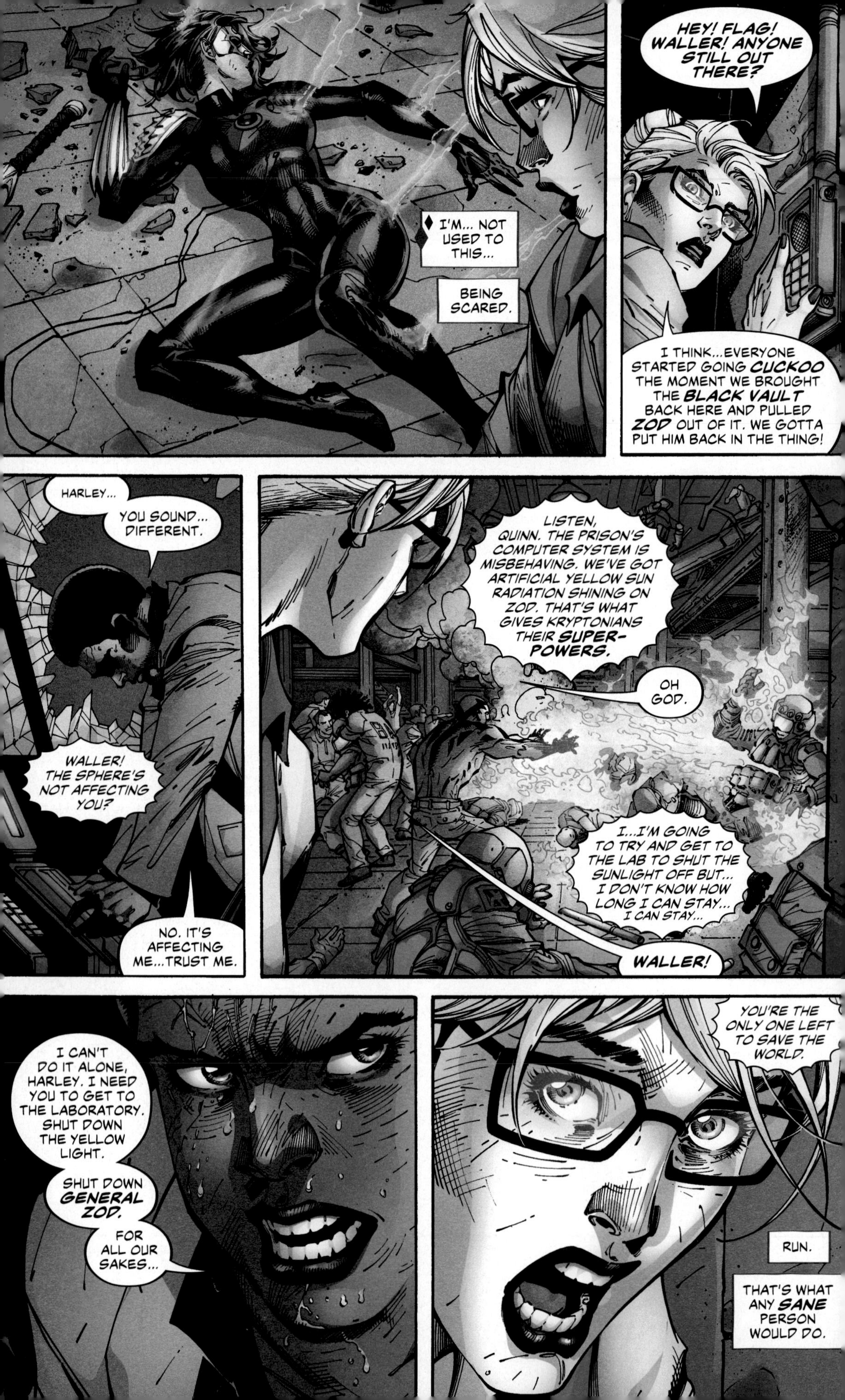

I'M... NOT USED TO THIS...
BEING SCARED.
HEY! FLAG! WALLER! ANYONE STILL OUT THERE?
I THINK...EVERYONE STARTED GOING CUCKOO THE MOMENT WE BROUGHT THE BLACK VAULT BACK HERE AND PULLED ZOD OUT OF IT. WE GOTTA PUT HIM BACK IN THE THING!
HARLEY...
YOU SOUND... DIFFERENT.
WALLER! THE SPHERE'S NOT AFFECTING YOU?
NO. IT'S AFFECTING ME...TRUST ME.
LISTEN, QUINN. THE PRISON'S COMPUTER SYSTEM IS MISBEHAVING. WE'VE GOT ARTIFICIAL YELLOW SUN RADIATION SHINING ON ZOD. THAT'S WHAT GIVES KRYPTONIANS THEIR SUPER-POWERS.
OH GOD.
I...I'M GOING TO TRY AND GET TO THE LAB TO SHUT THE SUNLIGHT OFF BUT... I DON'T KNOW HOW LONG I CAN STAY... I CAN STAY...
WALLER!
I CAN'T DO IT ALONE, HARLEY. I NEED YOU TO GET TO THE LABORATORY. SHUT DOWN THE YELLOW LIGHT.
SHUT DOWN GENERAL ZOD.
FOR ALL OUR SAKES...
YOU'RE THE ONLY ONE LEFT TO SAVE THE WORLD.
RUN.
THAT'S WHAT ANY SANE PERSON WOULD DO.

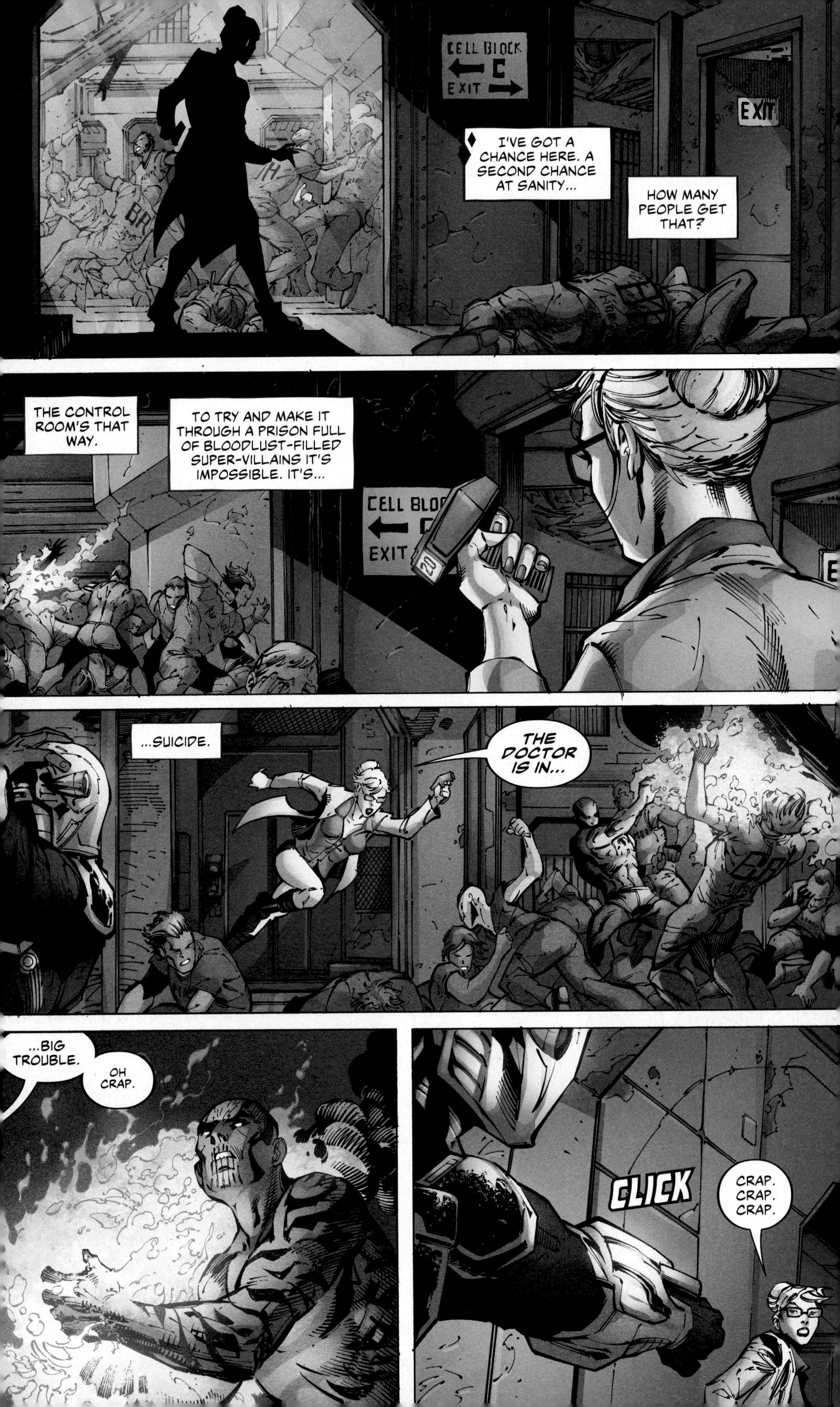
CELL BLOCK C
EXIT
EXIT
I'VE GOT A CHANCE HERE. A SECOND CHANCE AT SANITY...
HOW MANY PEOPLE GET THAT?
THE CONTROL ROOM'S THAT WAY.
TO TRY AND MAKE IT THROUGH A PRISON FULL OF BLOODLUST-FILLED SUPER-VILLAINS IT'S IMPOSSIBLE. IT'S...
...SUICIDE.
THE DOCTOR IS IN...
...BIG TROUBLE.
OH CRAP.
CLICK
CRAP. CRAP. CRAP.

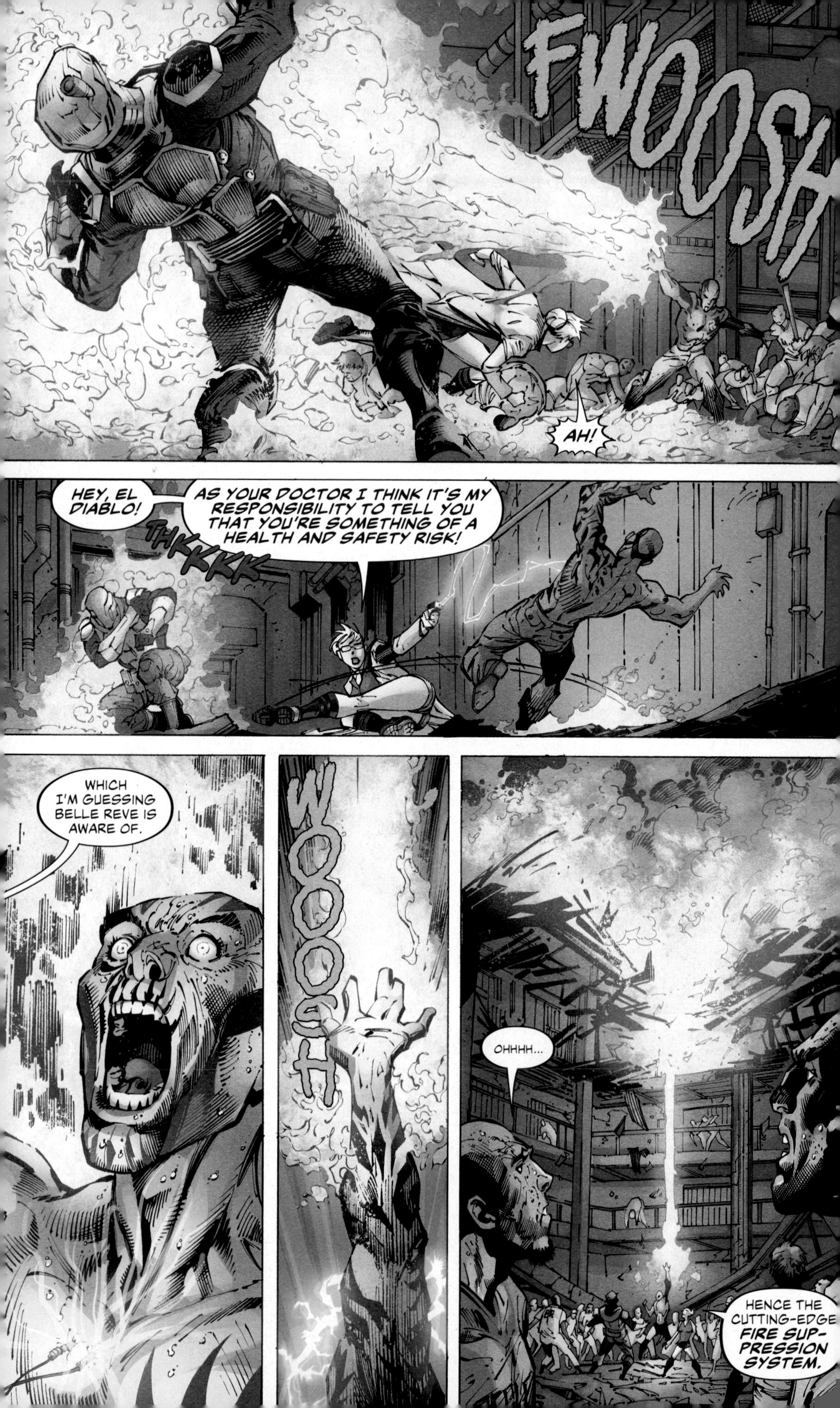

FWOOSH
AH!
HEY, EL DIABLO!
AS YOUR DOCTOR I THINK IT'S MY RESPONSIBILITY TO TELL YOU THAT YOU'RE SOMETHING OF A HEALTH AND SAFETY RISK!
THKKKK
WHICH I'M GUESSING BELLE REVE IS AWARE OF.
WOOOOSH
OHHHH...
HENCE THE CUTTING-EDGE FIRE SUPPRESSION SYSTEM.

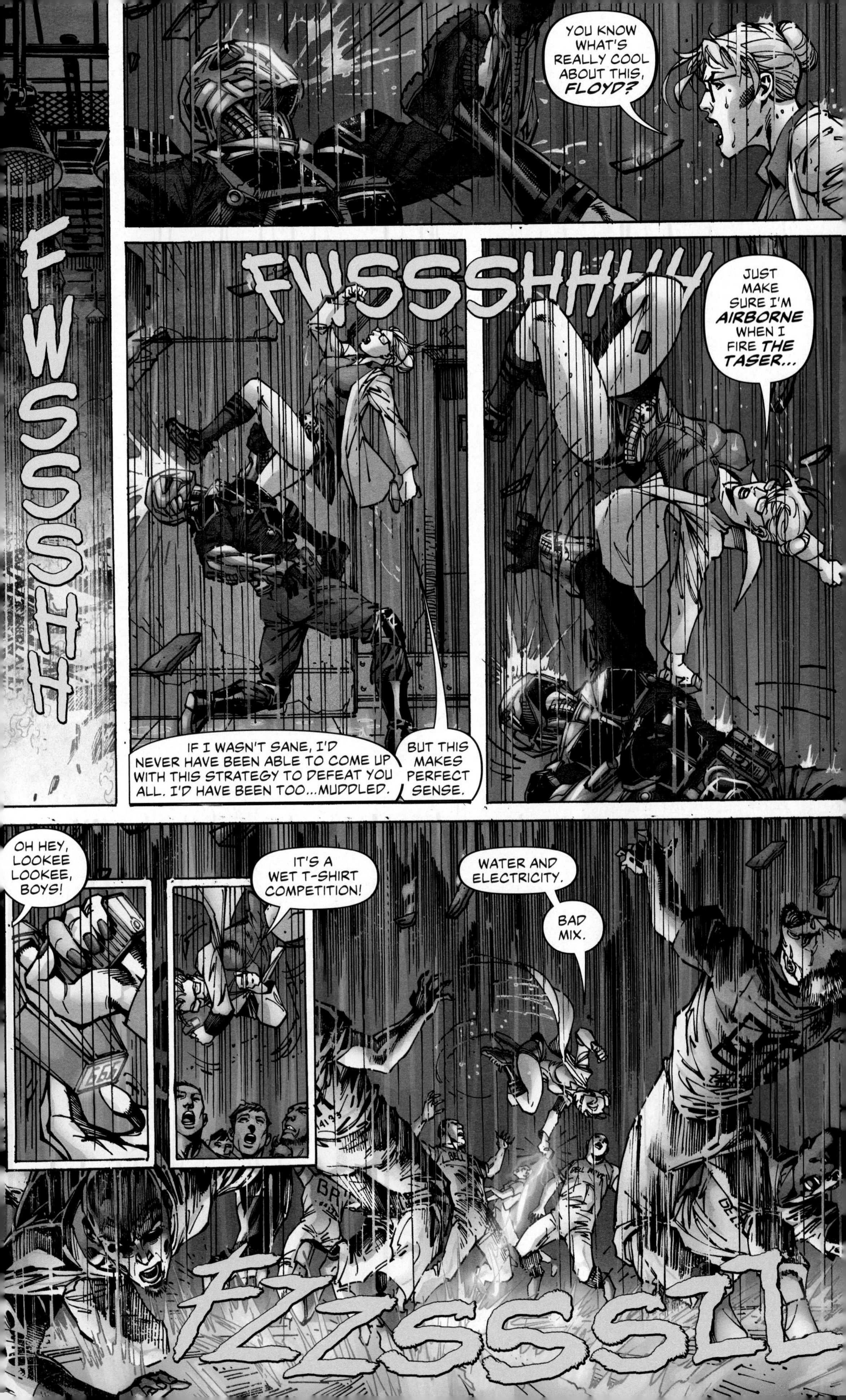
YOU KNOW WHAT'S REALLY COOL ABOUT THIS, FLOYD?
FWSSSHH
FWSSSHHH
JUST MAKE SURE I'M AIRBORNE WHEN I FIRE THE TASER...
IF I WASN'T SANE, I'D NEVER HAVE BEEN ABLE TO COME UP WITH THIS STRATEGY TO DEFEAT YOU ALL. I'D HAVE BEEN TOO...MUDDLED.
BUT THIS MAKES PERFECT SENSE.
OH HEY, LOOKEE LOOKEE, BOYS!
IT'S A WET T-SHIRT COMPETITION!
WATER AND ELECTRICITY.
BAD MIX.
FZZSSZT

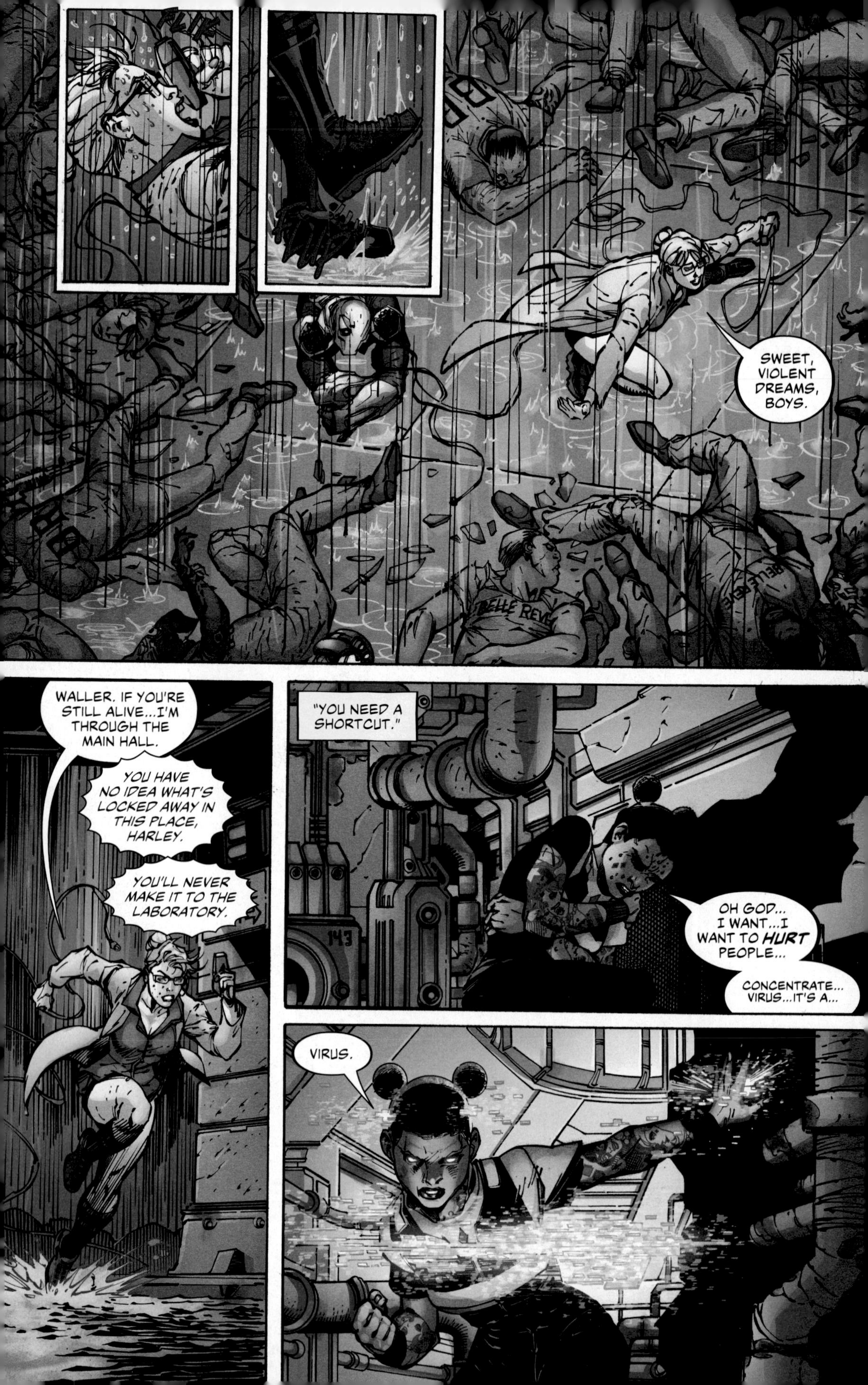
SWEET, VIOLENT DREAMS, BOYS.
WALLER. IF YOU'RE STILL ALIVE...I'M THROUGH THE MAIN HALL.
YOU HAVE NO IDEA WHAT'S LOCKED AWAY IN THIS PLACE, HARLEY.
YOU'LL NEVER MAKE IT TO THE LABORATORY.
"YOU NEED A SHORTCUT."
OH GOD... I WANT...I WANT TO HURT PEOPLE...
CONCENTRATE... VIRUS...IT'S A...
VIRUS.

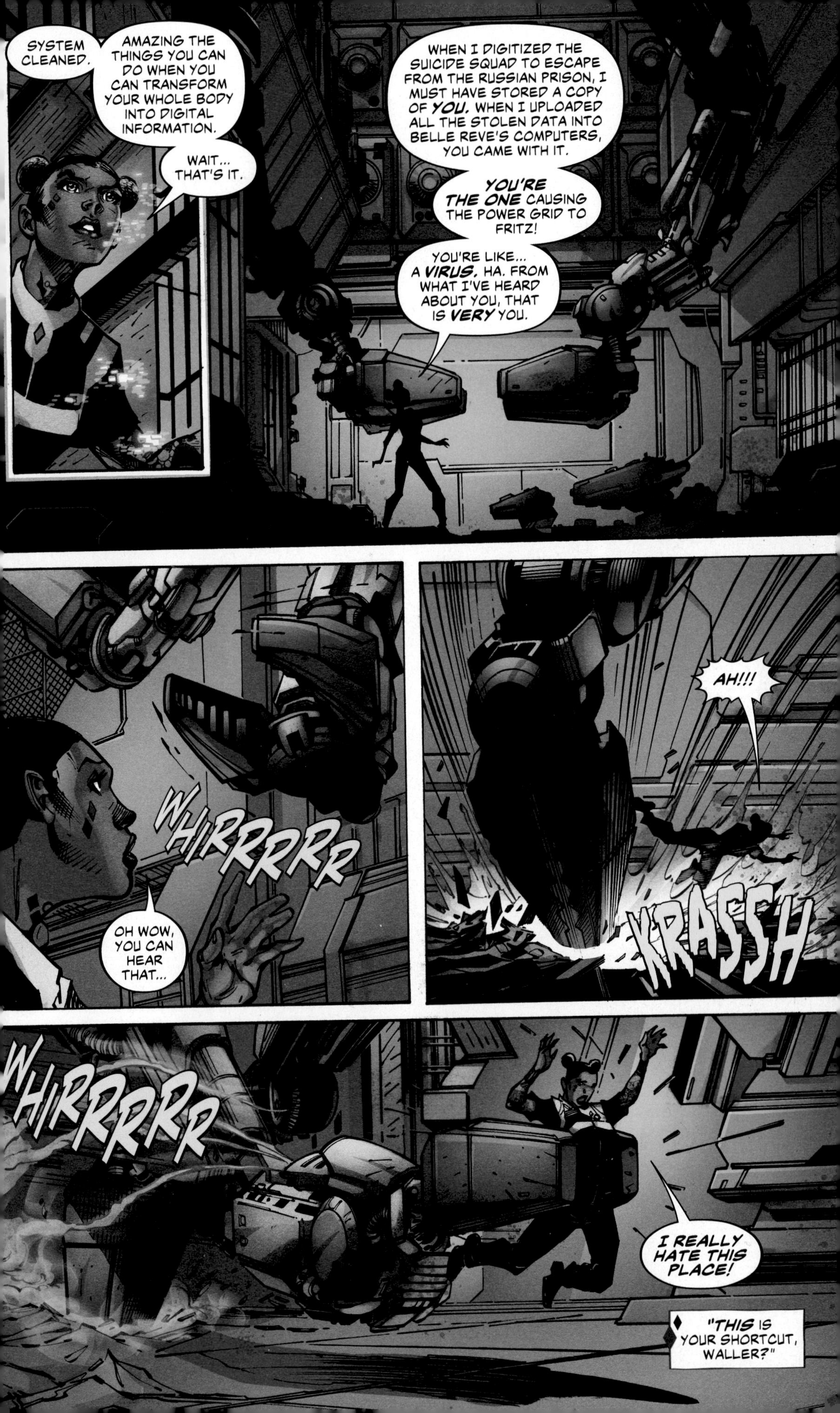
SYSTEM CLEANED.
AMAZING THE THINGS YOU CAN DO WHEN YOU CAN TRANSFORM YOUR WHOLE BODY INTO DIGITAL INFORMATION.
WAIT... THAT'S IT.
WHEN I DIGITIZED THE SUICIDE SQUAD TO ESCAPE FROM THE RUSSIAN PRISON, I MUST HAVE STORED A COPY OF YOU. WHEN I UPLOADED ALL THE STOLEN DATA INTO BELLE REVE'S COMPUTERS, YOU CAME WITH IT.
YOU'RE THE ONE CAUSING THE POWER GRID TO FRITZ!
YOU'RE LIKE... A VIRUS. HA. FROM WHAT I'VE HEARD ABOUT YOU, THAT IS VERY YOU.
WHIRRRRRR
OH WOW, YOU CAN HEAR THAT...
AH!!!
KRASSH
WHIRRRRRR
I REALLY HATE THIS PLACE!
"THIS IS YOUR SHORTCUT, WALLER?"

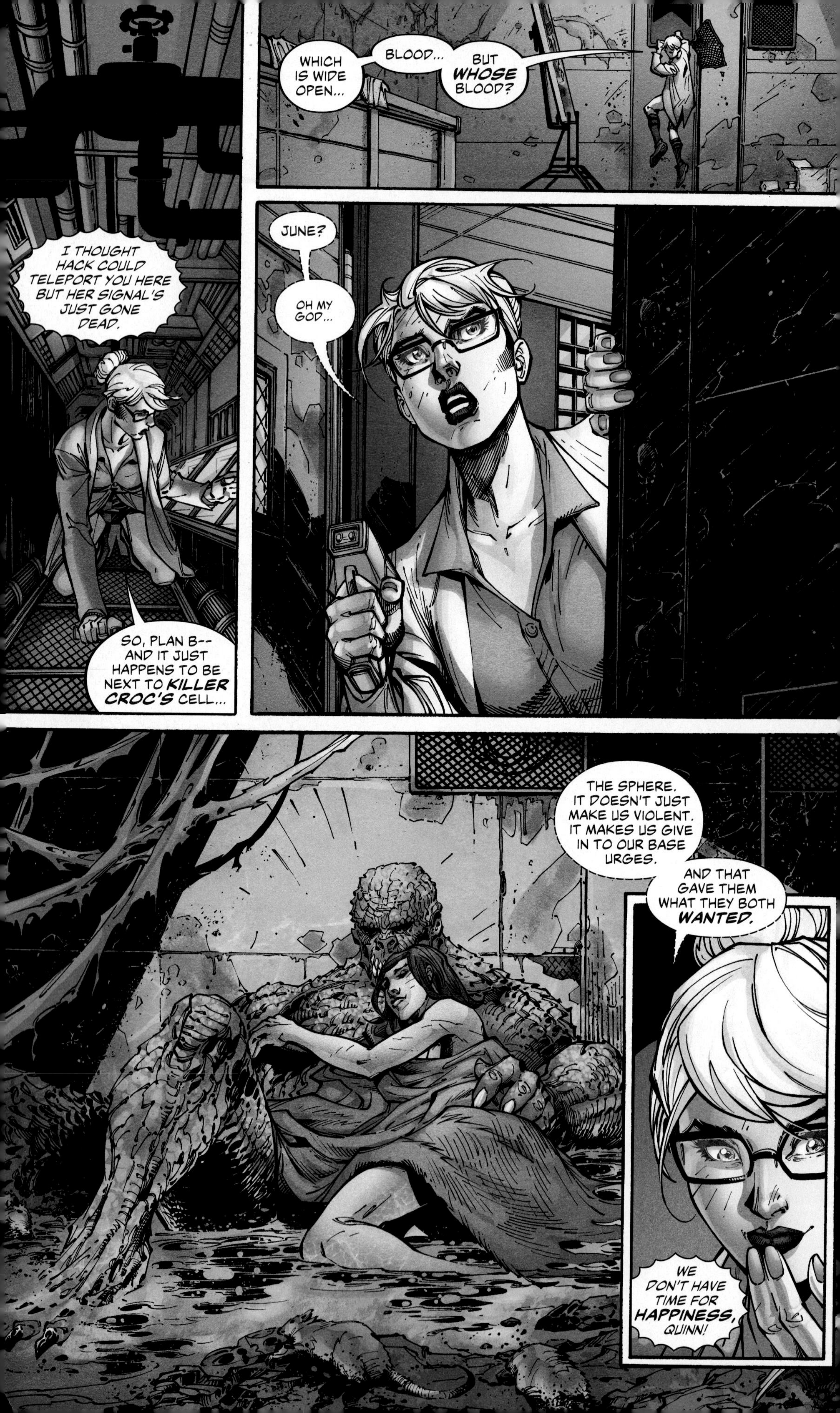
I THOUGHT HACK COULD TELEPORT YOU HERE BUT HER SIGNAL'S JUST GONE DEAD.
SO, PLAN B-- AND IT JUST HAPPENS TO BE NEXT TO KILLER CROC'S CELL...
WHICH IS WIDE OPEN...
BLOOD...
BUT WHOSE BLOOD?
JUNE?
OH MY GOD...
THE SPHERE. IT DOESN'T JUST MAKE US VIOLENT. IT MAKES US GIVE IN TO OUR BASE URGES.
AND THAT GAVE THEM WHAT THEY BOTH WANTED.
WE DON'T HAVE TIME FOR HAPPINESS, QUINN!

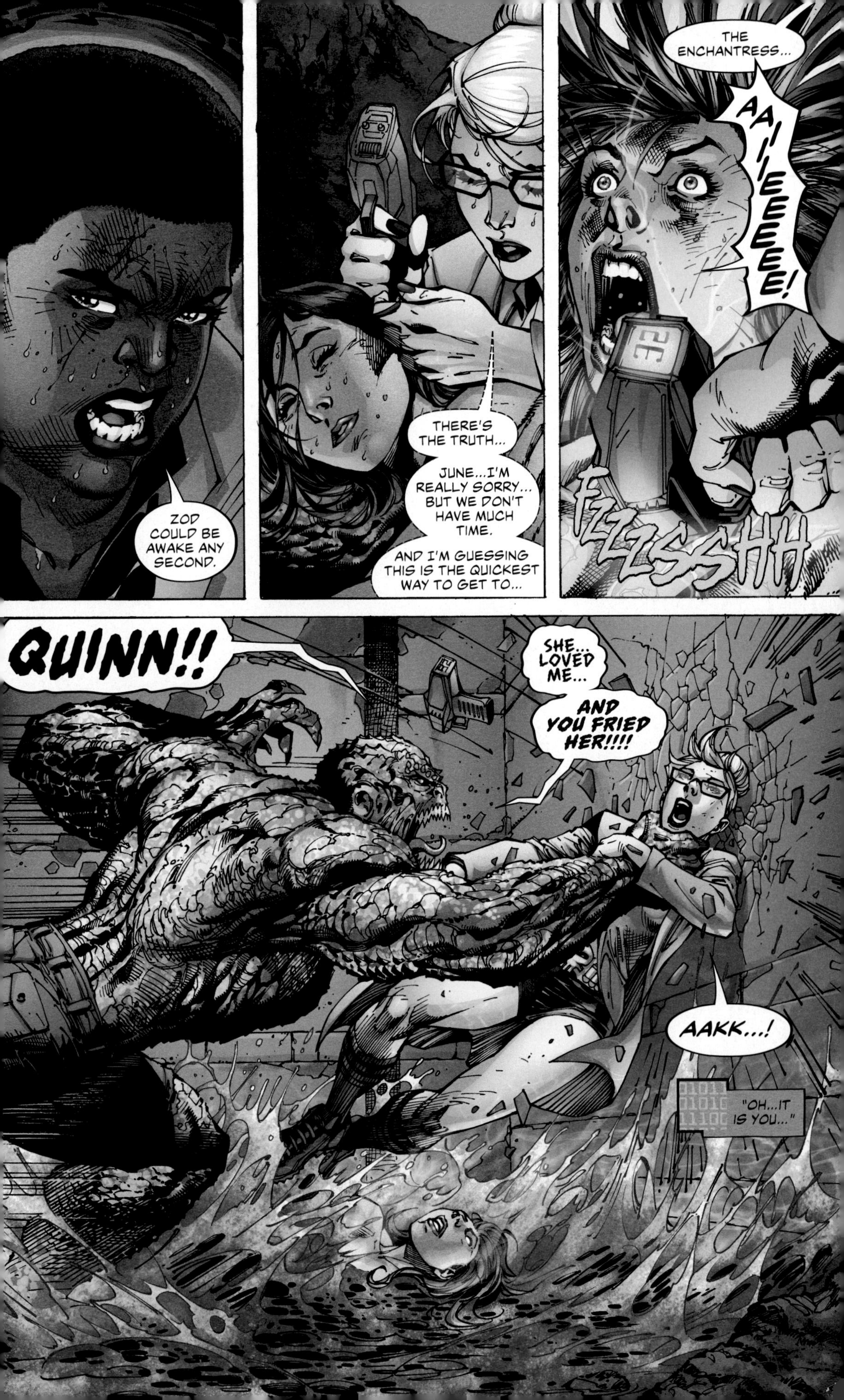
ZOD COULD BE AWAKE ANY SECOND.
THERE'S THE TRUTH...
JUNE...I'M REALLY SORRY... BUT WE DON'T HAVE MUCH TIME.
AND I'M GUESSING THIS IS THE QUICKEST WAY TO GET TO...
THE ENCHANTRESS...
AAIIIEEEEE!
FZZZSSHH
QUINN!!
SHE... LOVED ME...
AND YOU FRIED HER!!!!
AAKK...!
"OH...IT IS YOU..."

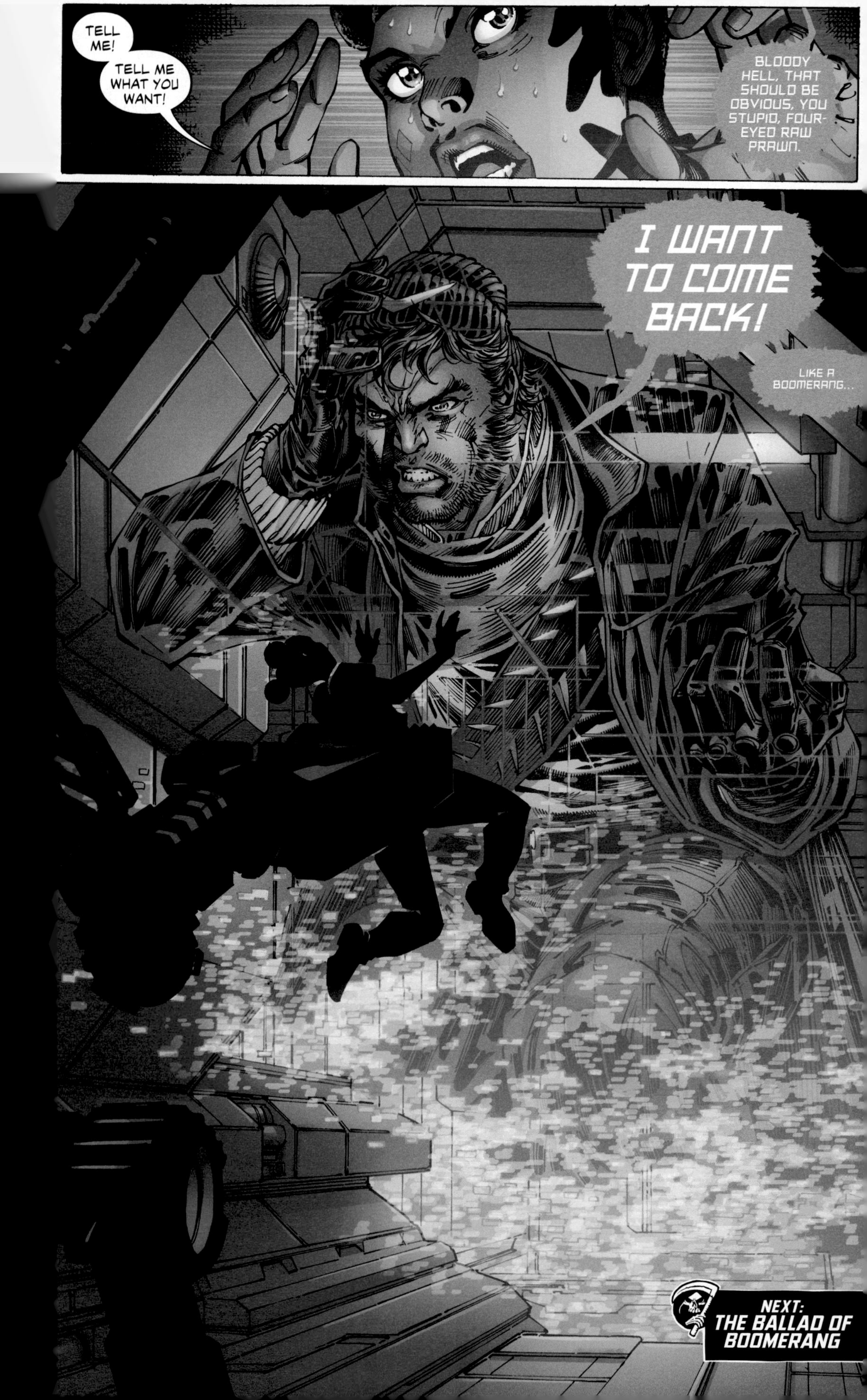
TELL ME!
TELL ME WHAT YOU WANT!
BLOODY HELL, THAT SHOULD BE OBVIOUS, YOU STUPID, FOUR-EYED RAW PRAWN.
I WANT TO COME BACK!
LIKE A BOOMERANG...
NEXT: THE BALLAD OF BOOMERANG

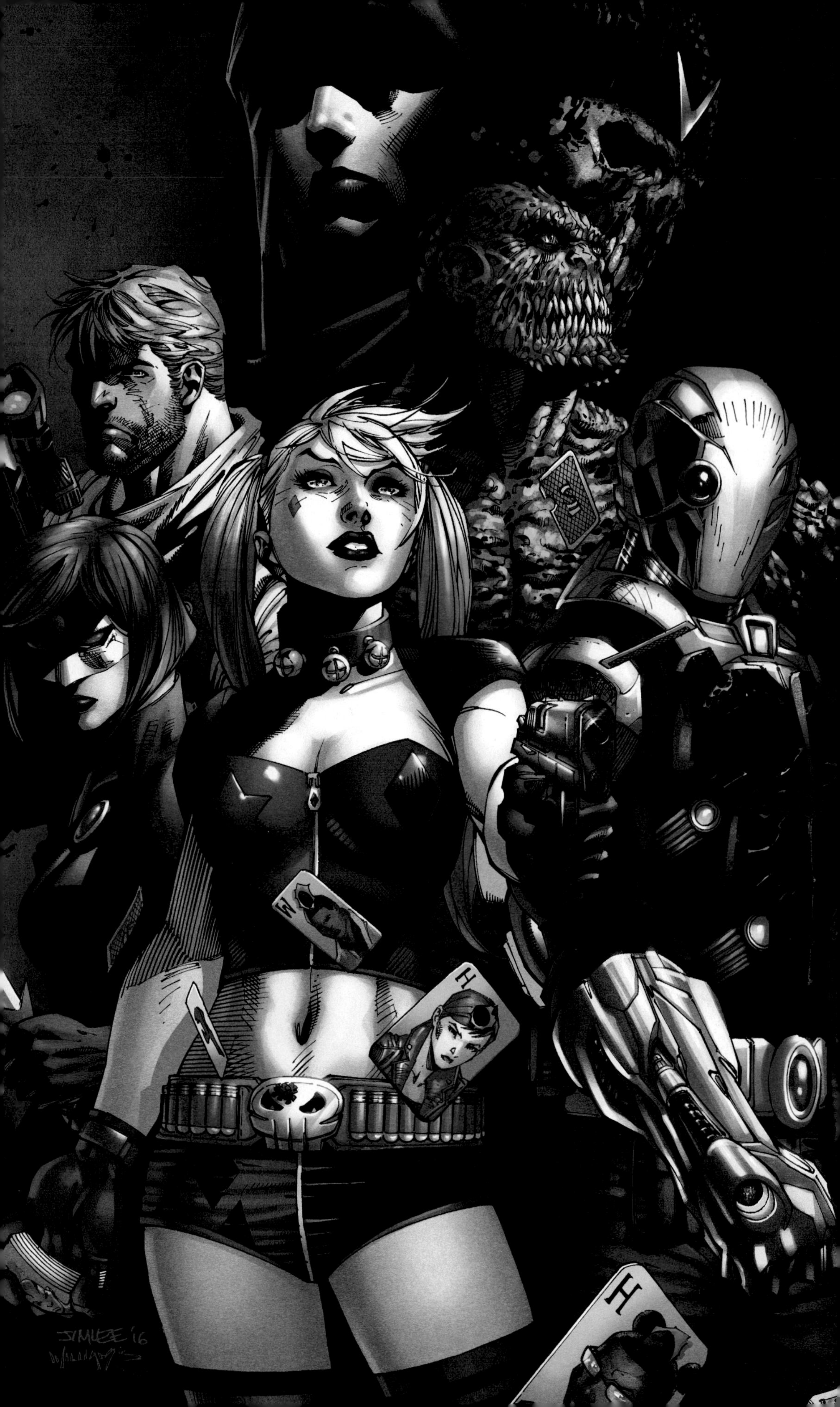
JIMLEE '16

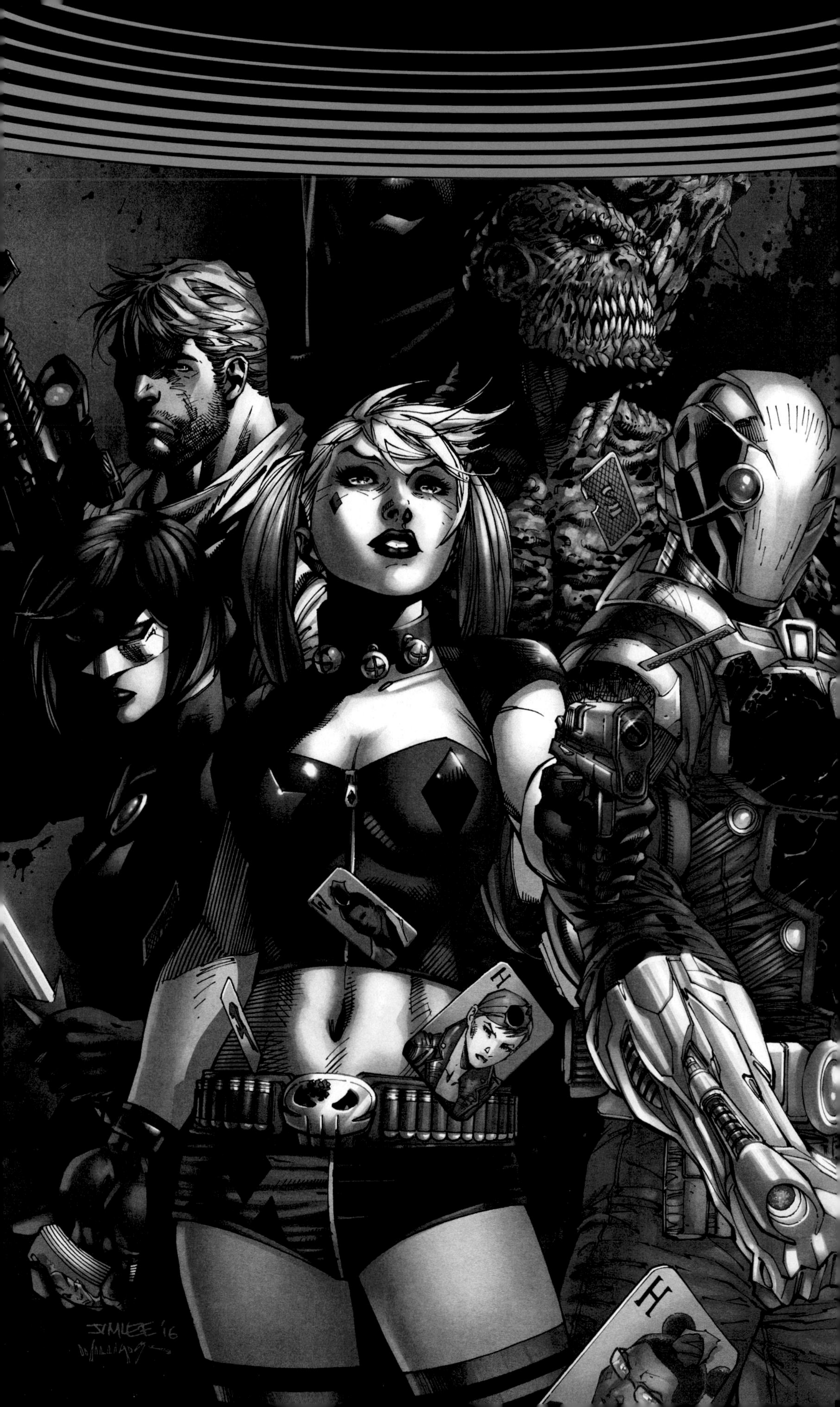

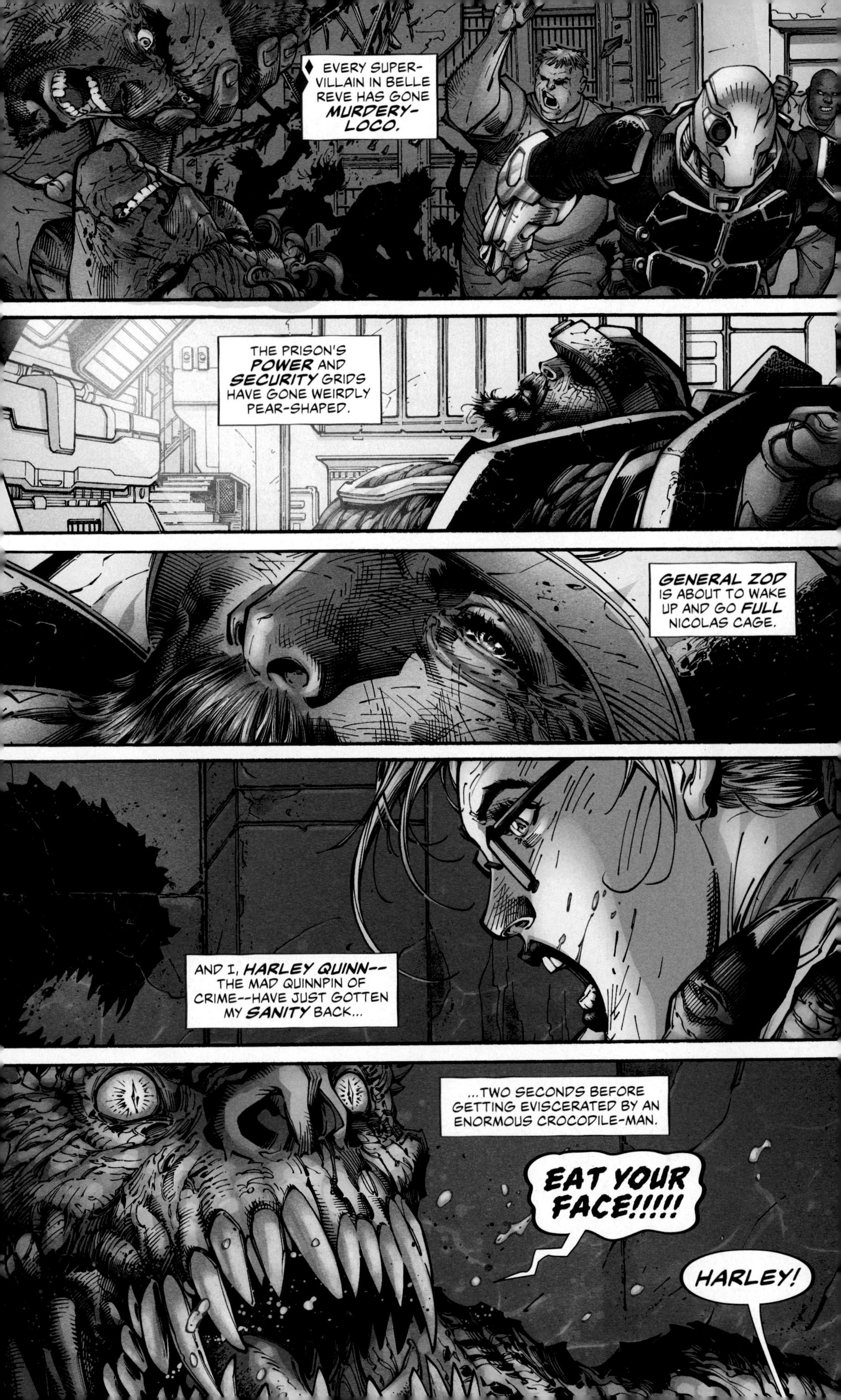
EVERY SUPER-VILLAIN IN BELLE REVE HAS GONE MURDERY-LOCO.
THE PRISON'S POWER AND SECURITY GRIDS HAVE GONE WEIRDLY PEAR-SHAPED.
GENERAL ZOD IS ABOUT TO WAKE UP AND GO FULL NICOLAS CAGE.
AND I, HARLEY QUINN--THE MAD QUINNPIN OF CRIME--HAVE JUST GOTTEN MY SANITY BACK...
...TWO SECONDS BEFORE GETTING EVISCERATED BY AN ENORMOUS CROCODILE-MAN.
EAT YOUR FACE!!!!!
HARLEY!

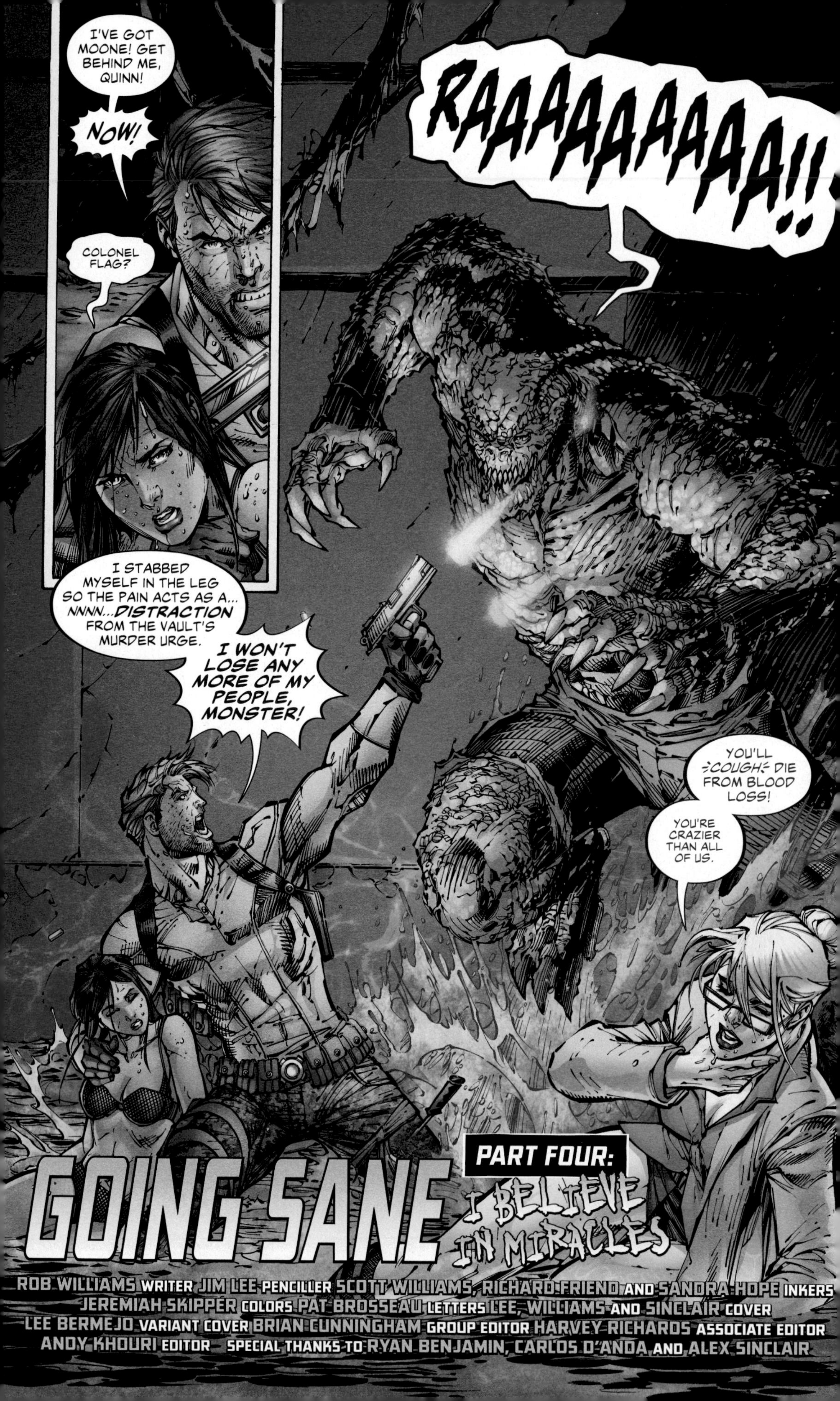
I'VE GOT MOONE! GET BEHIND ME, QUINN!
NOW!
COLONEL FLAG?
RAAAAAAAAAA!!
I STABBED MYSELF IN THE LEG SO THE PAIN ACTS AS A... NNNN...DISTRACTION FROM THE VAULT'S MURDER URGE.
I WON'T LOSE ANY MORE OF MY PEOPLE, MONSTER!
YOU'LL *COUGH* DIE FROM BLOOD LOSS!
YOU'RE CRAZIER THAN ALL OF US.
PART FOUR:
GOING SANE
I BELIEVE IN MIRACLES
ROB WILLIAMS WRITER JIM LEE PENCILLER SCOTT WILLIAMS, RICHARD FRIEND AND SANDRA HOPE INKERS
JEREMIAH SKIPPER COLORS PAT BROSSEAU LETTERS LEE, WILLIAMS AND SINCLAIR COVER
LEE BERMEJO VARIANT COVER BRIAN CUNNINGHAM GROUP EDITOR HARVEY RICHARDS ASSOCIATE EDITOR
ANDY KHOURI EDITOR SPECIAL THANKS TO RYAN BENJAMIN, CARLOS D'ANDA AND ALEX SINCLAIR

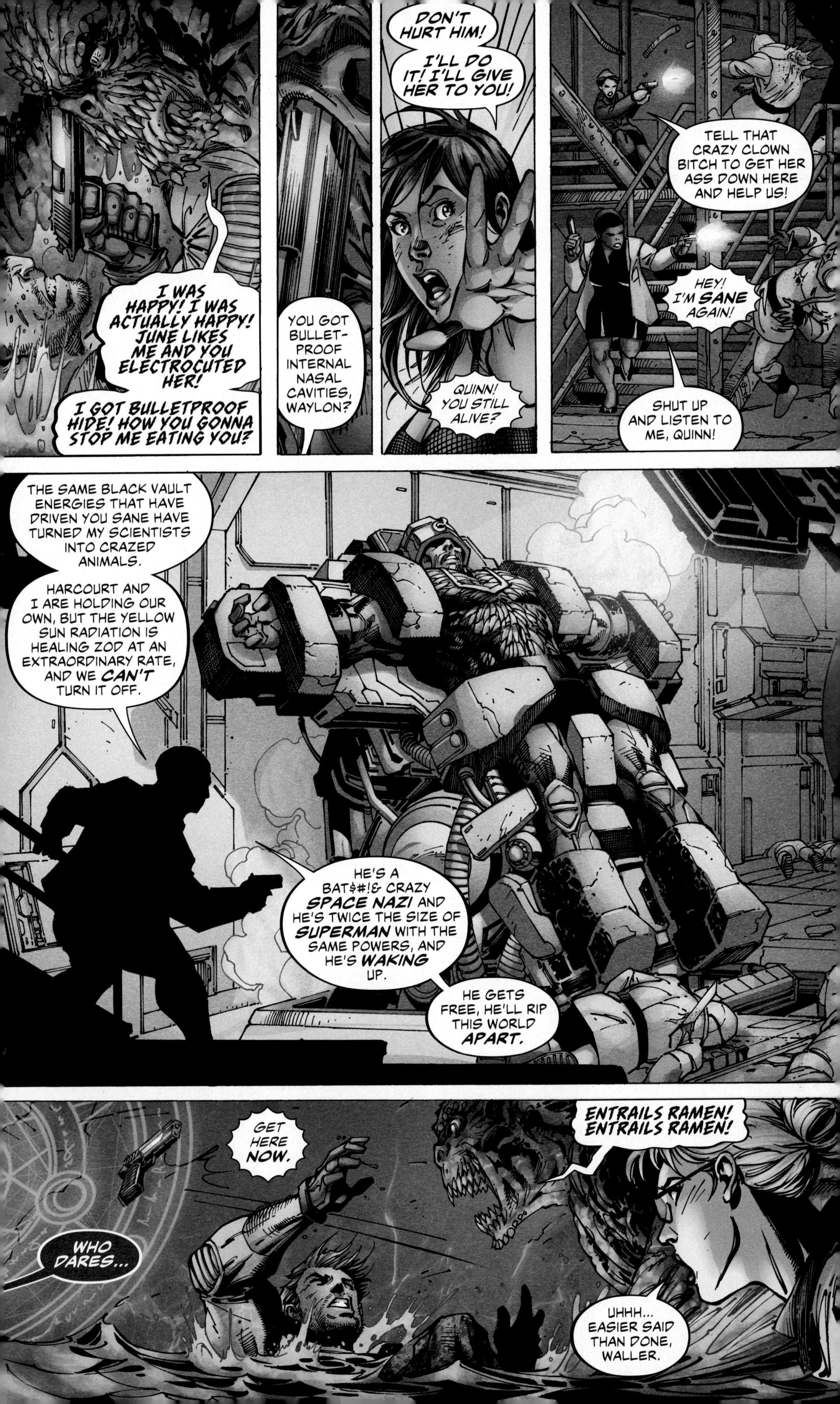

I WAS HAPPY! I WAS ACTUALLY HAPPY! JUNE LIKES ME AND YOU ELECTROCUTED HER!
I GOT BULLETPROOF HIDE! HOW YOU GONNA STOP ME EATING YOU?
YOU GOT BULLET-PROOF INTERNAL NASAL CAVITIES, WAYLON?
DON'T HURT HIM!
I'LL DO IT! I'LL GIVE HER TO YOU!
QUINN! YOU STILL ALIVE?
TELL THAT CRAZY CLOWN BITCH TO GET HER ASS DOWN HERE AND HELP US!
HEY! I'M SANE AGAIN!
SHUT UP AND LISTEN TO ME, QUINN!
THE SAME BLACK VAULT ENERGIES THAT HAVE DRIVEN YOU SANE HAVE TURNED MY SCIENTISTS INTO CRAZED ANIMALS.
HARCOURT AND I ARE HOLDING OUR OWN, BUT THE YELLOW SUN RADIATION IS HEALING ZOD AT AN EXTRAORDINARY RATE, AND WE CAN'T TURN IT OFF.
HE'S A BAT$#!& CRAZY SPACE NAZI AND HE'S TWICE THE SIZE OF SUPERMAN WITH THE SAME POWERS, AND HE'S WAKING UP.
HE GETS FREE, HE'LL RIP THIS WORLD APART.
GET HERE NOW.
ENTRAILS RAMEN! ENTRAILS RAMEN!
WHO DARES...
UHHH... EASIER SAID THAN DONE, WALLER.

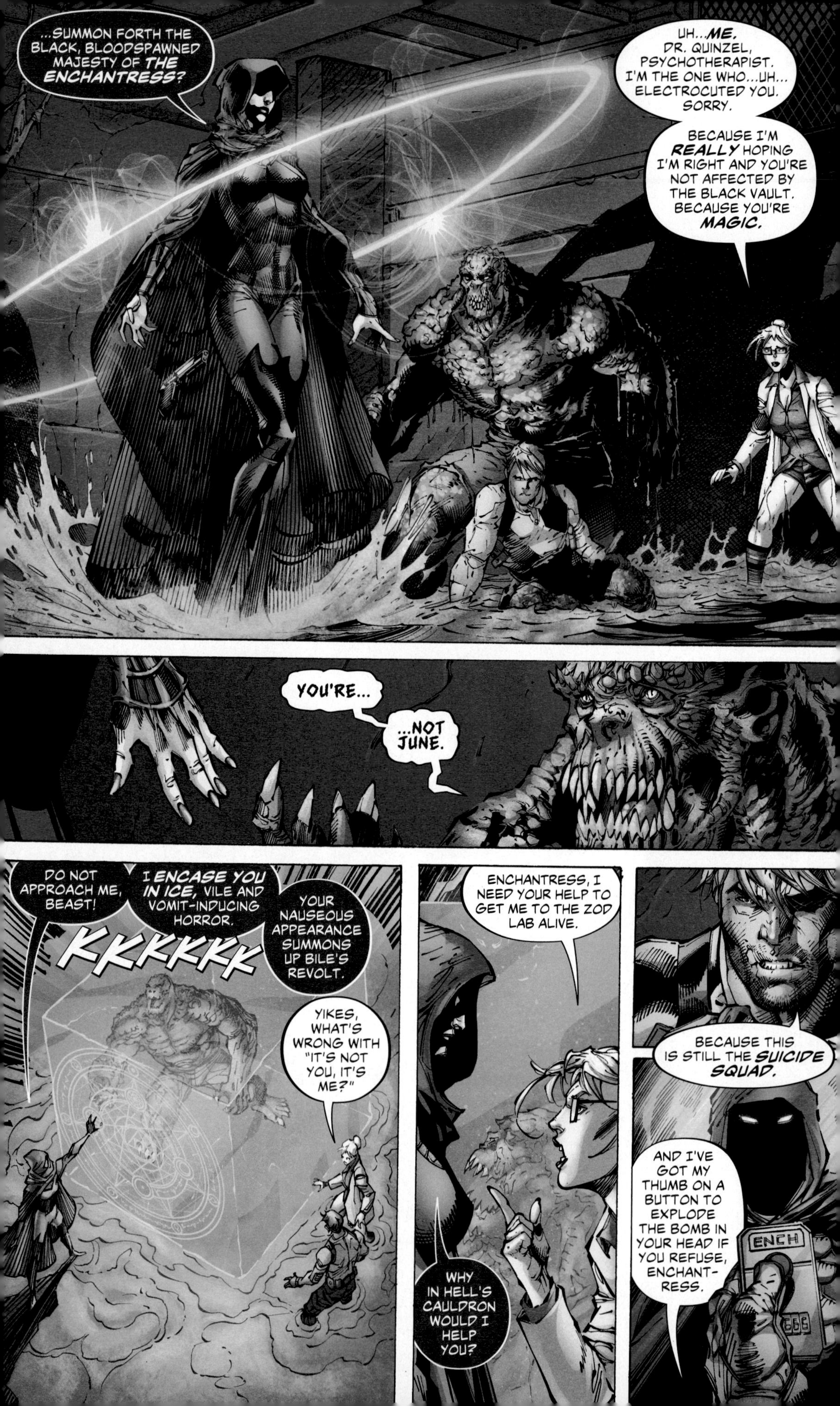

...SUMMON FORTH THE BLACK, BLOODSPAWNED MAJESTY OF THE ENCHANTRESS?
UH...ME. DR. QUINZEL, PSYCHOTHERAPIST. I'M THE ONE WHO...UH... ELECTROCUTED YOU. SORRY.
BECAUSE I'M REALLY HOPING I'M RIGHT AND YOU'RE NOT AFFECTED BY THE BLACK VAULT. BECAUSE YOU'RE MAGIC.
YOU'RE...
...NOT JUNE.
DO NOT APPROACH ME, BEAST!
I ENCASE YOU IN ICE, VILE AND VOMIT-INDUCING HORROR.
YOUR NAUSEOUS APPEARANCE SUMMONS UP BILE'S REVOLT.
KKKKKK
YIKES, WHAT'S WRONG WITH "IT'S NOT YOU, IT'S ME?"
ENCHANTRESS, I NEED YOUR HELP TO GET ME TO THE ZOD LAB ALIVE.
WHY IN HELL'S CAULDRON WOULD I HELP YOU?
BECAUSE THIS IS STILL THE SUICIDE SQUAD.
AND I'VE GOT MY THUMB ON A BUTTON TO EXPLODE THE BOMB IN YOUR HEAD IF YOU REFUSE, ENCHANT-RESS.
ENCH

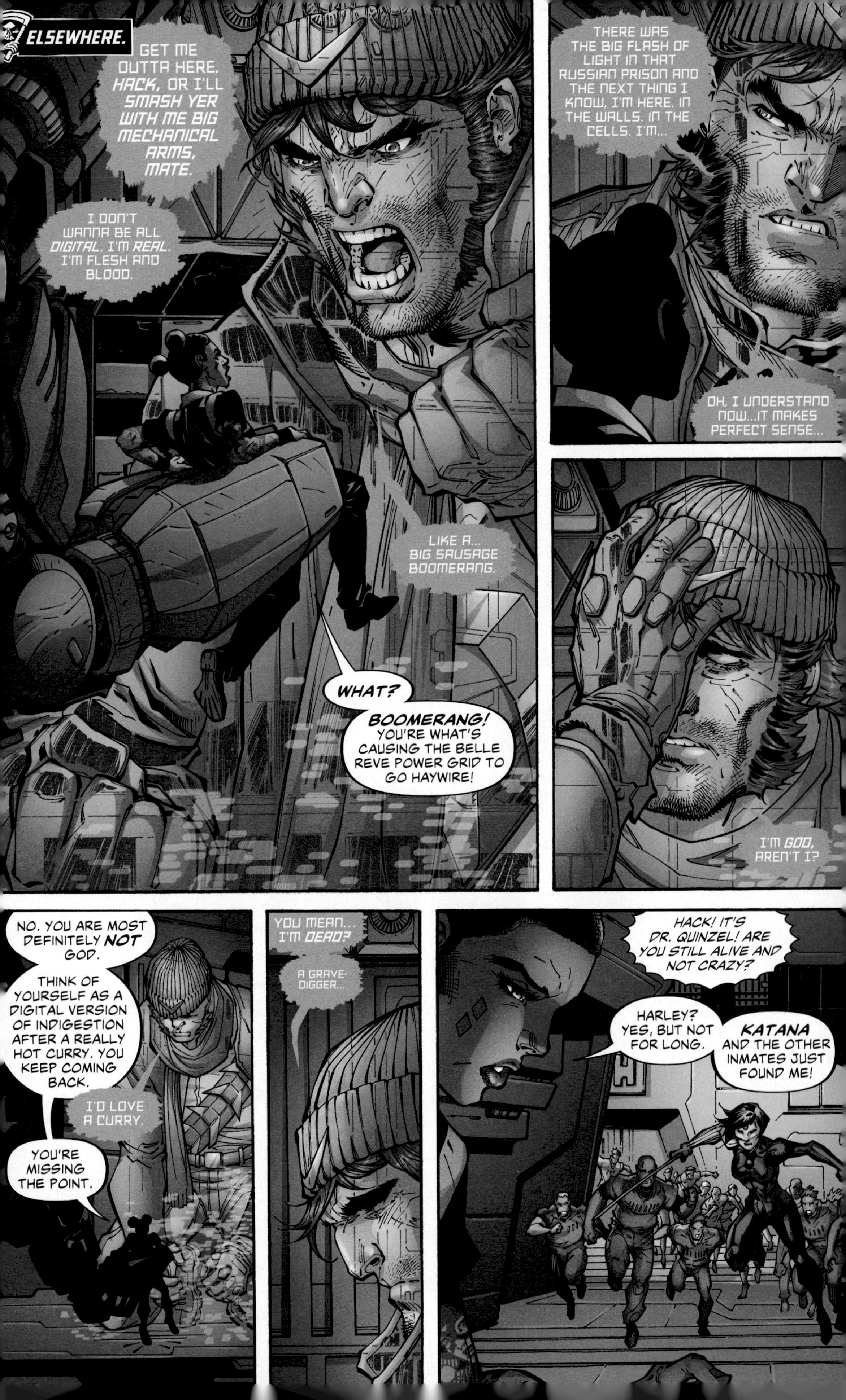
ELSEWHERE.
GET ME OUTTA HERE, HACK, OR I'LL SMASH YER WITH ME BIG MECHANICAL ARMS, MATE.
I DON'T WANNA BE ALL DIGITAL. I'M REAL. I'M FLESH AND BLOOD.
LIKE A... BIG SAUSAGE BOOMERANG.
WHAT?
BOOMERANG! YOU'RE WHAT'S CAUSING THE BELLE REVE POWER GRID TO GO HAYWIRE!
THERE WAS THE BIG FLASH OF LIGHT IN THAT RUSSIAN PRISON AND THE NEXT THING I KNOW, I'M HERE. IN THE WALLS. IN THE CELLS. I'M...
OH, I UNDERSTAND NOW...IT MAKES PERFECT SENSE...
I'M GOD, AREN'T I?
NO. YOU ARE MOST DEFINITELY NOT GOD.
THINK OF YOURSELF AS A DIGITAL VERSION OF INDIGESTION AFTER A REALLY HOT CURRY. YOU KEEP COMING BACK.
I'D LOVE A CURRY.
YOU'RE MISSING THE POINT.
YOU MEAN... I'M DEAD?
A GRAVE-DIGGER...
HACK! IT'S DR. QUINZEL! ARE YOU STILL ALIVE AND NOT CRAZY?
HARLEY? YES, BUT NOT FOR LONG.
KATANA AND THE OTHER INMATES JUST FOUND ME!

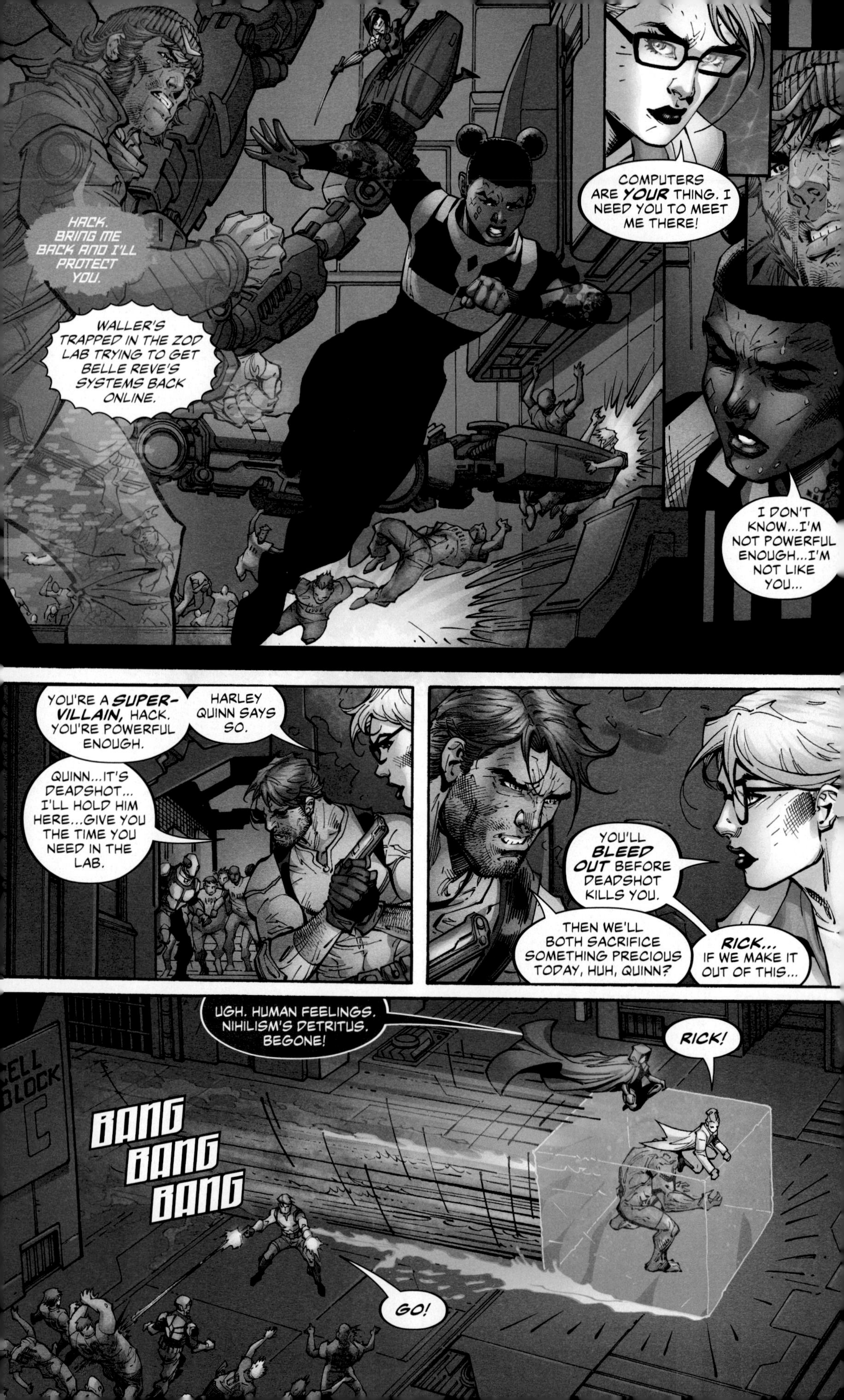

HACK. BRING ME BACK AND I'LL PROTECT YOU.
WALLER'S TRAPPED IN THE ZOD LAB TRYING TO GET BELLE REVE'S SYSTEMS BACK ONLINE.
COMPUTERS ARE YOUR THING. I NEED YOU TO MEET ME THERE!
I DON'T KNOW...I'M NOT POWERFUL ENOUGH...I'M NOT LIKE YOU...
YOU'RE A SUPER-VILLAIN, HACK. YOU'RE POWERFUL ENOUGH.
HARLEY QUINN SAYS SO.
QUINN...IT'S DEADSHOT... I'LL HOLD HIM HERE...GIVE YOU THE TIME YOU NEED IN THE LAB.
YOU'LL BLEED OUT BEFORE DEADSHOT KILLS YOU.
THEN WE'LL BOTH SACRIFICE SOMETHING PRECIOUS TODAY, HUH, QUINN?
RICK... IF WE MAKE IT OUT OF THIS...
UGH. HUMAN FEELINGS. NIHILISM'S DETRITUS. BEGONE!
RICK!
CELL BLOCK C
BANG BANG BANG
GO!

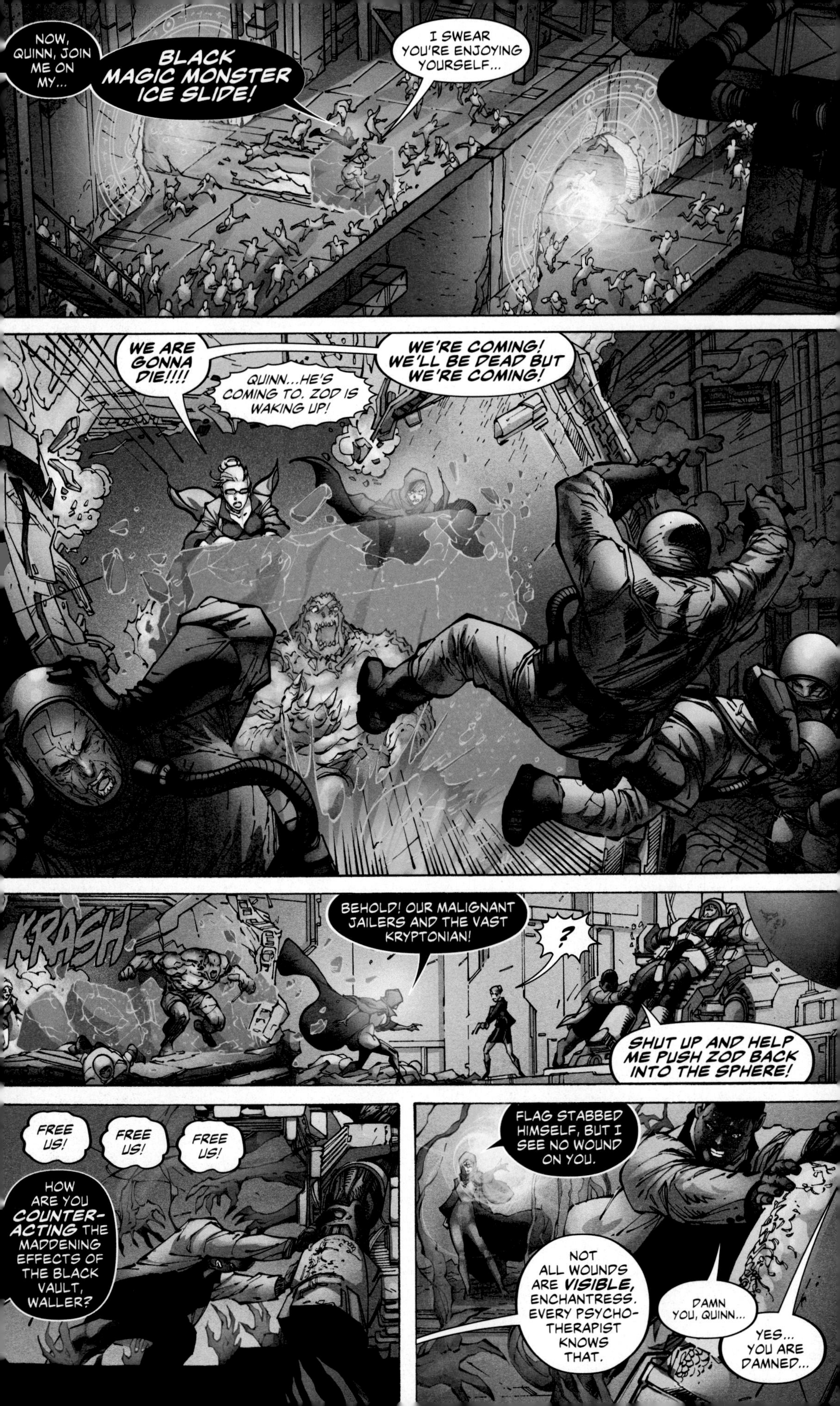
NOW, QUINN, JOIN ME ON MY...
BLACK MAGIC MONSTER ICE SLIDE!
I SWEAR YOU'RE ENJOYING YOURSELF...
WE ARE GONNA DIE!!!!
WE'RE COMING! WE'LL BE DEAD BUT WE'RE COMING!
QUINN...HE'S COMING TO. ZOD IS WAKING UP!
KRASH
BEHOLD! OUR MALIGNANT JAILERS AND THE VAST KRYPTONIAN!
?
SHUT UP AND HELP ME PUSH ZOD BACK INTO THE SPHERE!
FREE US!
FREE US!
FREE US!
HOW ARE YOU COUNTER-ACTING THE MADDENING EFFECTS OF THE BLACK VAULT, WALLER?
FLAG STABBED HIMSELF, BUT I SEE NO WOUND ON YOU.
NOT ALL WOUNDS ARE VISIBLE, ENCHANTRESS. EVERY PSYCHO-THERAPIST KNOWS THAT.
DAMN YOU, QUINN...
YES... YOU ARE DAMNED...

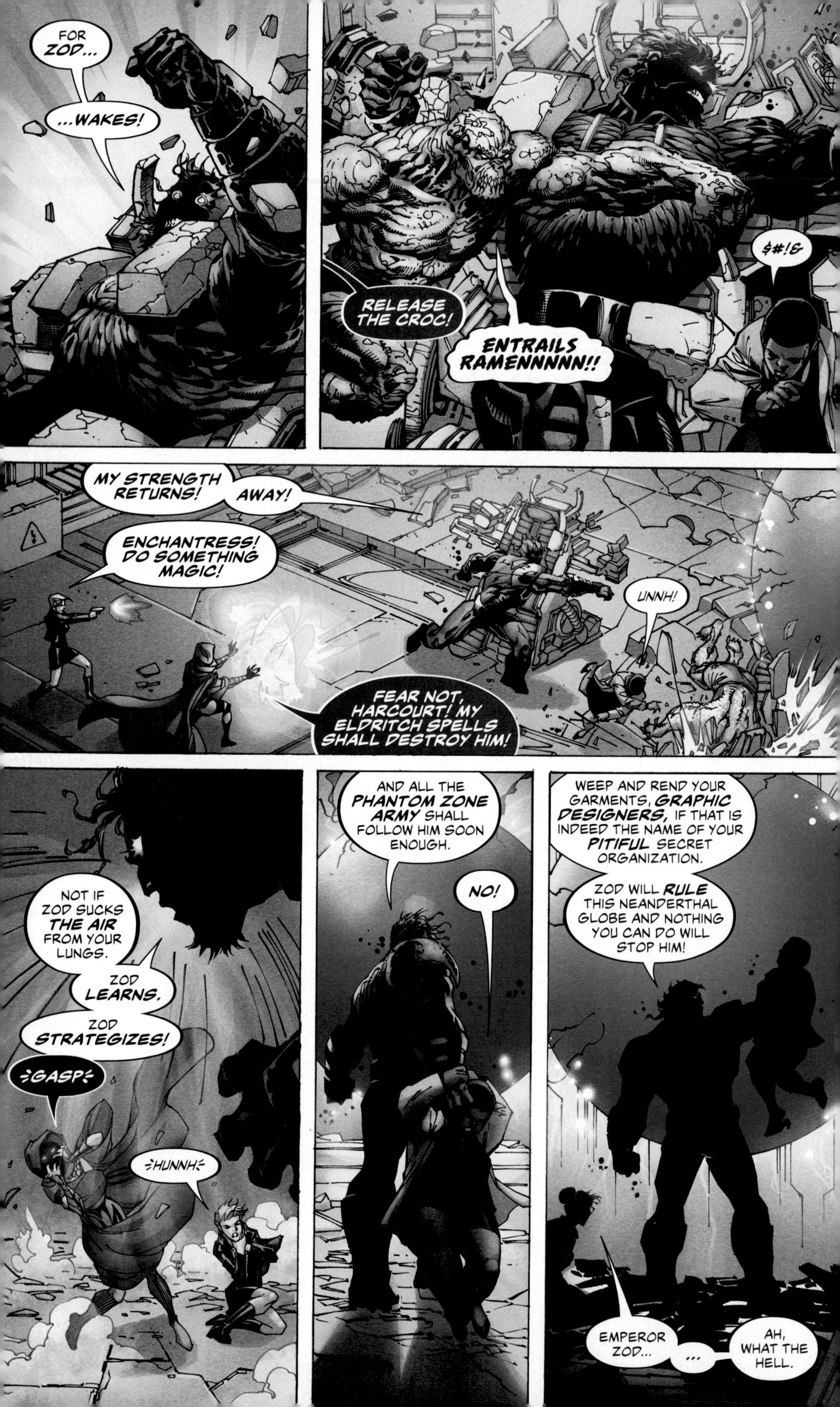
FOR ZOD...
...WAKES!
RELEASE THE CROC!
ENTRAILS RAMENNNNN!!
$#!&
MY STRENGTH RETURNS!
AWAY!
ENCHANTRESS! DO SOMETHING MAGIC!
UNNH!
FEAR NOT, HARCOURT! MY ELDRITCH SPELLS SHALL DESTROY HIM!
NOT IF ZOD SUCKS THE AIR FROM YOUR LUNGS.
ZOD LEARNS.
ZOD STRATEGIZES!
GASP
HUNNH
AND ALL THE PHANTOM ZONE ARMY SHALL FOLLOW HIM SOON ENOUGH.
NO!
WEEP AND REND YOUR GARMENTS, GRAPHIC DESIGNERS, IF THAT IS INDEED THE NAME OF YOUR PITIFUL SECRET ORGANIZATION.
ZOD WILL RULE THIS NEANDERTHAL GLOBE AND NOTHING YOU CAN DO WILL STOP HIM!
EMPEROR ZOD...
...
AH, WHAT THE HELL.

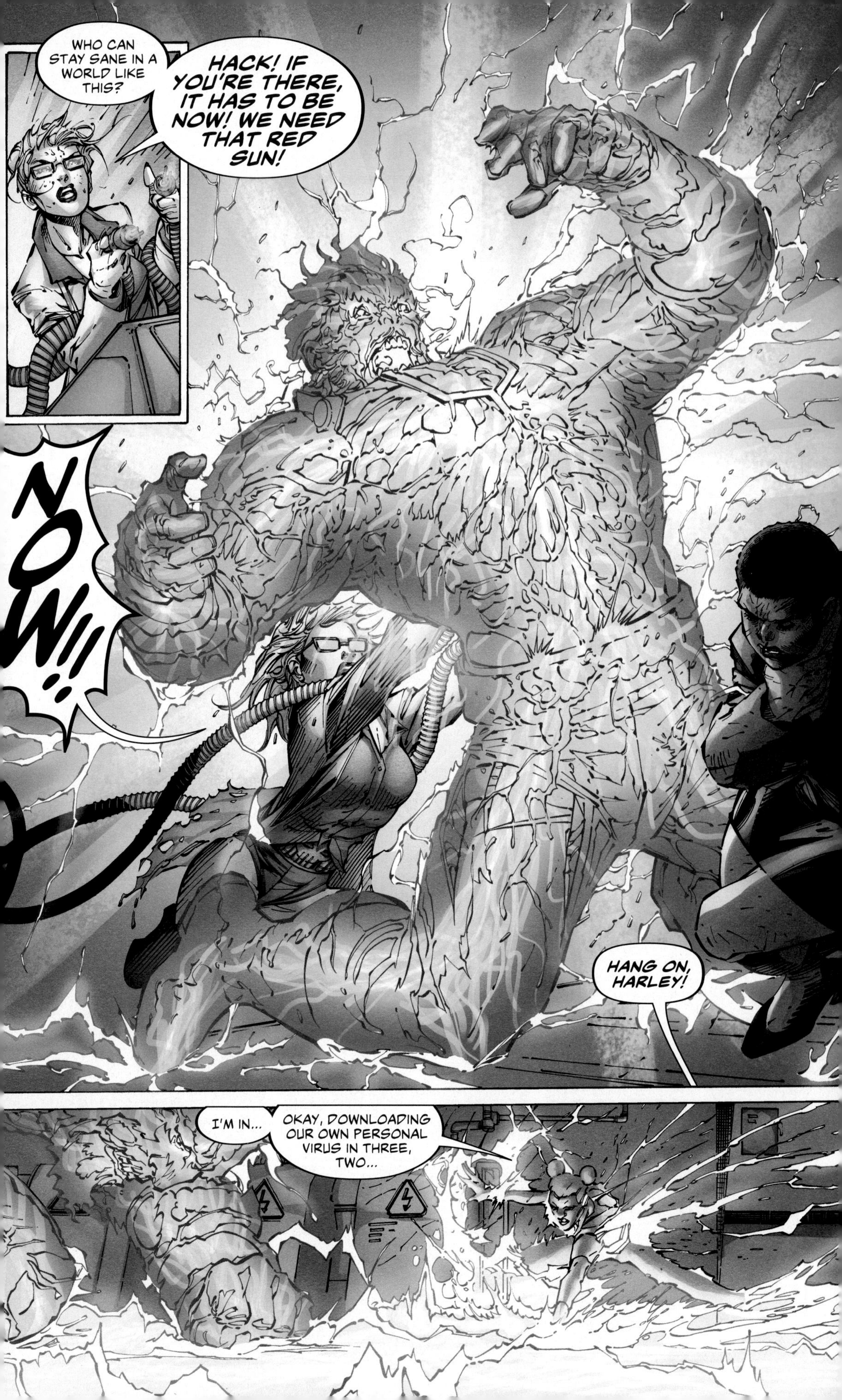
WHO CAN STAY SANE IN A WORLD LIKE THIS?
HACK! IF YOU'RE THERE, IT HAS TO BE NOW! WE NEED THAT RED SUN!
NOW!!!
HANG ON, HARLEY!
I'M IN...
OKAY, DOWNLOADING OUR OWN PERSONAL VIRUS IN THREE, TWO...

ROARRRRR!!

OI, OI... SUPERMAN'S DIRTY UNCLE OR WHATEVER YOU ARE...

FZZZSSHH

REMEMBER ME?

FZZZSSHH

NOOOOOO!!!

...

HE'S DEAD ON HIS FEET! HACK, WHAT DID YOU JUST HIT HIM WITH?

WITH...A... BOOMERANG!

WHAT?!!

HE WAS THE TURD IN THE MACHINE!

AND WE JUST FLUSHED HIM OUT!

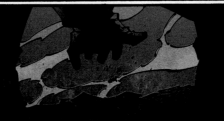

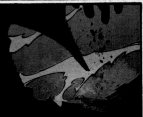

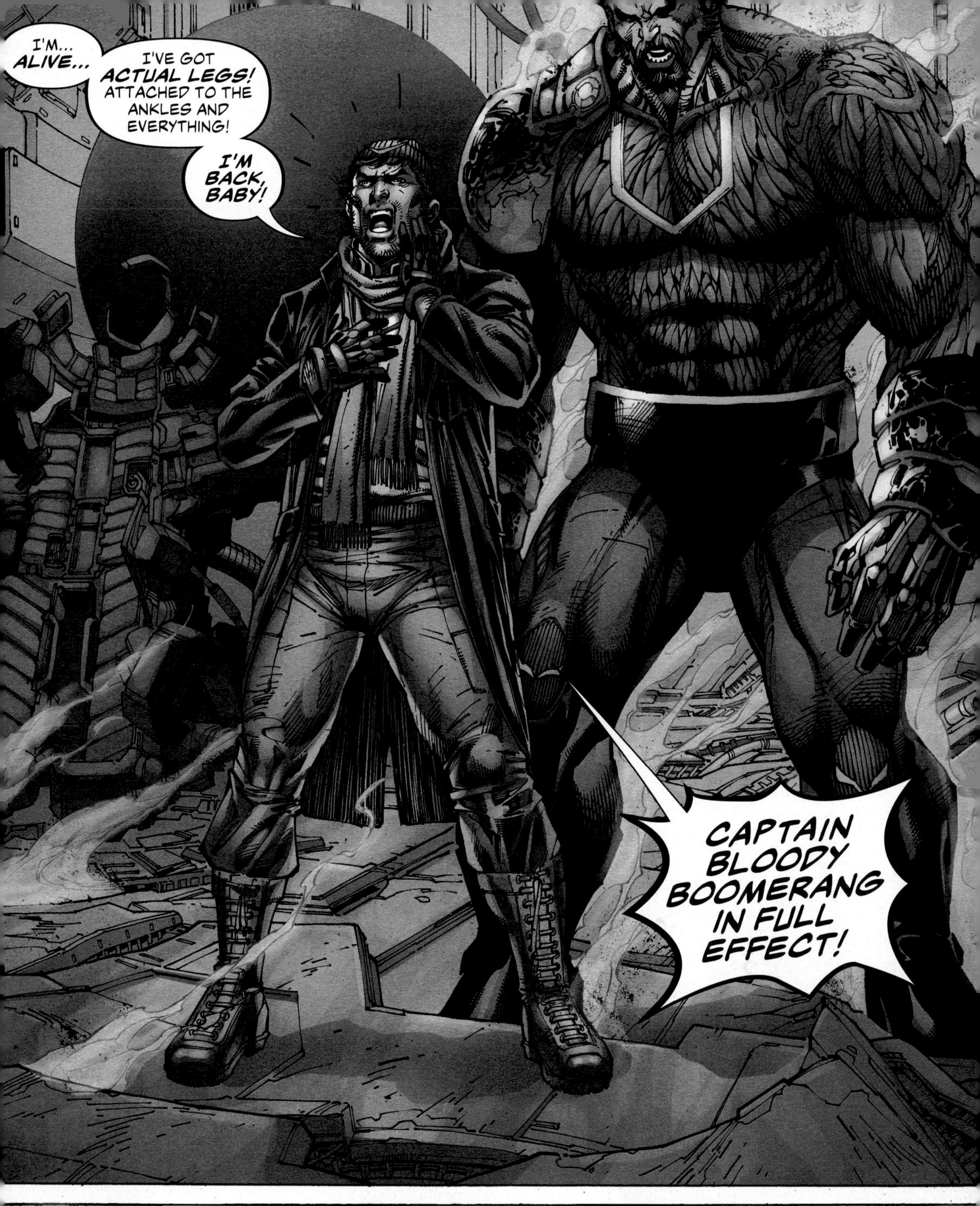
I'M... ALIVE...
I'VE GOT ACTUAL LEGS! ATTACHED TO THE ANKLES AND EVERYTHING!
I'M BACK, BABY!
CAPTAIN BLOODY BOOMERANG IN FULL EFFECT!
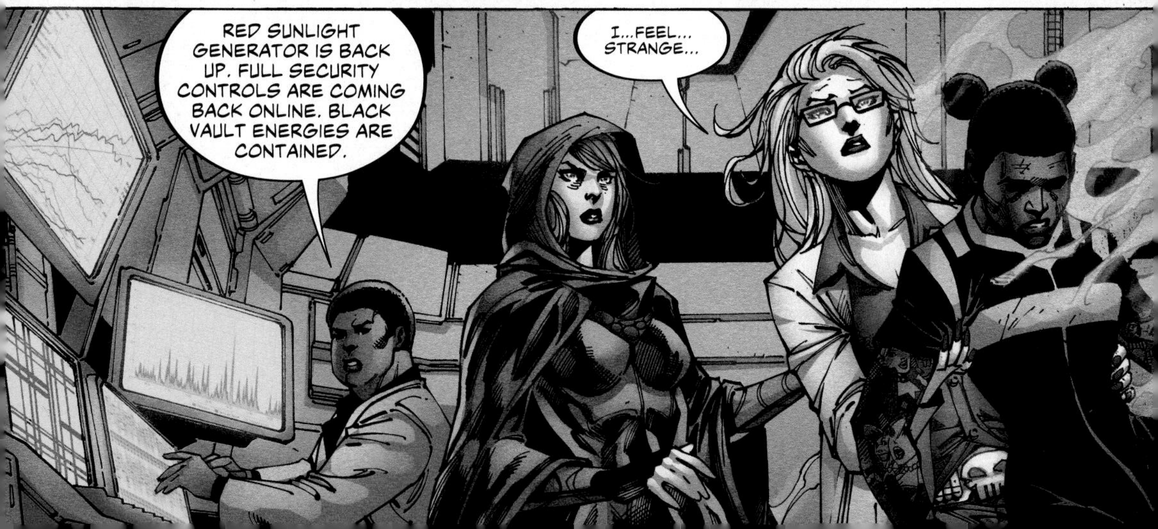
RED SUNLIGHT GENERATOR IS BACK UP. FULL SECURITY CONTROLS ARE COMING BACK ONLINE. BLACK VAULT ENERGIES ARE CONTAINED.
I...FEEL... STRANGE...

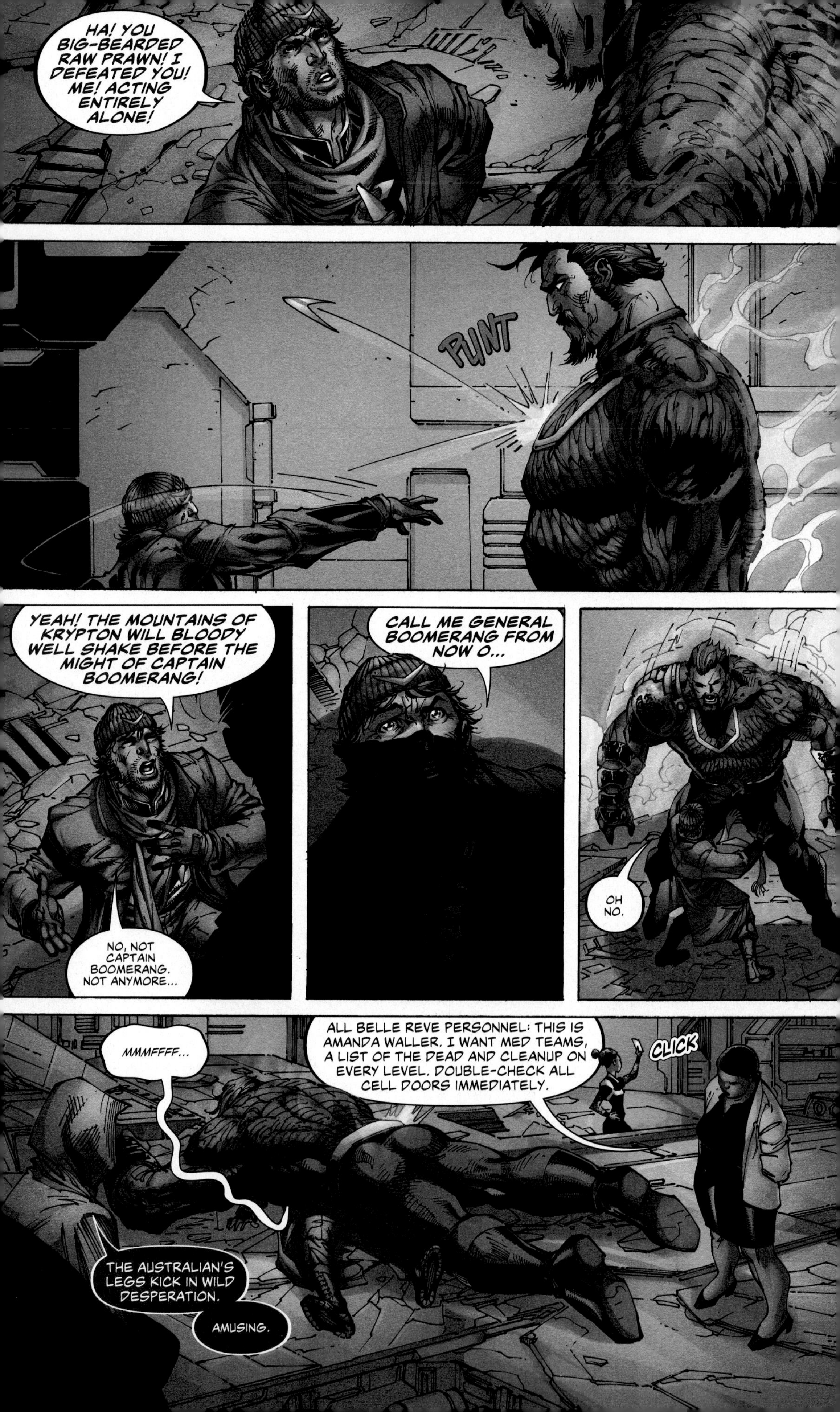
HA! YOU BIG-BEARDED RAW PRAWN! I DEFEATED YOU! ME! ACTING ENTIRELY ALONE!
PUNT
YEAH! THE MOUNTAINS OF KRYPTON WILL BLOODY WELL SHAKE BEFORE THE MIGHT OF CAPTAIN BOOMERANG!
NO, NOT CAPTAIN BOOMERANG. NOT ANYMORE...
CALL ME GENERAL BOOMERANG FROM NOW O...
OH NO.
MMMFFFF...
ALL BELLE REVE PERSONNEL: THIS IS AMANDA WALLER. I WANT MED TEAMS, A LIST OF THE DEAD AND CLEANUP ON EVERY LEVEL. DOUBLE-CHECK ALL CELL DOORS IMMEDIATELY.
CLICK
THE AUSTRALIAN'S LEGS KICK IN WILD DESPERATION.
AMUSING.

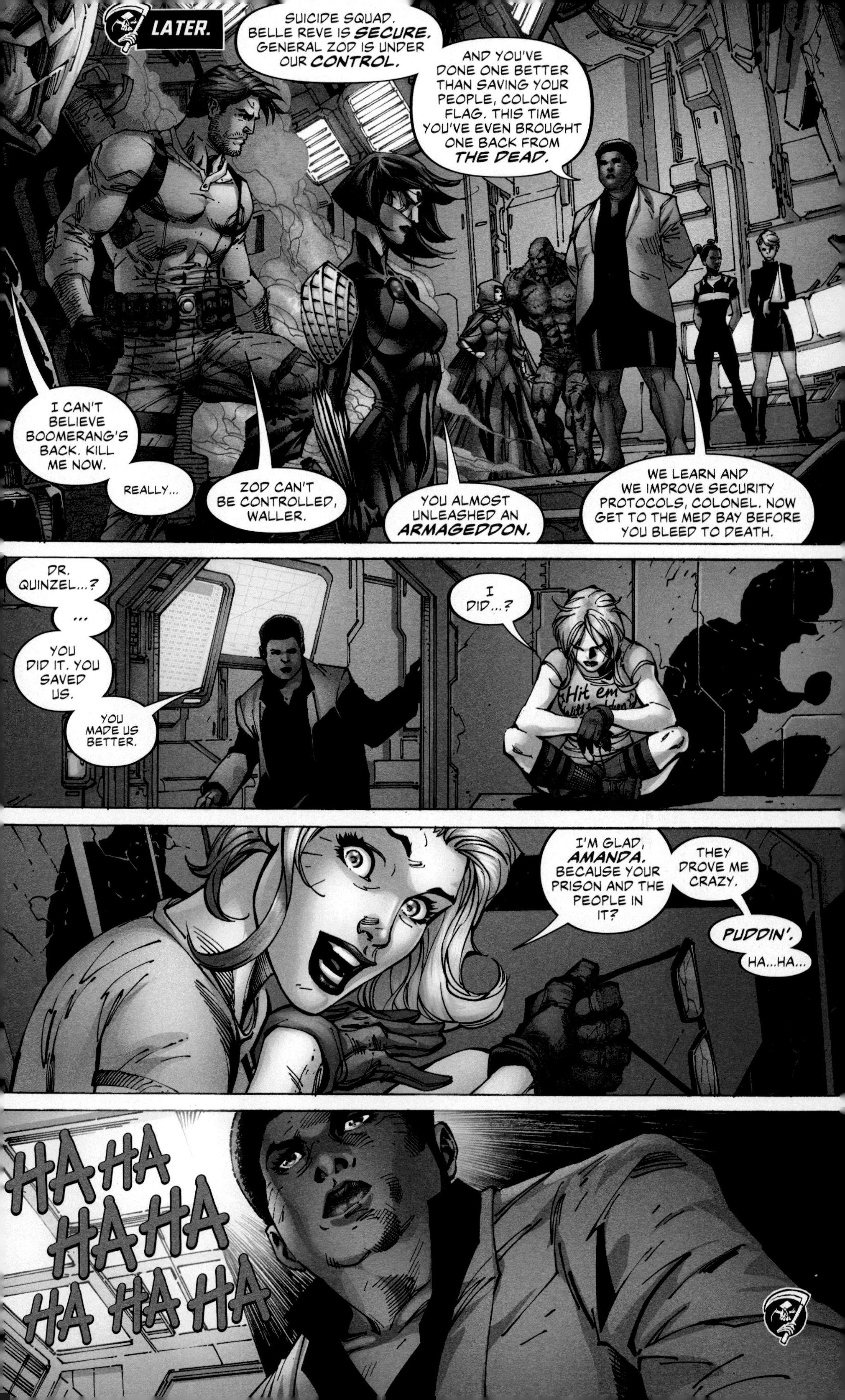
LATER.
SUICIDE SQUAD. BELLE REVE IS SECURE. GENERAL ZOD IS UNDER OUR CONTROL.
AND YOU'VE DONE ONE BETTER THAN SAVING YOUR PEOPLE, COLONEL FLAG. THIS TIME YOU'VE EVEN BROUGHT ONE BACK FROM THE DEAD.
I CAN'T BELIEVE BOOMERANG'S BACK. KILL ME NOW.
REALLY...
ZOD CAN'T BE CONTROLLED, WALLER.
YOU ALMOST UNLEASHED AN ARMAGEDDON.
WE LEARN AND WE IMPROVE SECURITY PROTOCOLS, COLONEL. NOW GET TO THE MED BAY BEFORE YOU BLEED TO DEATH.
DR. QUINZEL...?
...
YOU DID IT. YOU SAVED US.
YOU MADE US BETTER.
I DID...?
I'M GLAD, AMANDA. BECAUSE YOUR PRISON AND THE PEOPLE IN IT?
THEY DROVE ME CRAZY.
PUDDIN'.
HA...HA...
HA HA HA HA HA HA HA

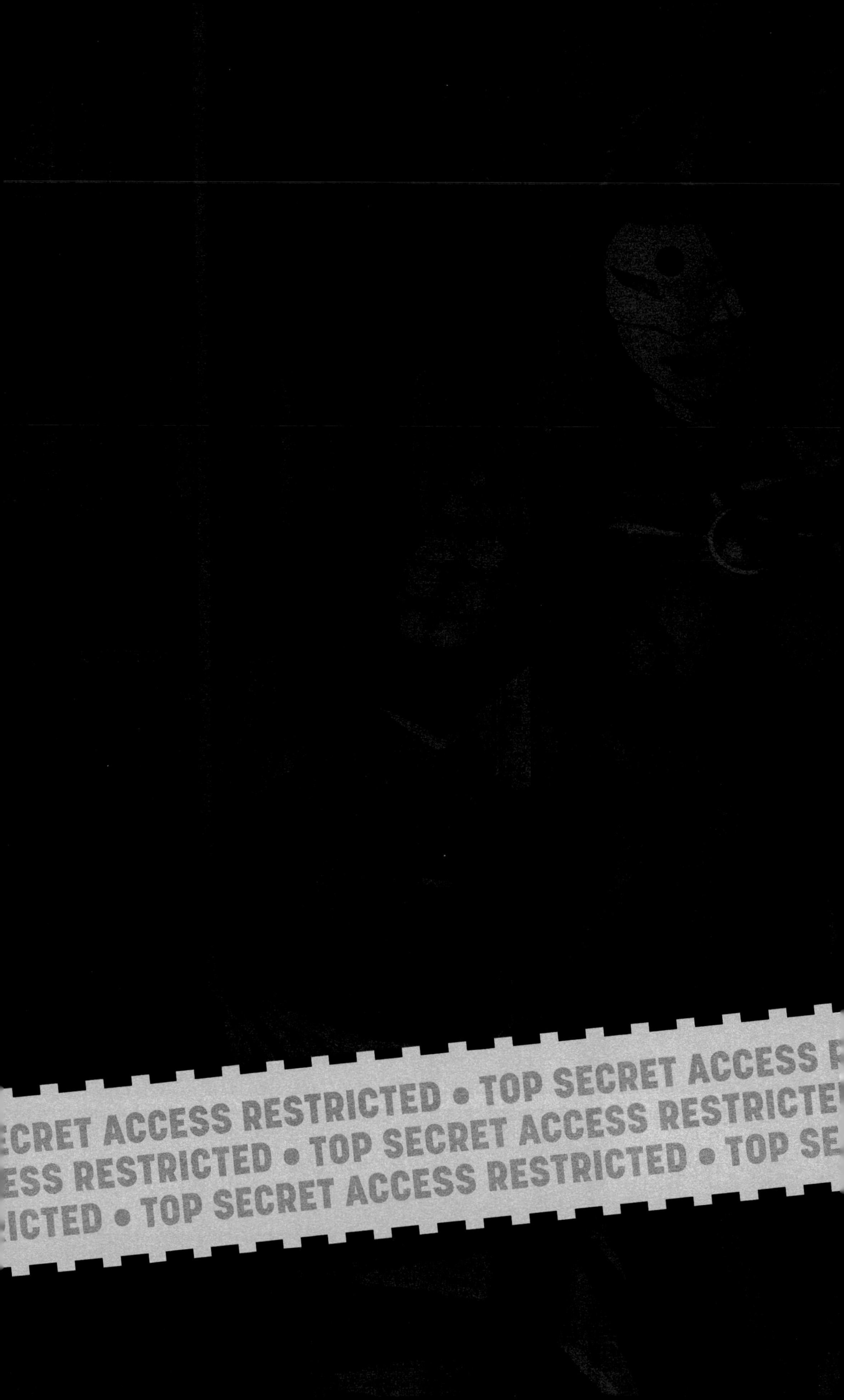
ACCESS RESTRICTED • TOP SECRET ACCESS
RESTRICTED • TOP SECRET ACCESS
TOP SECRET ACCESS RESTRICTED • TOP

TASK FORCE X
PERSONNEL FILES

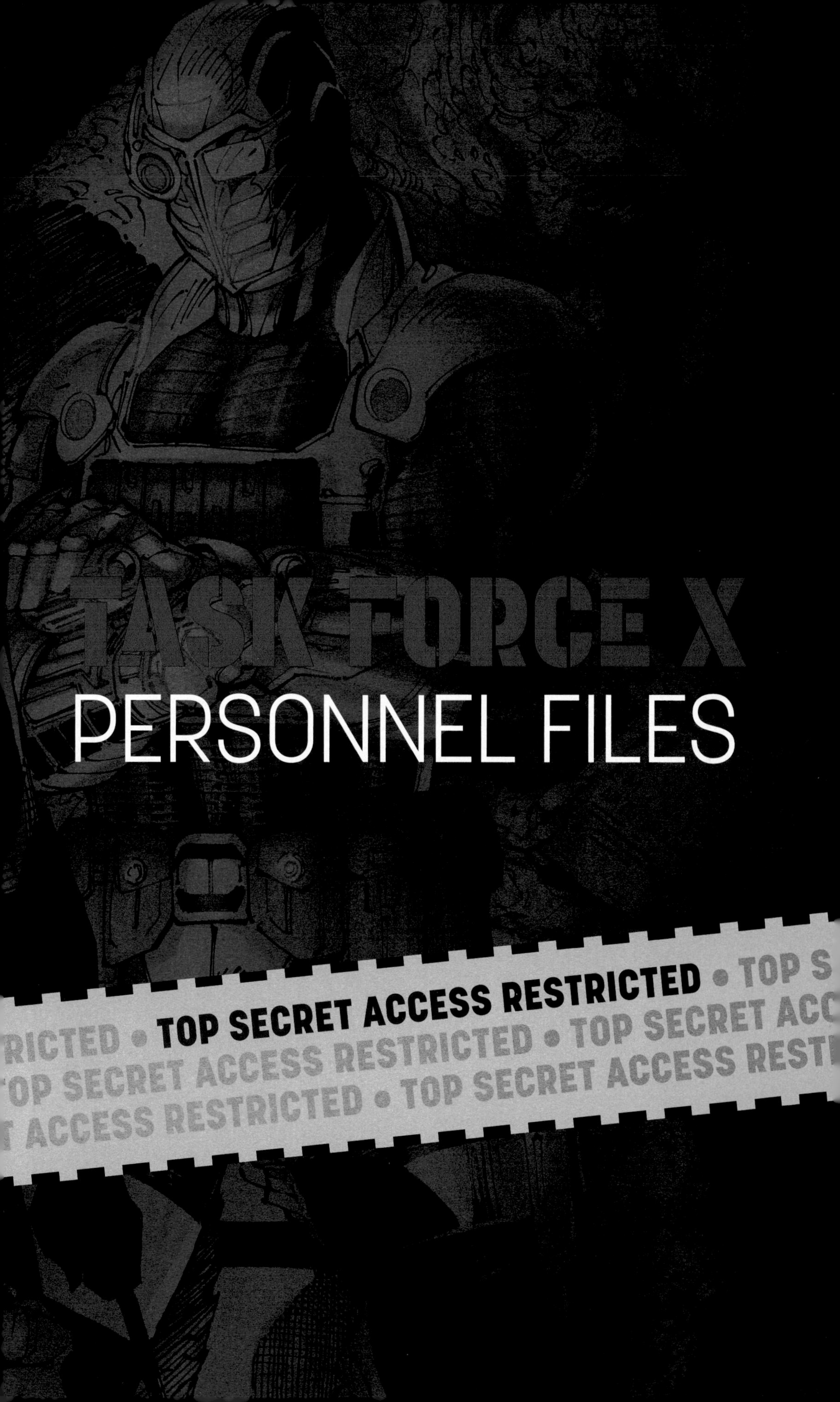
TOP SECRET ACCESS RESTRICTED

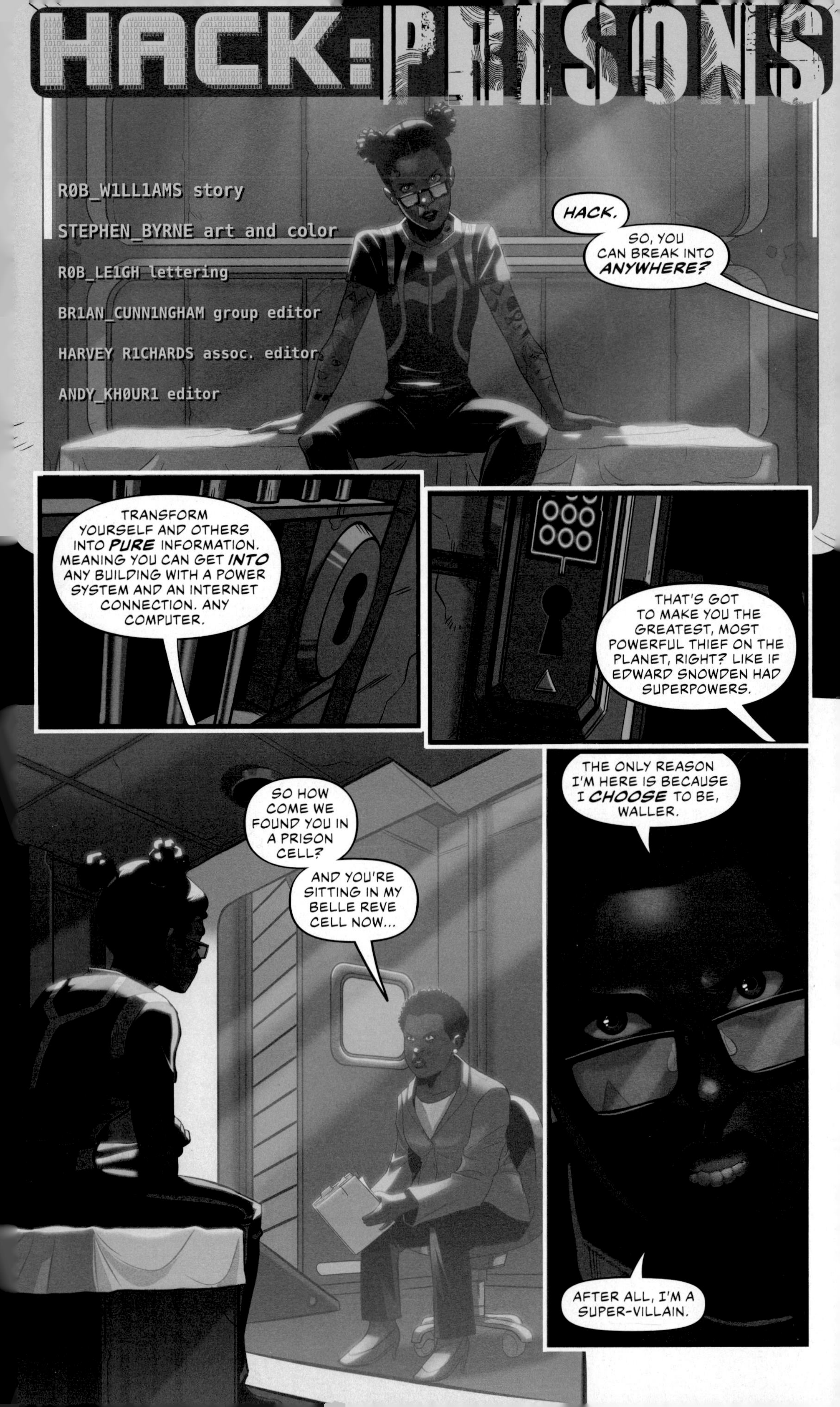

HACK: PRISONS
R0B_W1LL1AMS story
STEPHEN_BYRNE art and color
R0B_LE1GH lettering
BR1AN_CUNN1NGHAM group editor
HARVEY R1CHARDS assoc. editor
ANDY_KH0UR1 editor
HACK.
SO, YOU CAN BREAK INTO ANYWHERE?
TRANSFORM YOURSELF AND OTHERS INTO PURE INFORMATION. MEANING YOU CAN GET INTO ANY BUILDING WITH A POWER SYSTEM AND AN INTERNET CONNECTION. ANY COMPUTER.
THAT'S GOT TO MAKE YOU THE GREATEST, MOST POWERFUL THIEF ON THE PLANET, RIGHT? LIKE IF EDWARD SNOWDEN HAD SUPERPOWERS.
SO HOW COME WE FOUND YOU IN A PRISON CELL?
AND YOU'RE SITTING IN MY BELLE REVE CELL NOW...
THE ONLY REASON I'M HERE IS BECAUSE I CHOOSE TO BE, WALLER.
AFTER ALL, I'M A SUPER-VILLAIN.

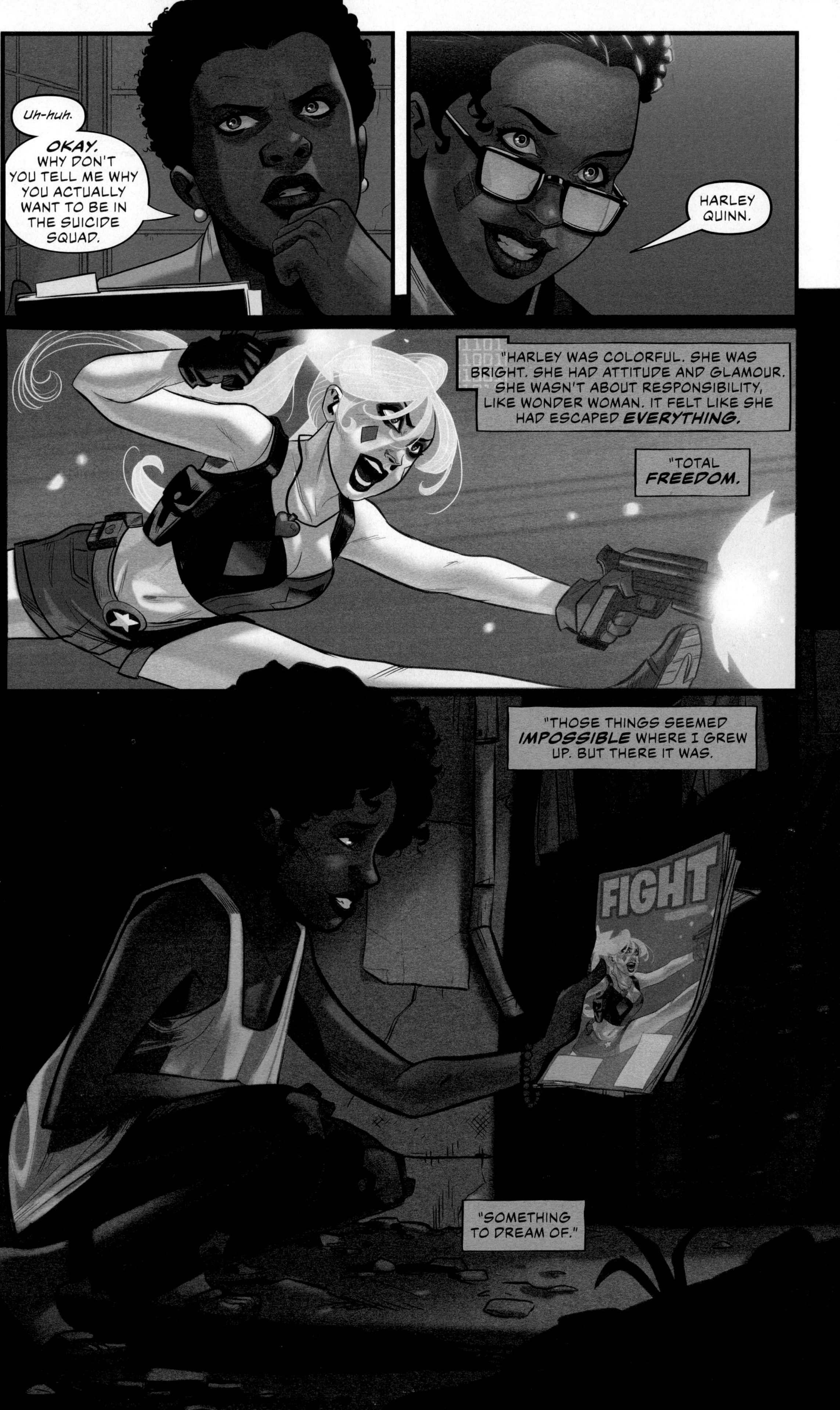
Uh-huh.
OKAY. WHY DON'T YOU TELL ME WHY YOU ACTUALLY WANT TO BE IN THE SUICIDE SQUAD.
HARLEY QUINN.
"HARLEY WAS COLORFUL. SHE WAS BRIGHT. SHE HAD ATTITUDE AND GLAMOUR. SHE WASN'T ABOUT RESPONSIBILITY, LIKE WONDER WOMAN. IT FELT LIKE SHE HAD ESCAPED EVERYTHING.
"TOTAL FREEDOM.
"THOSE THINGS SEEMED IMPOSSIBLE WHERE I GREW UP. BUT THERE IT WAS.
FIGHT
"SOMETHING TO DREAM OF."

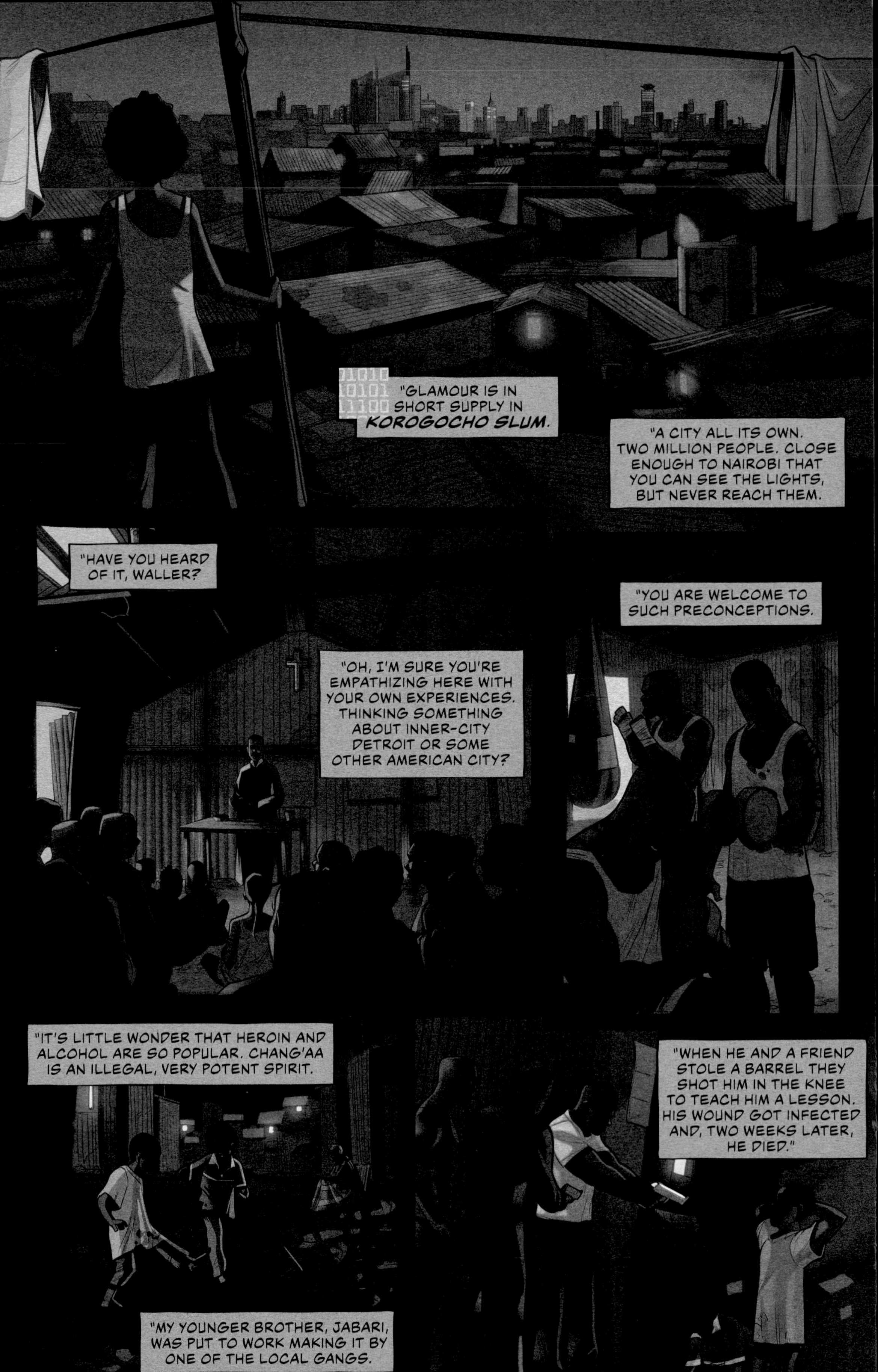
01010 10101 11100
"GLAMOUR IS IN SHORT SUPPLY IN *KOROGOCHO SLUM*.
"A CITY ALL ITS OWN. TWO MILLION PEOPLE. CLOSE ENOUGH TO NAIROBI THAT YOU CAN SEE THE LIGHTS, BUT NEVER REACH THEM.
"HAVE YOU HEARD OF IT, WALLER?
"OH, I'M SURE YOU'RE EMPATHIZING HERE WITH YOUR OWN EXPERIENCES. THINKING SOMETHING ABOUT INNER-CITY DETROIT OR SOME OTHER AMERICAN CITY?
"YOU ARE WELCOME TO SUCH PRECONCEPTIONS.
"IT'S LITTLE WONDER THAT HEROIN AND ALCOHOL ARE SO POPULAR. CHANG'AA IS AN ILLEGAL, VERY POTENT SPIRIT.
"MY YOUNGER BROTHER, JABARI, WAS PUT TO WORK MAKING IT BY ONE OF THE LOCAL GANGS.
"WHEN HE AND A FRIEND STOLE A BARREL THEY SHOT HIM IN THE KNEE TO TEACH HIM A LESSON. HIS WOUND GOT INFECTED AND, TWO WEEKS LATER, HE DIED."

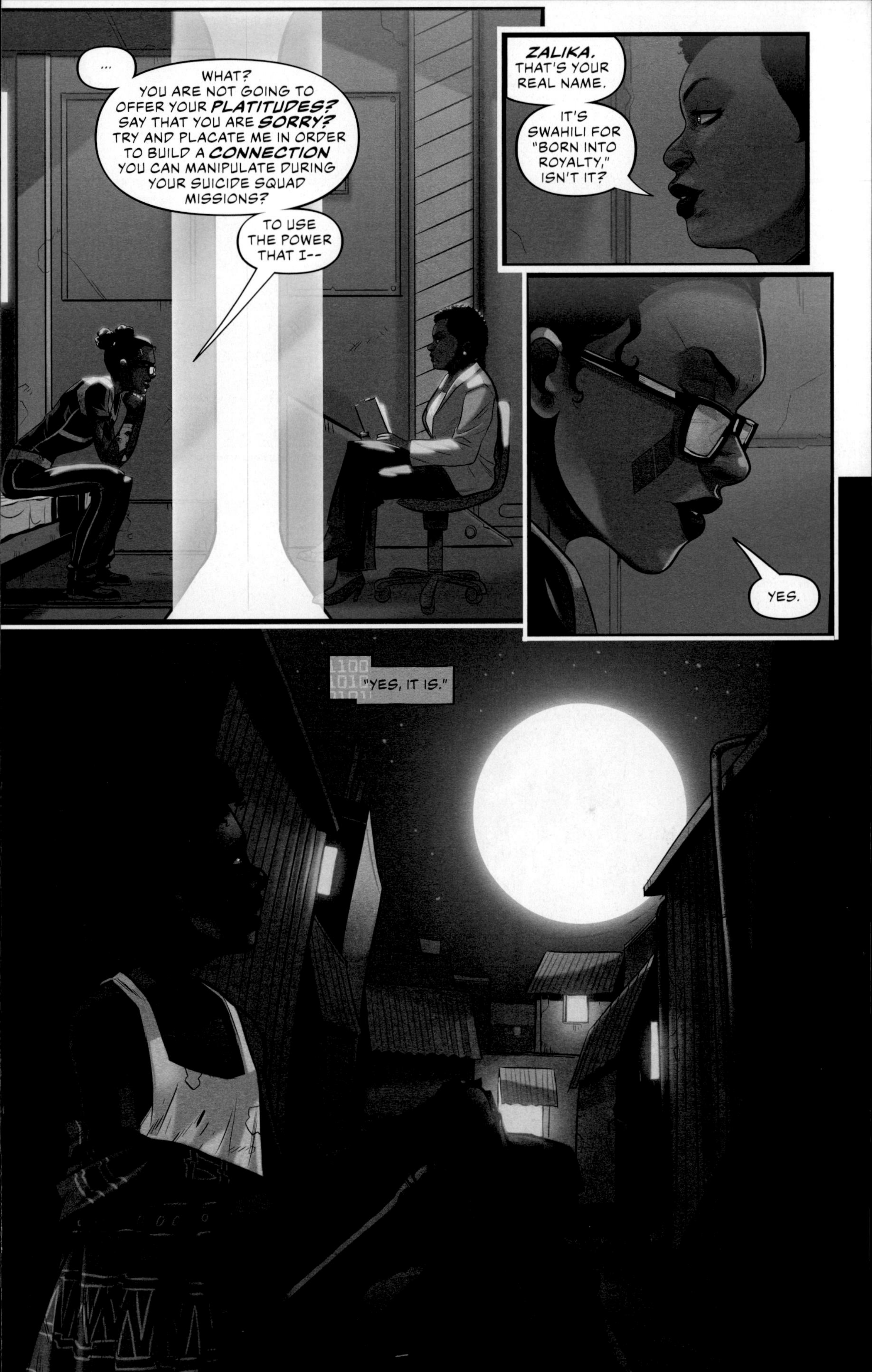
...
WHAT? YOU ARE NOT GOING TO OFFER YOUR PLATITUDES? SAY THAT YOU ARE SORRY? TRY AND PLACATE ME IN ORDER TO BUILD A CONNECTION YOU CAN MANIPULATE DURING YOUR SUICIDE SQUAD MISSIONS?
TO USE THE POWER THAT I--
ZALIKA. THAT'S YOUR REAL NAME.
IT'S SWAHILI FOR "BORN INTO ROYALTY," ISN'T IT?
YES.
"YES, IT IS."

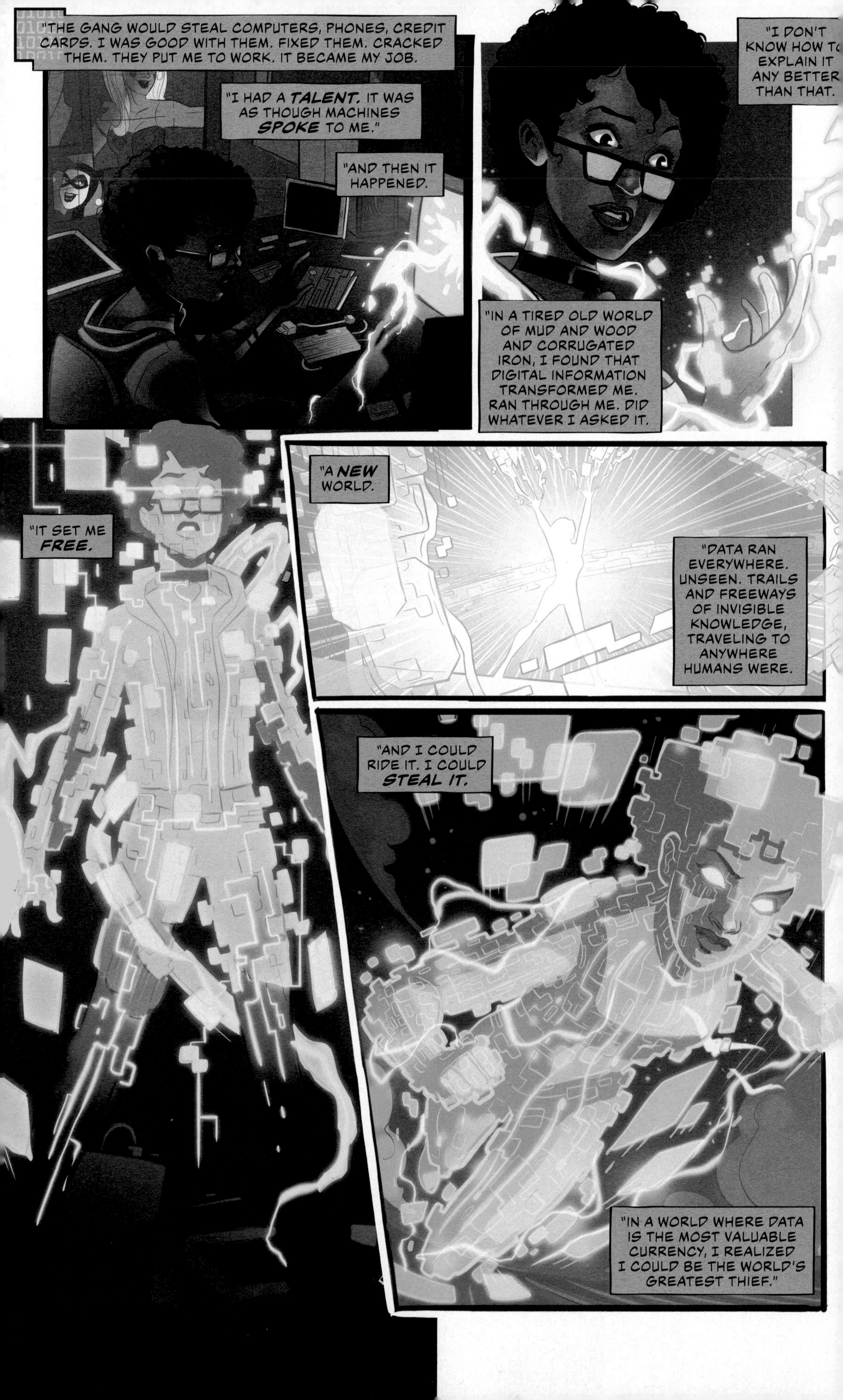
"THE GANG WOULD STEAL COMPUTERS, PHONES, CREDIT CARDS. I WAS GOOD WITH THEM. FIXED THEM. CRACKED THEM. THEY PUT ME TO WORK. IT BECAME MY JOB.
"I HAD A **TALENT.** IT WAS AS THOUGH MACHINES **SPOKE** TO ME."
"AND THEN IT HAPPENED.
"I DON'T KNOW HOW TO EXPLAIN IT ANY BETTER THAN THAT.
"IN A TIRED OLD WORLD OF MUD AND WOOD AND CORRUGATED IRON, I FOUND THAT DIGITAL INFORMATION TRANSFORMED ME. RAN THROUGH ME. DID WHATEVER I ASKED IT.
"IT SET ME **FREE.**
"A **NEW** WORLD.
"DATA RAN EVERYWHERE. UNSEEN. TRAILS AND FREEWAYS OF INVISIBLE KNOWLEDGE, TRAVELING TO ANYWHERE HUMANS WERE.
"AND I COULD RIDE IT. I COULD **STEAL IT.**
"IN A WORLD WHERE DATA IS THE MOST VALUABLE CURRENCY, I REALIZED I COULD BE THE WORLD'S GREATEST THIEF."

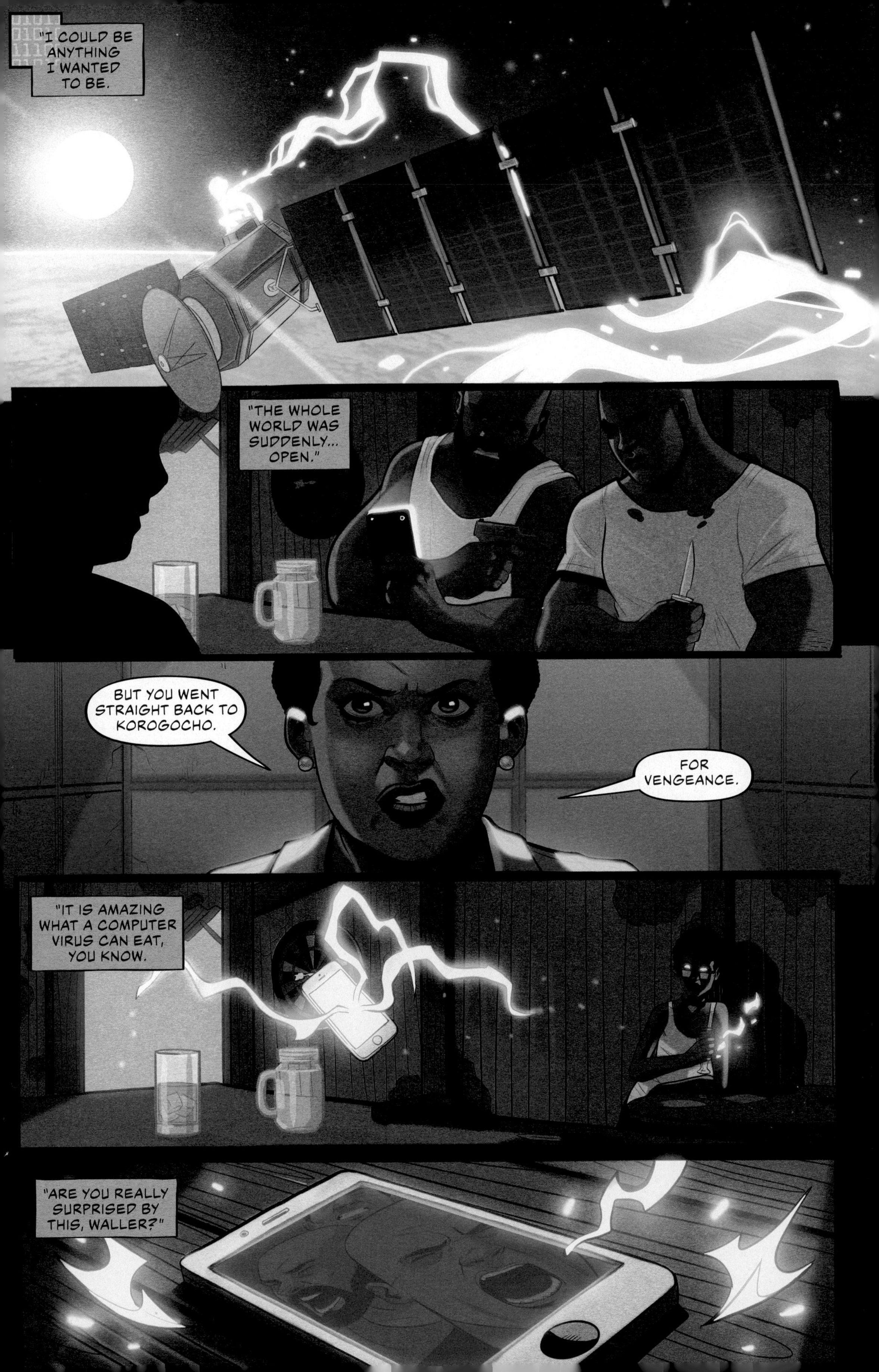
"I COULD BE ANYTHING I WANTED TO BE.
"THE WHOLE WORLD WAS SUDDENLY... OPEN."
BUT YOU WENT STRAIGHT BACK TO KOROGOCHO.
FOR VENGEANCE.
"IT IS AMAZING WHAT A COMPUTER VIRUS CAN EAT, YOU KNOW.
"ARE YOU REALLY SURPRISED BY THIS, WALLER?"

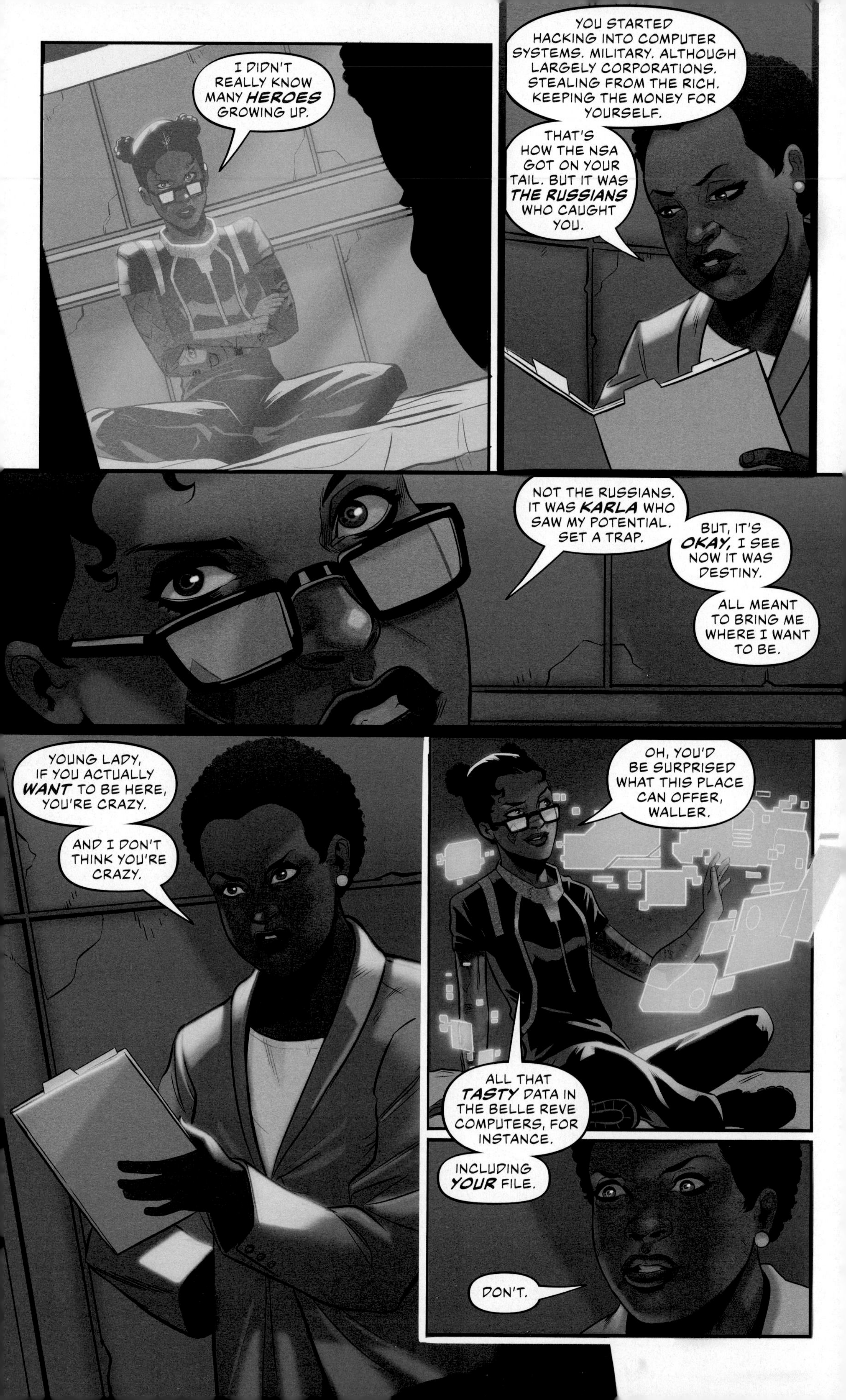

I DIDN'T REALLY KNOW MANY HEROES GROWING UP.
YOU STARTED HACKING INTO COMPUTER SYSTEMS. MILITARY. ALTHOUGH LARGELY CORPORATIONS. STEALING FROM THE RICH. KEEPING THE MONEY FOR YOURSELF.
THAT'S HOW THE NSA GOT ON YOUR TAIL. BUT IT WAS THE RUSSIANS WHO CAUGHT YOU.
NOT THE RUSSIANS. IT WAS KARLA WHO SAW MY POTENTIAL. SET A TRAP.
BUT, IT'S OKAY, I SEE NOW IT WAS DESTINY.
ALL MEANT TO BRING ME WHERE I WANT TO BE.
YOUNG LADY, IF YOU ACTUALLY WANT TO BE HERE, YOU'RE CRAZY.
AND I DON'T THINK YOU'RE CRAZY.
OH, YOU'D BE SURPRISED WHAT THIS PLACE CAN OFFER, WALLER.
ALL THAT TASTY DATA IN THE BELLE REVE COMPUTERS, FOR INSTANCE.
INCLUDING YOUR FILE.
DON'T.

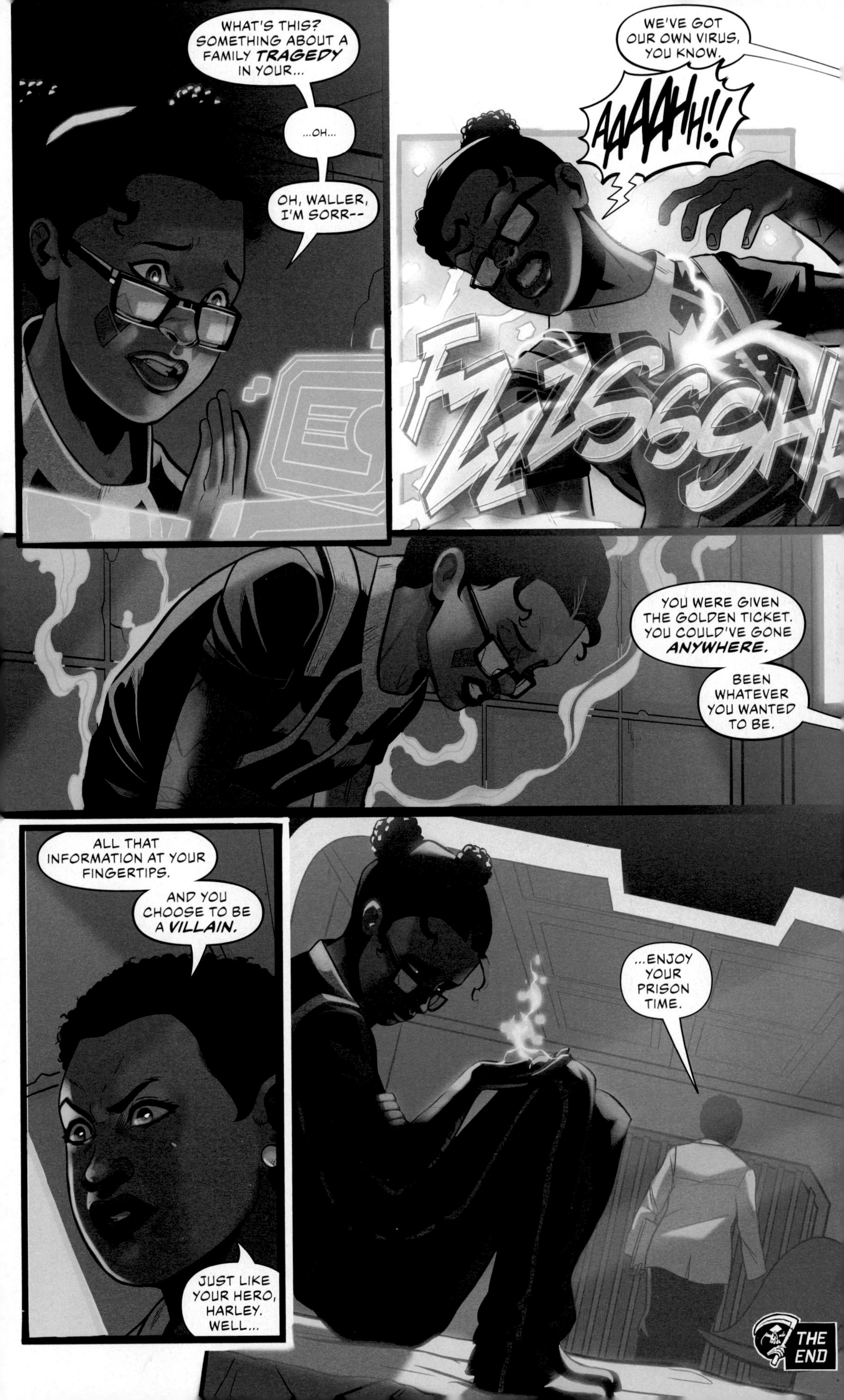
WHAT'S THIS? SOMETHING ABOUT A FAMILY TRAGEDY IN YOUR...
...OH...
OH, WALLER, I'M SORR--
WE'VE GOT OUR OWN VIRUS, YOU KNOW.
AAAAHH!!
FZZSSCHH
YOU WERE GIVEN THE GOLDEN TICKET. YOU COULD'VE GONE ANYWHERE.
BEEN WHATEVER YOU WANTED TO BE.
ALL THAT INFORMATION AT YOUR FINGERTIPS.
AND YOU CHOOSE TO BE A VILLAIN.
JUST LIKE YOUR HERO, HARLEY. WELL...
...ENJOY YOUR PRISON TIME.
THE END

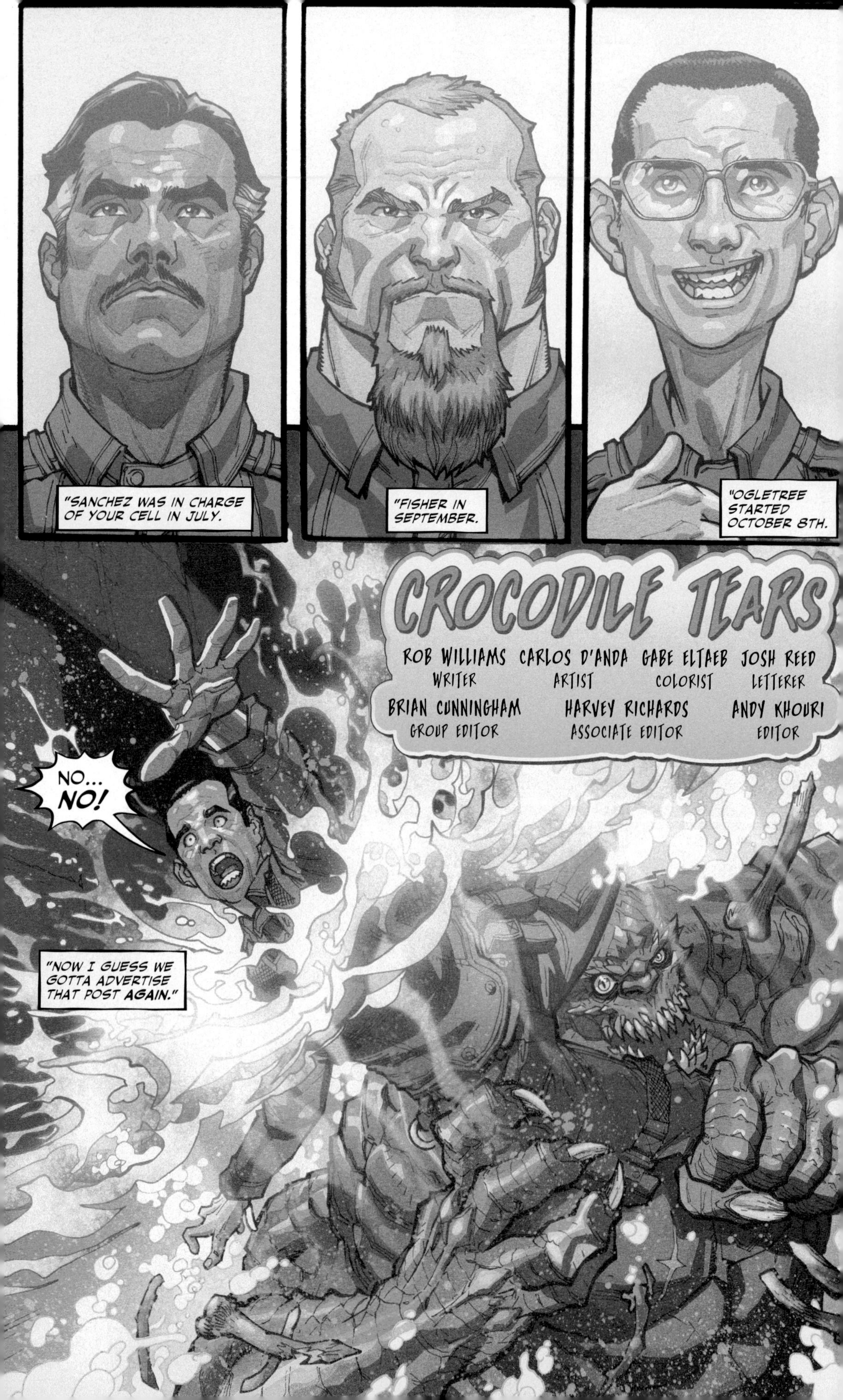
"SANCHEZ WAS IN CHARGE OF YOUR CELL IN JULY.
"FISHER IN SEPTEMBER.
"OGLETREE STARTED OCTOBER 8TH.
CROCODILE TEARS
ROB WILLIAMS WRITER
CARLOS D'ANDA ARTIST
GABE ELTAEB COLORIST
JOSH REED LETTERER
BRIAN CUNNINGHAM GROUP EDITOR
HARVEY RICHARDS ASSOCIATE EDITOR
ANDY KHOURI EDITOR
NO... NO!
"NOW I GUESS WE GOTTA ADVERTISE THAT POST AGAIN."

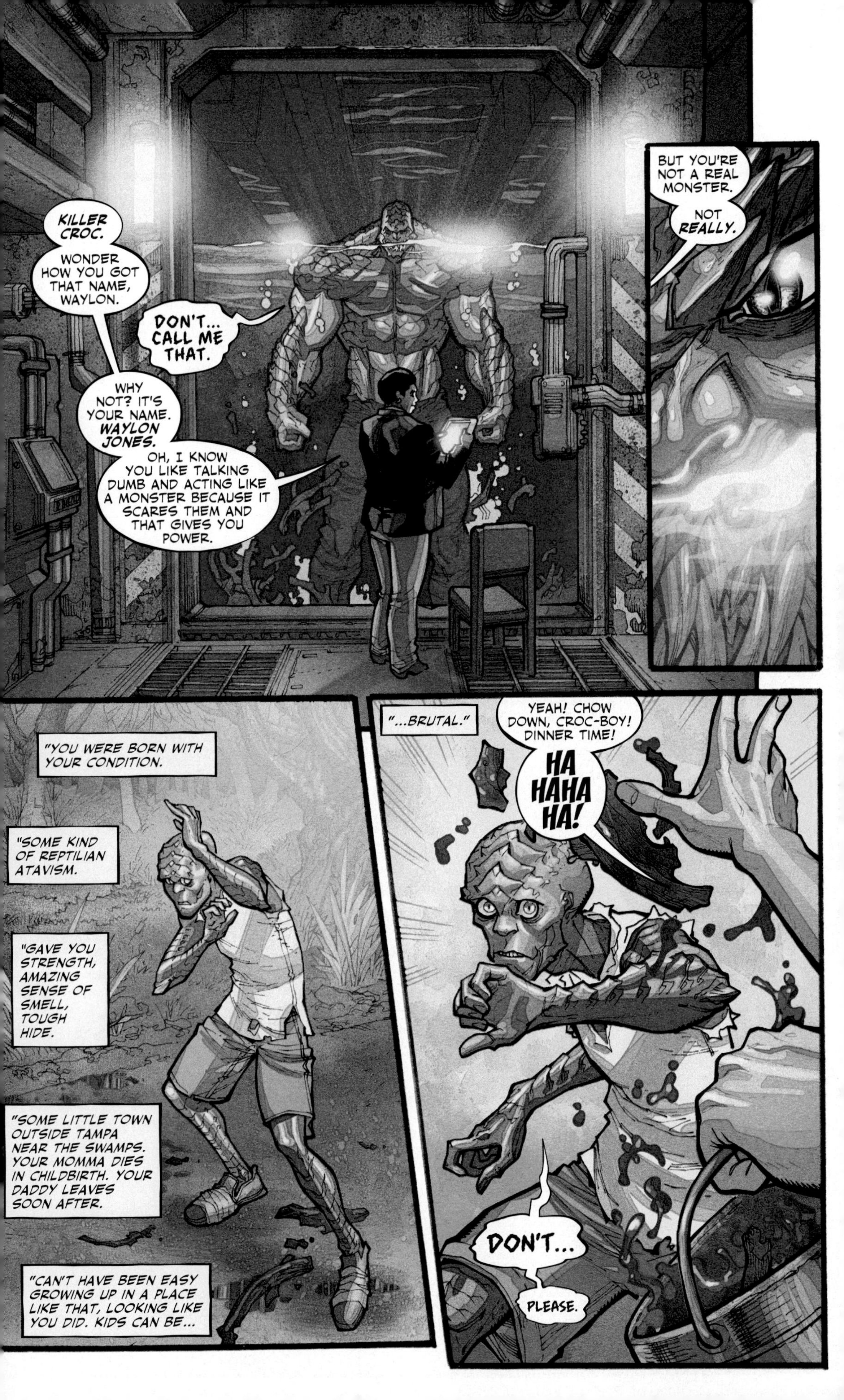
KILLER CROC.
WONDER HOW YOU GOT THAT NAME, WAYLON.
DON'T... CALL ME THAT.
WHY NOT? IT'S YOUR NAME. WAYLON JONES.
OH, I KNOW YOU LIKE TALKING DUMB AND ACTING LIKE A MONSTER BECAUSE IT SCARES THEM AND THAT GIVES YOU POWER.
BUT YOU'RE NOT A REAL MONSTER.
NOT REALLY.
"YOU WERE BORN WITH YOUR CONDITION.
"SOME KIND OF REPTILIAN ATAVISM.
"GAVE YOU STRENGTH, AMAZING SENSE OF SMELL, TOUGH HIDE.
"SOME LITTLE TOWN OUTSIDE TAMPA NEAR THE SWAMPS. YOUR MOMMA DIES IN CHILDBIRTH. YOUR DADDY LEAVES SOON AFTER.
"CAN'T HAVE BEEN EASY GROWING UP IN A PLACE LIKE THAT, LOOKING LIKE YOU DID. KIDS CAN BE...
"...BRUTAL."
YEAH! CHOW DOWN, CROC-BOY! DINNER TIME!
HA HAHA HA!
DON'T...
PLEASE.

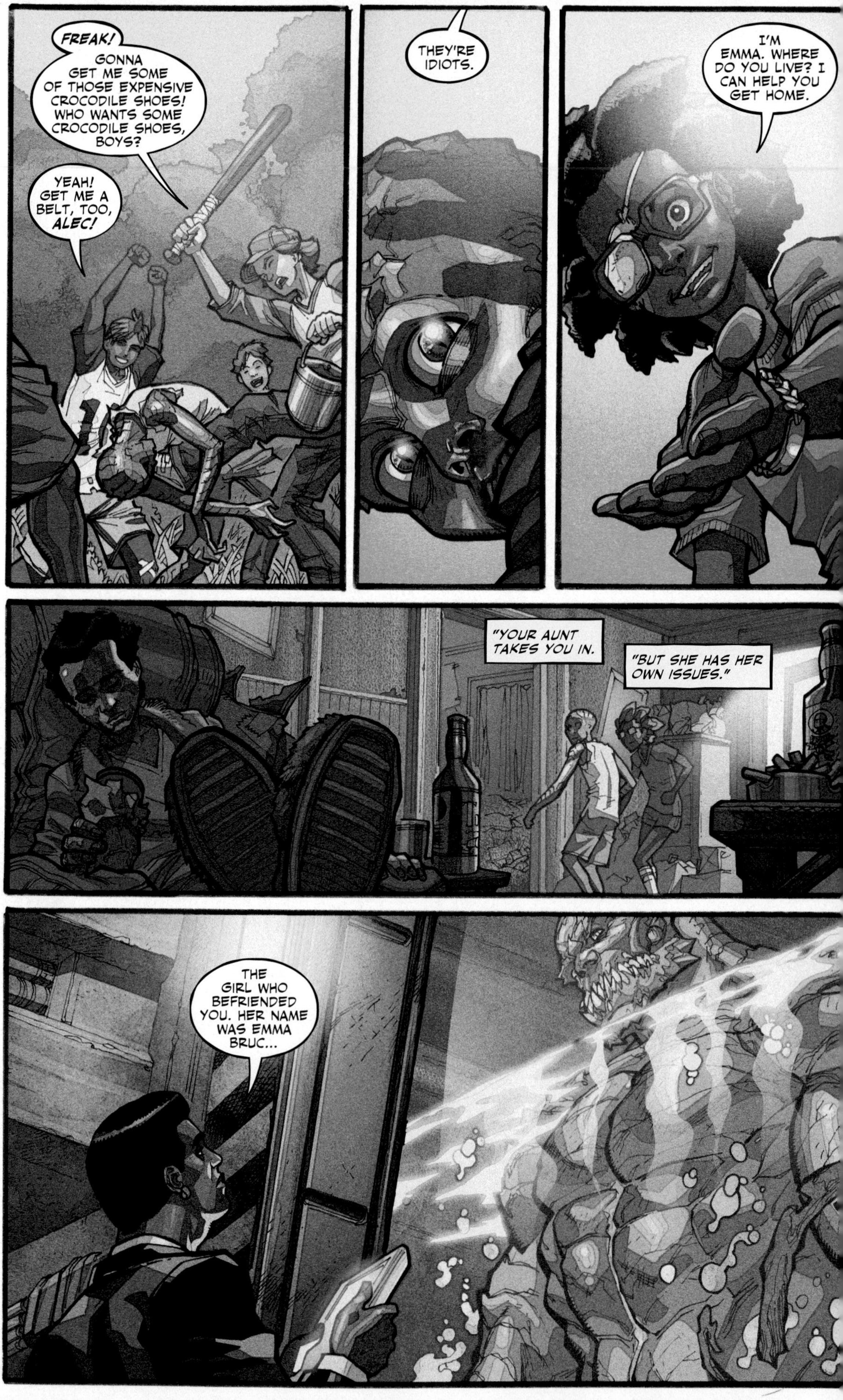
FREAK!
GONNA GET ME SOME OF THOSE EXPENSIVE CROCODILE SHOES! WHO WANTS SOME CROCODILE SHOES, BOYS?
YEAH! GET ME A BELT, TOO, ALEC!
THEY'RE IDIOTS.
I'M EMMA. WHERE DO YOU LIVE? I CAN HELP YOU GET HOME.
"YOUR AUNT TAKES YOU IN.
"BUT SHE HAS HER OWN ISSUES."
THE GIRL WHO BEFRIENDED YOU. HER NAME WAS EMMA BRUC...

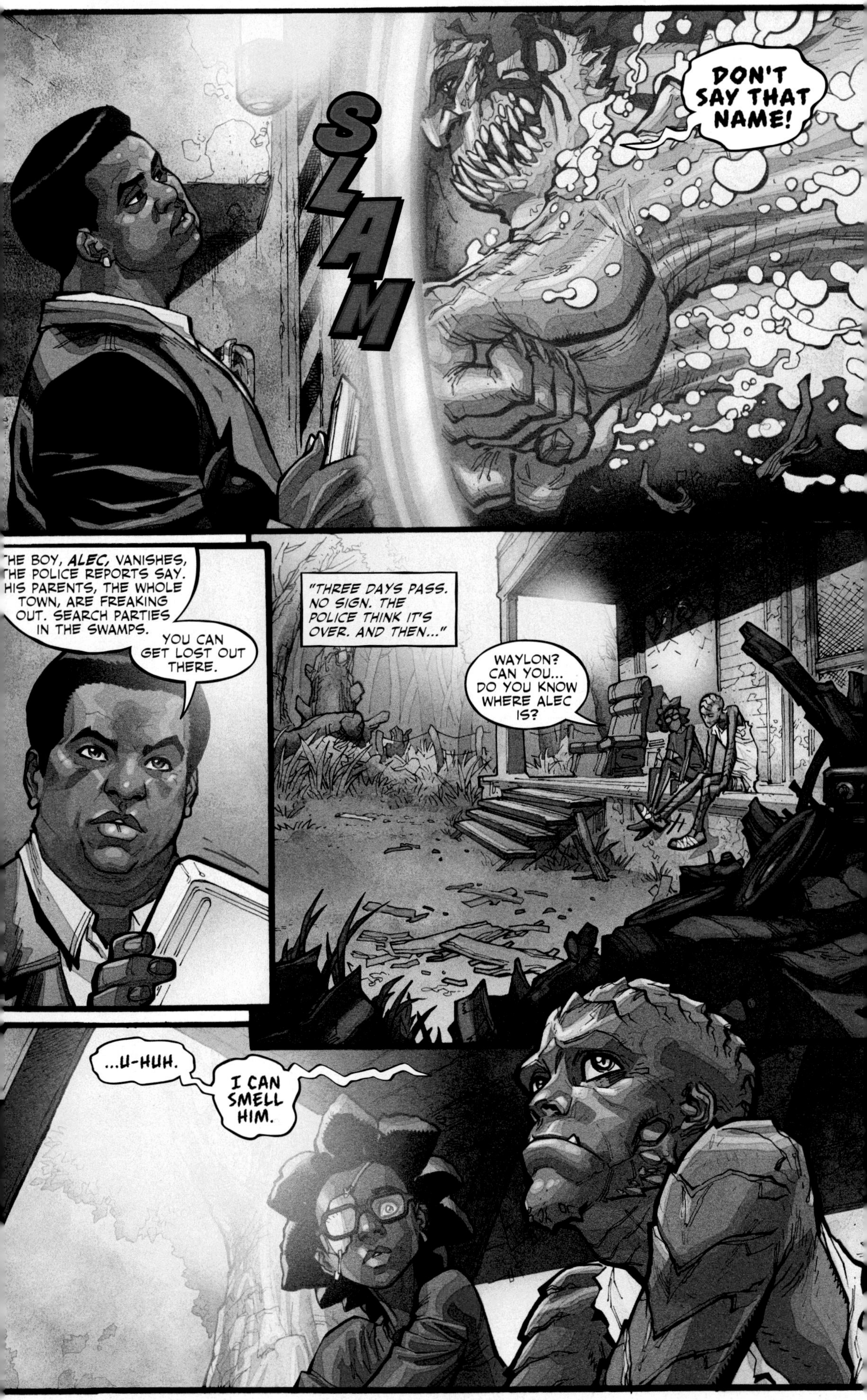
SLAM
DON'T SAY THAT NAME!
THE BOY, ALEC, VANISHES, THE POLICE REPORTS SAY. HIS PARENTS, THE WHOLE TOWN, ARE FREAKING OUT. SEARCH PARTIES IN THE SWAMPS.
YOU CAN GET LOST OUT THERE.
"THREE DAYS PASS. NO SIGN. THE POLICE THINK IT'S OVER. AND THEN..."
WAYLON? CAN YOU... DO YOU KNOW WHERE ALEC IS?
...U-HUH.
I CAN SMELL HIM.

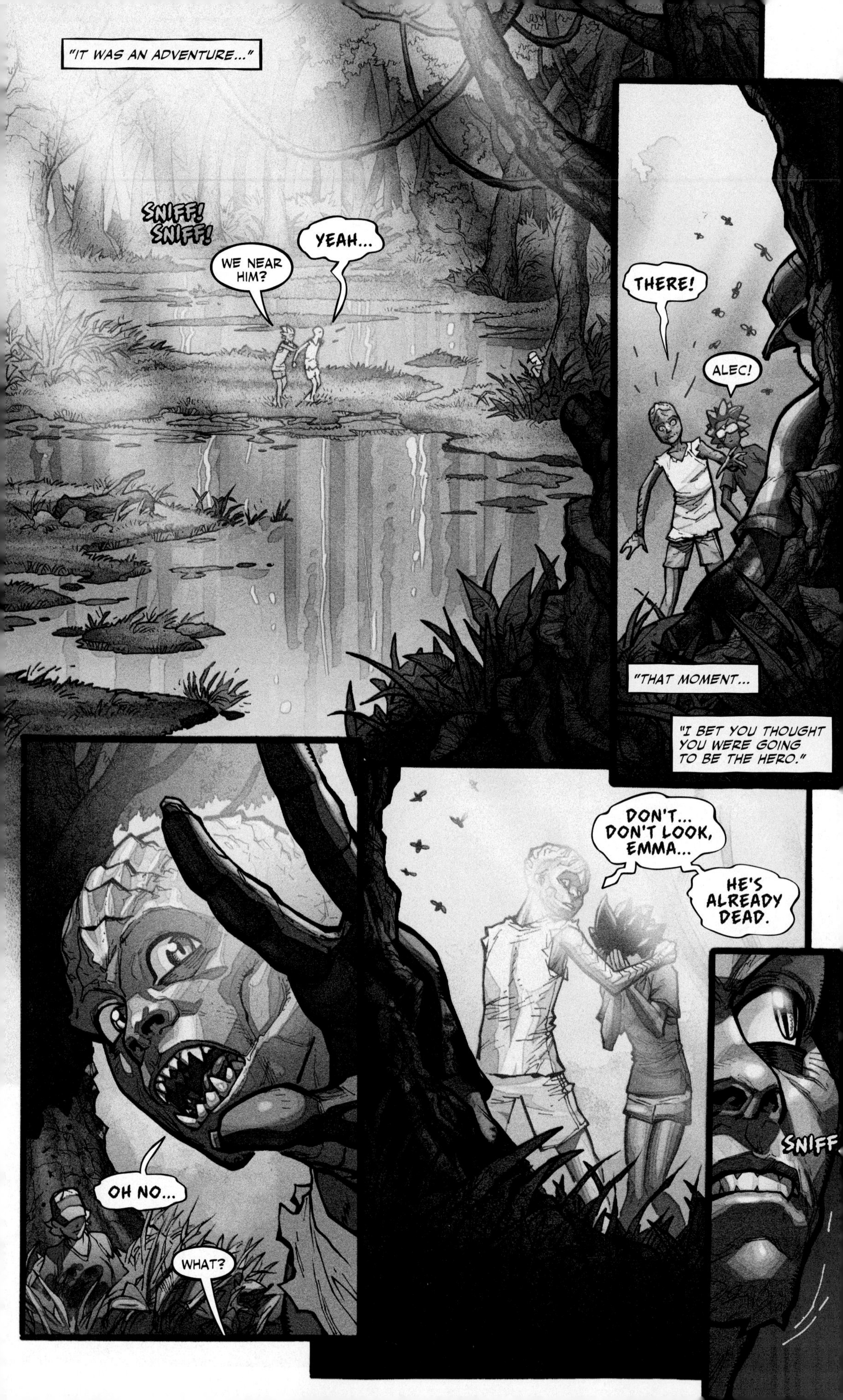
"IT WAS AN ADVENTURE..."
SNIFF! SNIFF!
WE NEAR HIM?
YEAH...
THERE!
ALEC!
"THAT MOMENT...
"I BET YOU THOUGHT YOU WERE GOING TO BE THE HERO."
OH NO...
WHAT?
DON'T... DON'T LOOK, EMMA...
HE'S ALREADY DEAD.
SNIFF

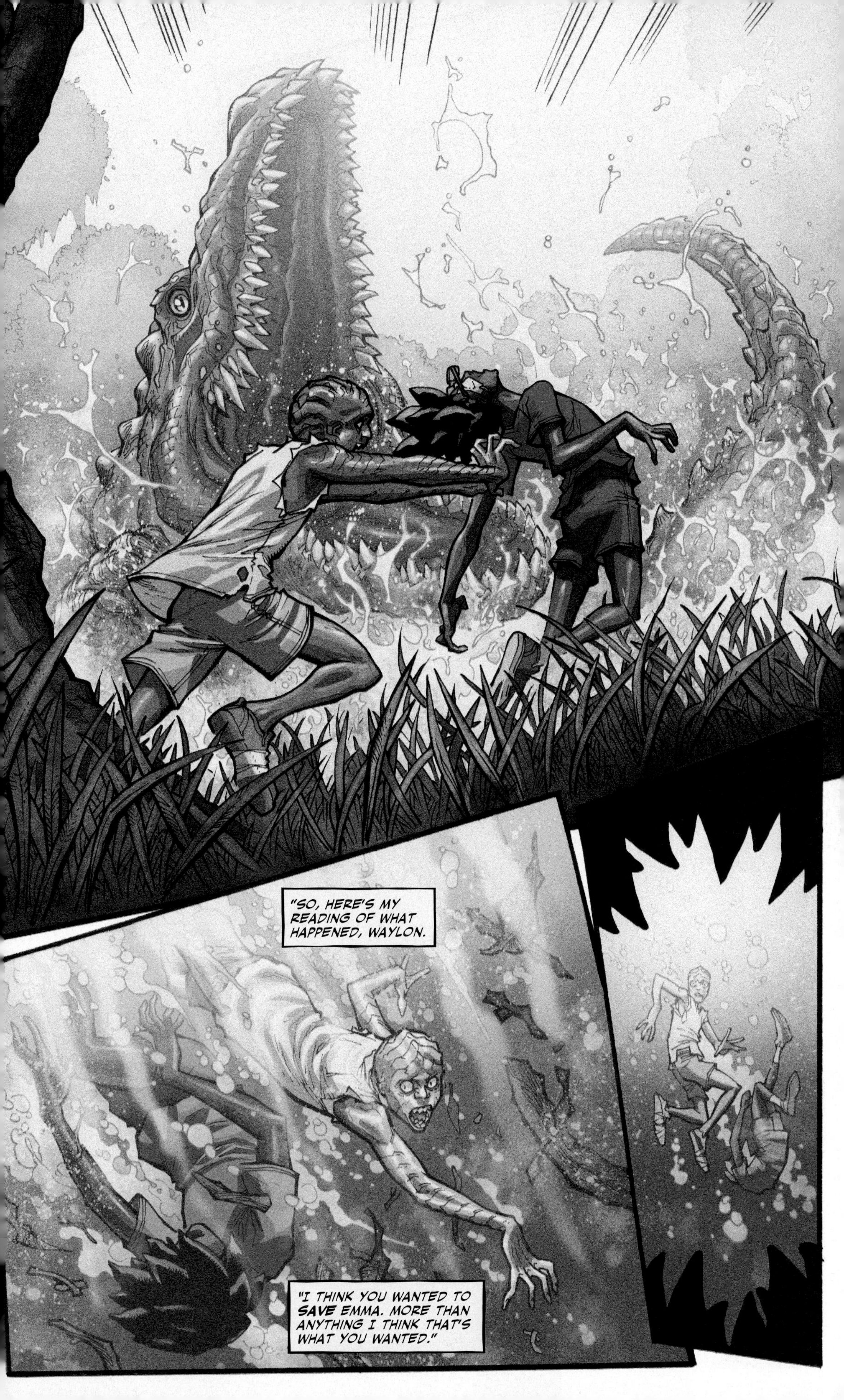
"SO, HERE'S MY READING OF WHAT HAPPENED, WAYLON.
"I THINK YOU WANTED TO SAVE EMMA. MORE THAN ANYTHING I THINK THAT'S WHAT YOU WANTED."

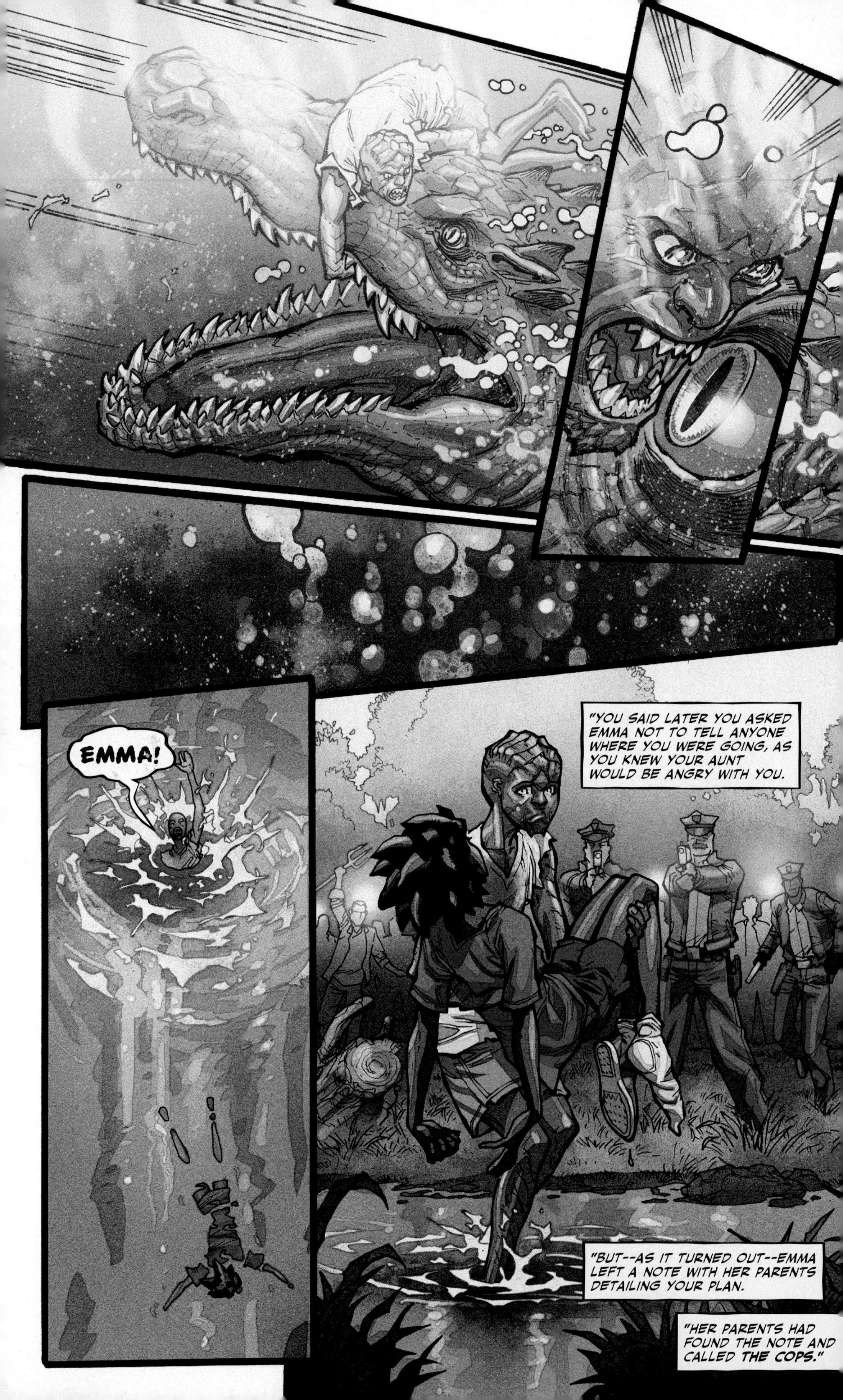
EMMA!
"YOU SAID LATER YOU ASKED EMMA NOT TO TELL ANYONE WHERE YOU WERE GOING, AS YOU KNEW YOUR AUNT WOULD BE ANGRY WITH YOU.
"BUT--AS IT TURNED OUT--EMMA LEFT A NOTE WITH HER PARENTS DETAILING YOUR PLAN.
"HER PARENTS HAD FOUND THE NOTE AND CALLED THE COPS."

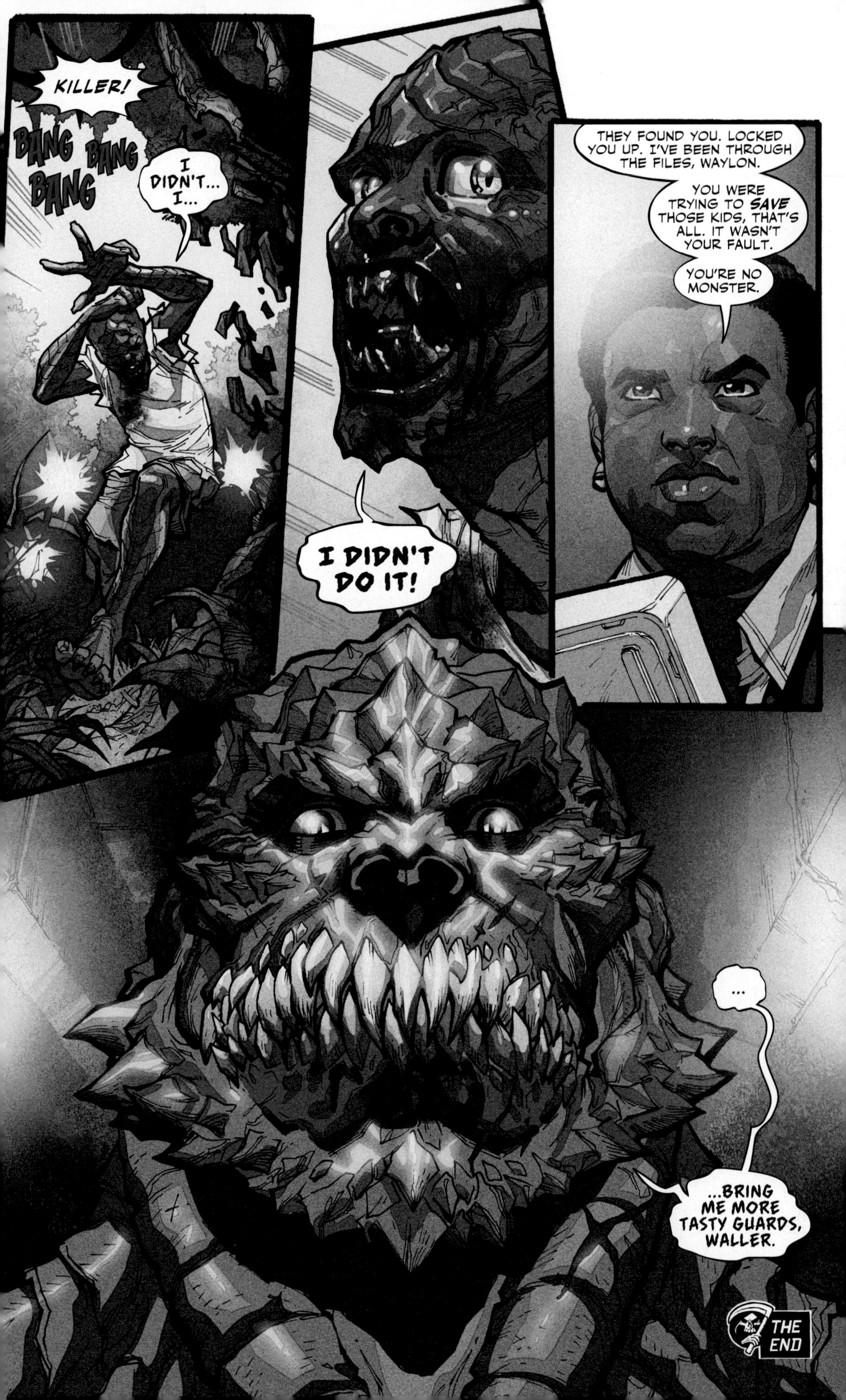
KILLER!
BANG BANG BANG
I DIDN'T... I...
I DIDN'T DO IT!
THEY FOUND YOU. LOCKED YOU UP. I'VE BEEN THROUGH THE FILES, WAYLON.
YOU WERE TRYING TO SAVE THOSE KIDS, THAT'S ALL. IT WASN'T YOUR FAULT.
YOU'RE NO MONSTER.
...
...BRING ME MORE TASTY GUARDS, WALLER.
THE END

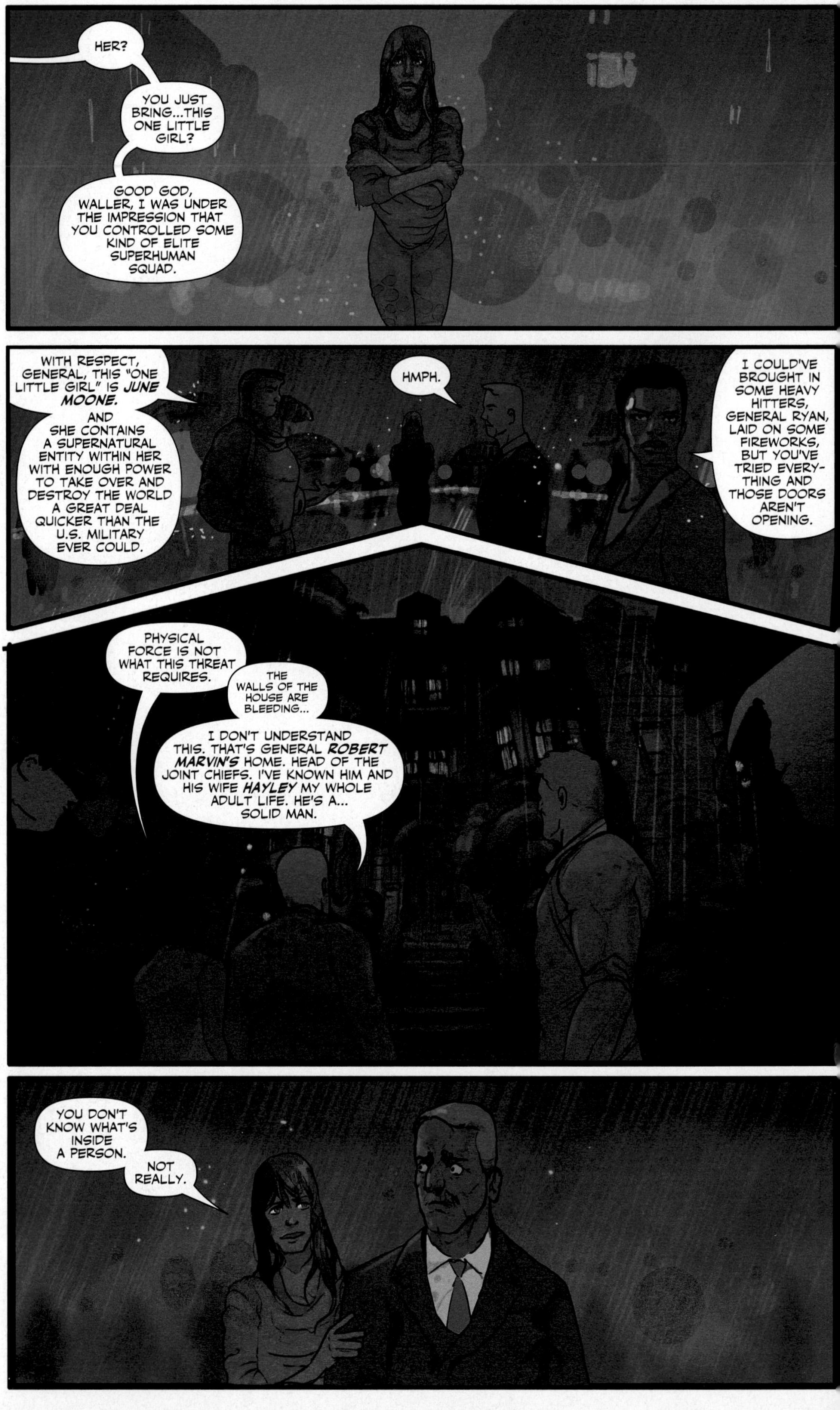
HER?
YOU JUST BRING...THIS ONE LITTLE GIRL?
GOOD GOD, WALLER, I WAS UNDER THE IMPRESSION THAT YOU CONTROLLED SOME KIND OF ELITE SUPERHUMAN SQUAD.
WITH RESPECT, GENERAL, THIS "ONE LITTLE GIRL" IS JUNE MOONE.
AND SHE CONTAINS A SUPERNATURAL ENTITY WITHIN HER WITH ENOUGH POWER TO TAKE OVER AND DESTROY THE WORLD A GREAT DEAL QUICKER THAN THE U.S. MILITARY EVER COULD.
HMPH.
I COULD'VE BROUGHT IN SOME HEAVY HITTERS, GENERAL RYAN, LAID ON SOME FIREWORKS, BUT YOU'VE TRIED EVERYTHING AND THOSE DOORS AREN'T OPENING.
PHYSICAL FORCE IS NOT WHAT THIS THREAT REQUIRES.
THE WALLS OF THE HOUSE ARE BLEEDING...
I DON'T UNDERSTAND THIS. THAT'S GENERAL ROBERT MARVIN'S HOME. HEAD OF THE JOINT CHIEFS. I'VE KNOWN HIM AND HIS WIFE HAYLEY MY WHOLE ADULT LIFE. HE'S A... SOLID MAN.
YOU DON'T KNOW WHAT'S INSIDE A PERSON.
NOT REALLY.

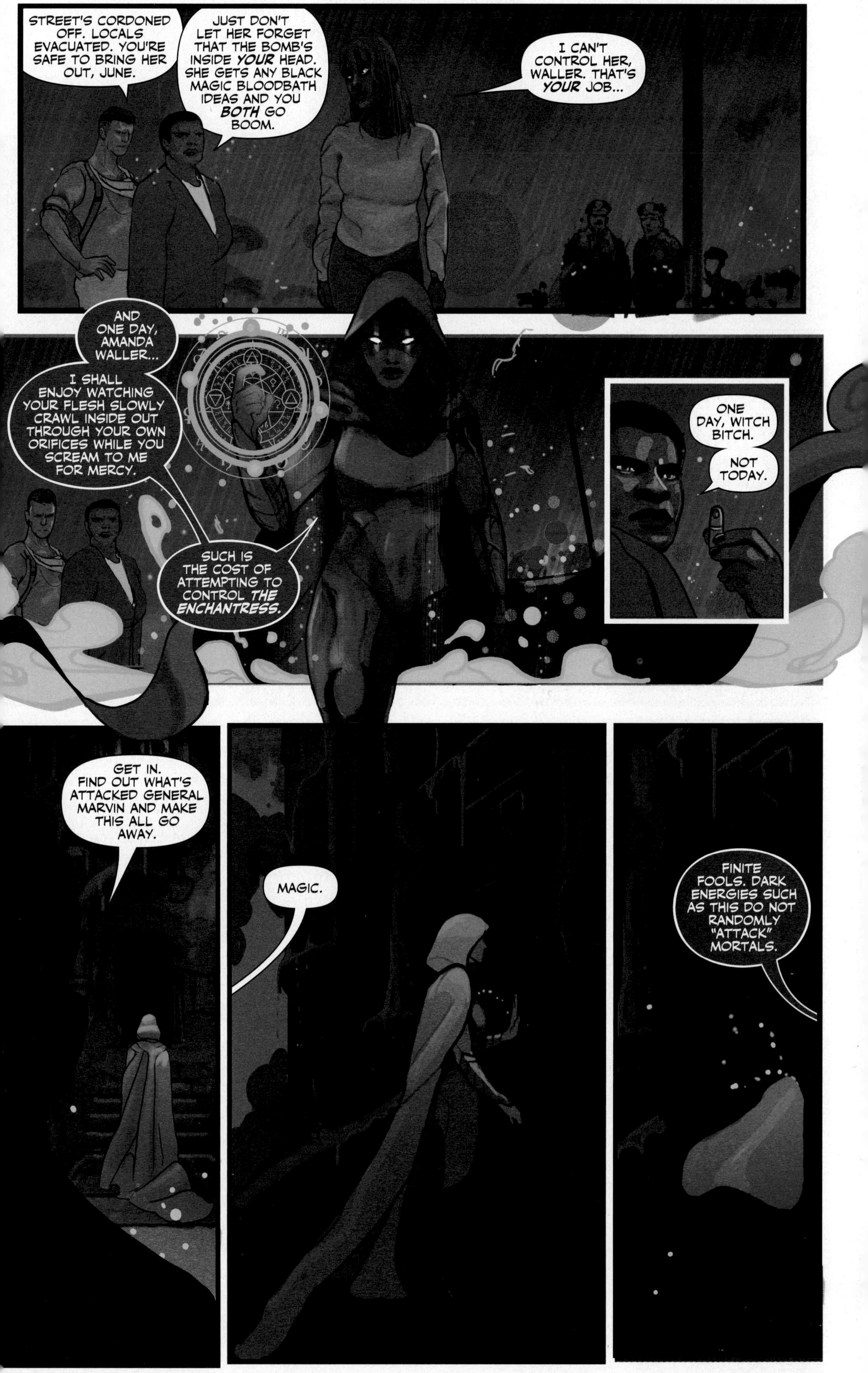
STREET'S CORDONED OFF. LOCALS EVACUATED. YOU'RE SAFE TO BRING HER OUT, JUNE.
JUST DON'T LET HER FORGET THAT THE BOMB'S INSIDE *YOUR* HEAD. SHE GETS ANY BLACK MAGIC BLOODBATH IDEAS AND YOU *BOTH* GO BOOM.
I CAN'T CONTROL HER, WALLER. THAT'S *YOUR* JOB...
AND ONE DAY, AMANDA WALLER...
I SHALL ENJOY WATCHING YOUR FLESH SLOWLY CRAWL INSIDE OUT THROUGH YOUR OWN ORIFICES WHILE YOU SCREAM TO ME FOR MERCY.
SUCH IS THE COST OF ATTEMPTING TO CONTROL *THE ENCHANTRESS.*
ONE DAY, WITCH BITCH.
NOT TODAY.
GET IN. FIND OUT WHAT'S ATTACKED GENERAL MARVIN AND MAKE THIS ALL GO AWAY.
MAGIC.
FINITE FOOLS. DARK ENERGIES SUCH AS THIS DO NOT RANDOMLY "ATTACK" MORTALS.

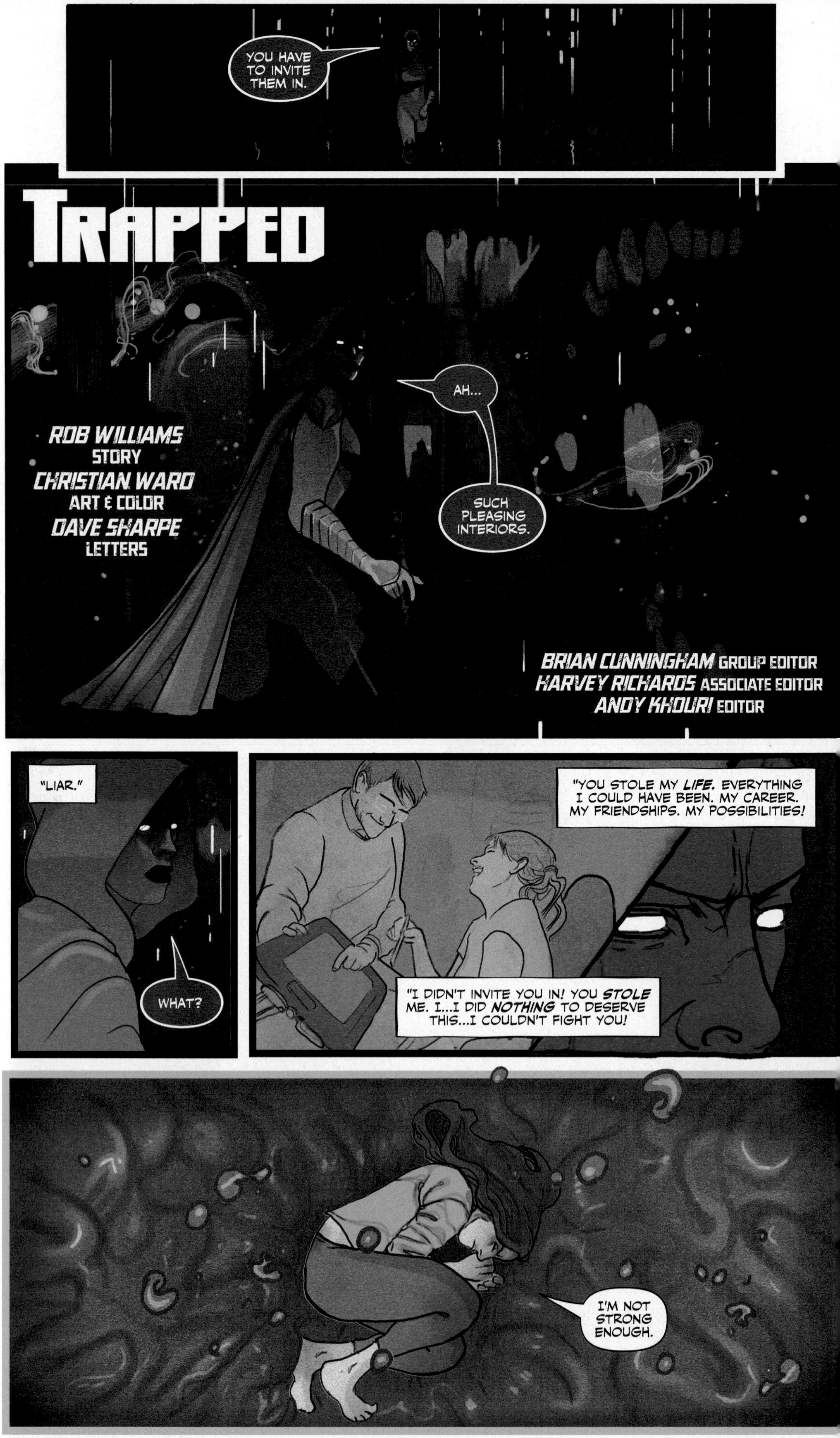
YOU HAVE TO INVITE THEM IN.
TRAPPED
AH...
SUCH PLEASING INTERIORS.
ROB WILLIAMS STORY
CHRISTIAN WARD ART & COLOR
DAVE SHARPE LETTERS
BRIAN CUNNINGHAM GROUP EDITOR
HARVEY RICHARDS ASSOCIATE EDITOR
ANDY KHOURI EDITOR
"LIAR."
WHAT?
"YOU STOLE MY LIFE. EVERYTHING I COULD HAVE BEEN. MY CAREER. MY FRIENDSHIPS. MY POSSIBILITIES!
"I DIDN'T INVITE YOU IN! YOU STOLE ME. I...I DID NOTHING TO DESERVE THIS...I COULDN'T FIGHT YOU!
I'M NOT STRONG ENOUGH.

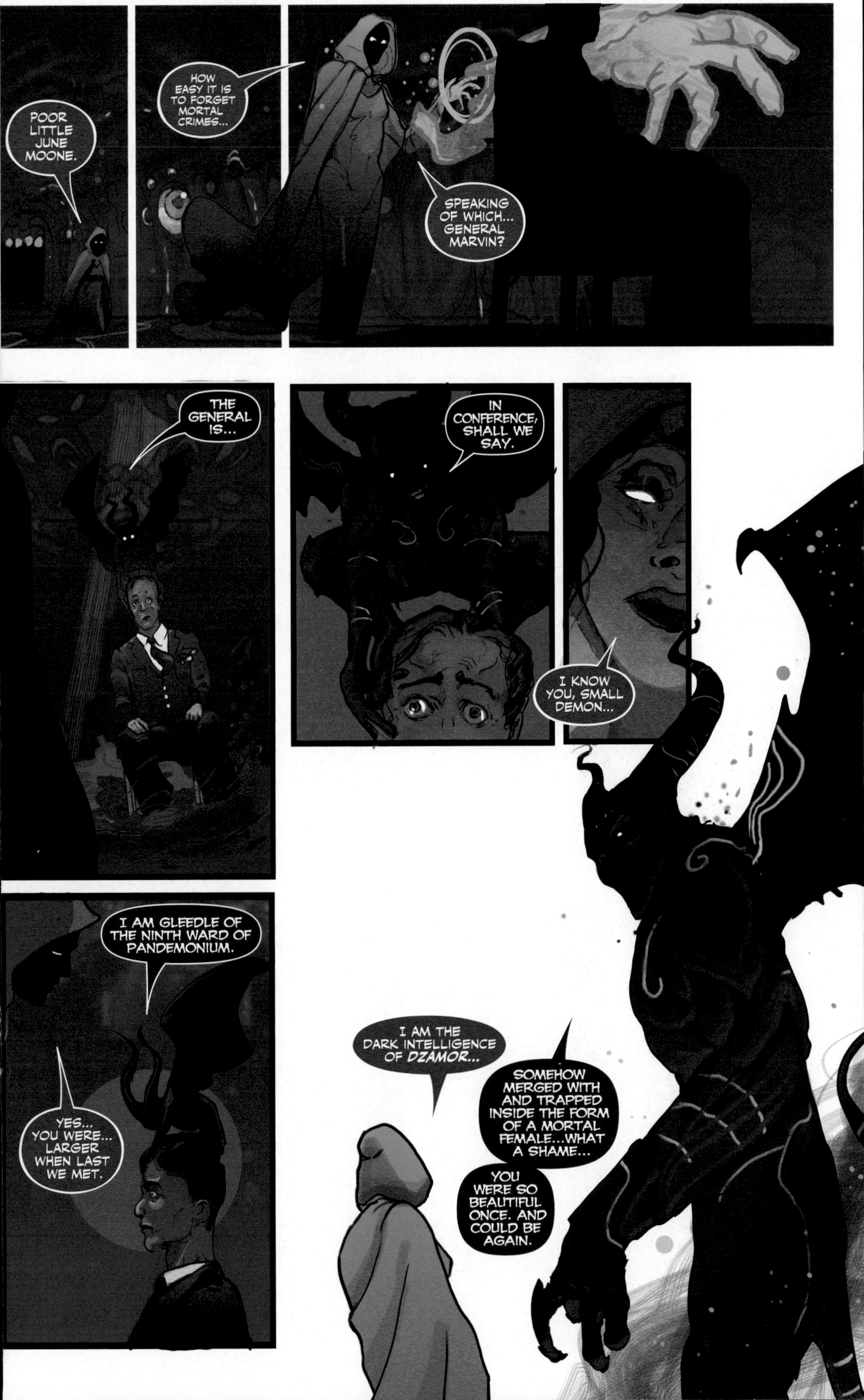
POOR LITTLE JUNE MOONE.
HOW EASY IT IS TO FORGET MORTAL CRIMES...
SPEAKING OF WHICH... GENERAL MARVIN?
THE GENERAL IS...
IN CONFERENCE, SHALL WE SAY.
I KNOW YOU, SMALL DEMON...
I AM GLEEDLE OF THE NINTH WARD OF PANDEMONIUM.
YES... YOU WERE... LARGER WHEN LAST WE MET.
I AM THE DARK INTELLIGENCE OF *DZAMOR*...
SOMEHOW MERGED WITH AND TRAPPED INSIDE THE FORM OF A MORTAL FEMALE...WHAT A SHAME...
YOU WERE SO BEAUTIFUL ONCE. AND COULD BE AGAIN.

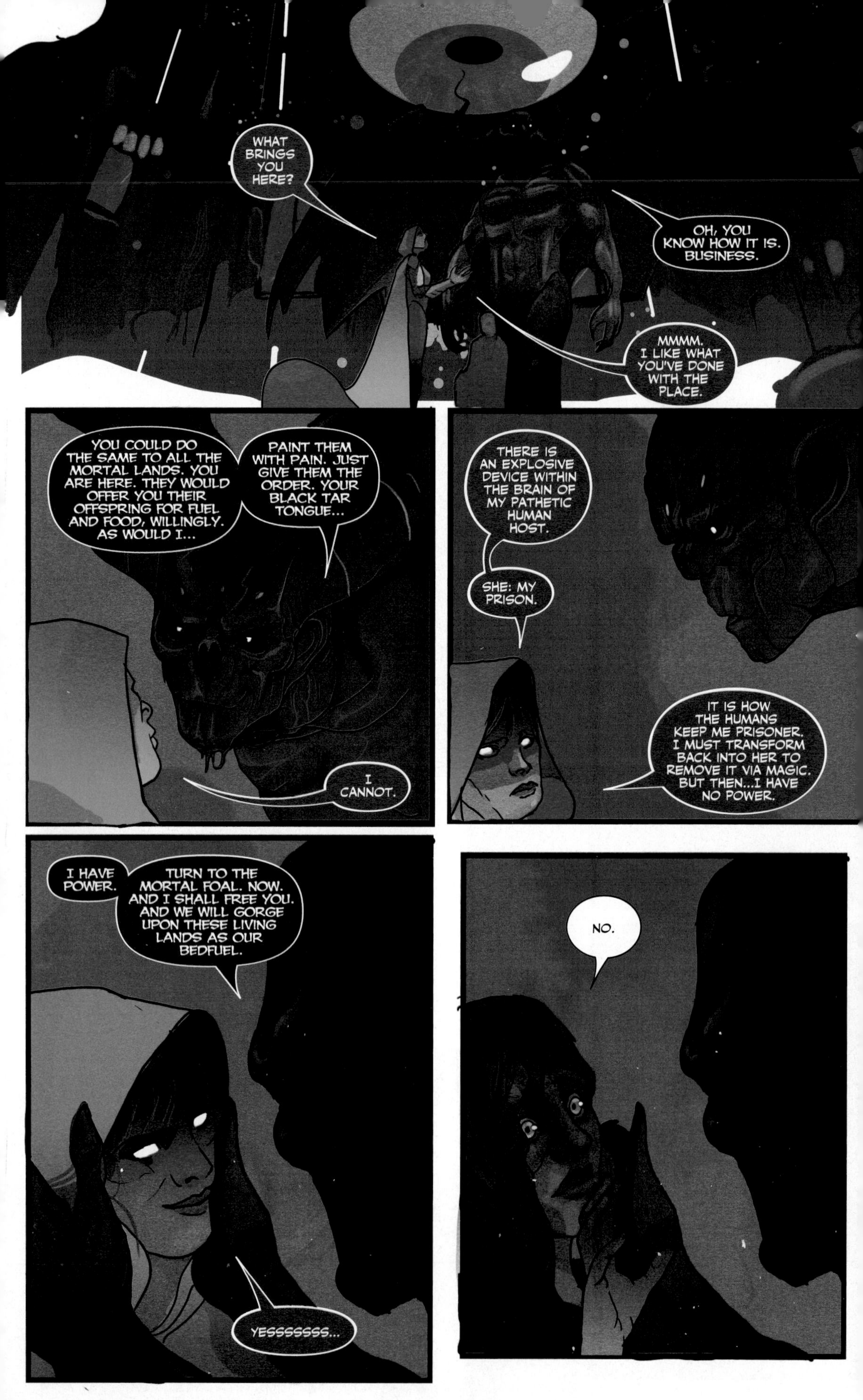
WHAT BRINGS YOU HERE?
OH, YOU KNOW HOW IT IS. BUSINESS.
MMMM. I LIKE WHAT YOU'VE DONE WITH THE PLACE.
YOU COULD DO THE SAME TO ALL THE MORTAL LANDS. YOU ARE HERE. THEY WOULD OFFER YOU THEIR OFFSPRING FOR FUEL AND FOOD, WILLINGLY. AS WOULD I...
PAINT THEM WITH PAIN. JUST GIVE THEM THE ORDER. YOUR BLACK TAR TONGUE...
I CANNOT.
THERE IS AN EXPLOSIVE DEVICE WITHIN THE BRAIN OF MY PATHETIC HUMAN HOST.
SHE: MY PRISON.
IT IS HOW THE HUMANS KEEP ME PRISONER. I MUST TRANSFORM BACK INTO HER TO REMOVE IT VIA MAGIC. BUT THEN...I HAVE NO POWER.
I HAVE POWER.
TURN TO THE MORTAL FOAL. NOW. AND I SHALL FREE YOU. AND WE WILL GORGE UPON THESE LIVING LANDS AS OUR BEDFUEL.
YESSSSSSS...
NO.

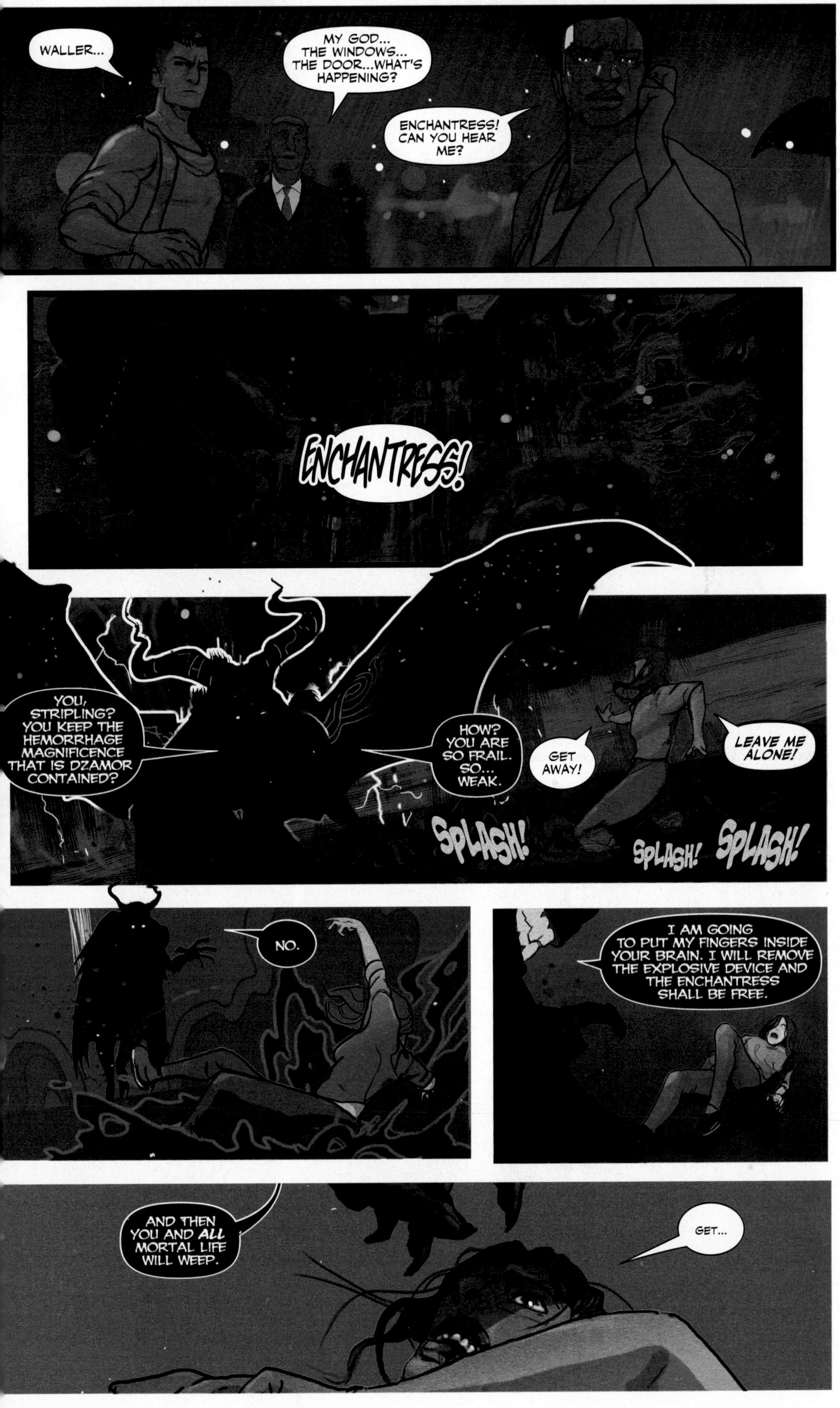
WALLER...
MY GOD... THE WINDOWS... THE DOOR...WHAT'S HAPPENING?
ENCHANTRESS! CAN YOU HEAR ME?
ENCHANTRESS!
YOU, STRIPLING? YOU KEEP THE HEMORRHAGE MAGNIFICENCE THAT IS DZAMOR CONTAINED?
HOW? YOU ARE SO FRAIL. SO... WEAK.
GET AWAY!
LEAVE ME ALONE!
SPLASH!
SPLASH!
SPLASH!
NO.
I AM GOING TO PUT MY FINGERS INSIDE YOUR BRAIN. I WILL REMOVE THE EXPLOSIVE DEVICE AND THE ENCHANTRESS SHALL BE FREE.
AND THEN YOU AND ALL MORTAL LIFE WILL WEEP.
GET...

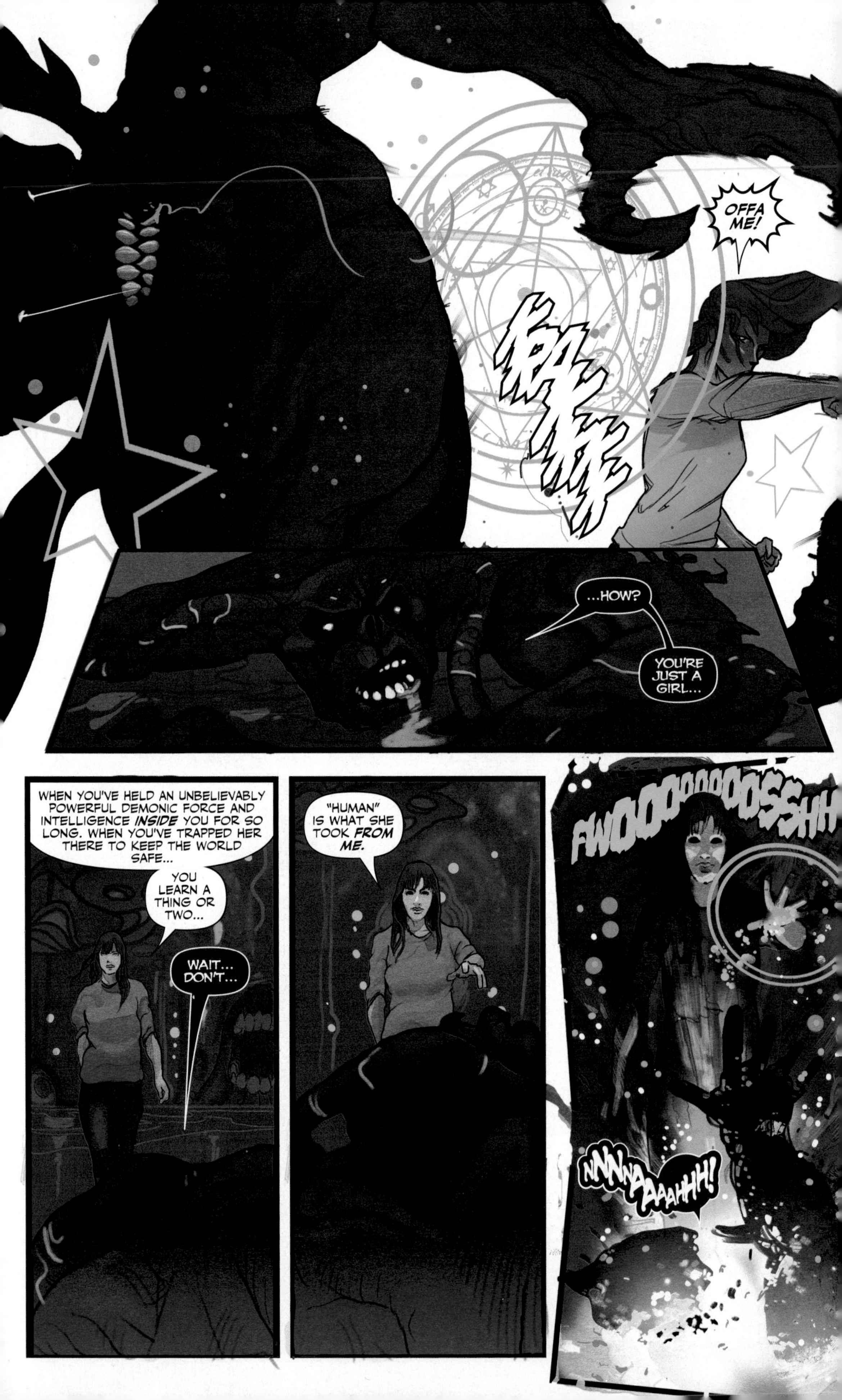
OFFA ME!
...HOW?
YOU'RE JUST A GIRL...
WHEN YOU'VE HELD AN UNBELIEVABLY POWERFUL DEMONIC FORCE AND INTELLIGENCE *INSIDE* YOU FOR SO LONG. WHEN YOU'VE TRAPPED HER THERE TO KEEP THE WORLD SAFE...
YOU LEARN A THING OR TWO...
WAIT... DON'T...
"HUMAN" IS WHAT SHE TOOK *FROM ME.*
FWOOOOOOOOSSHH
NNNNAAAAHHH!

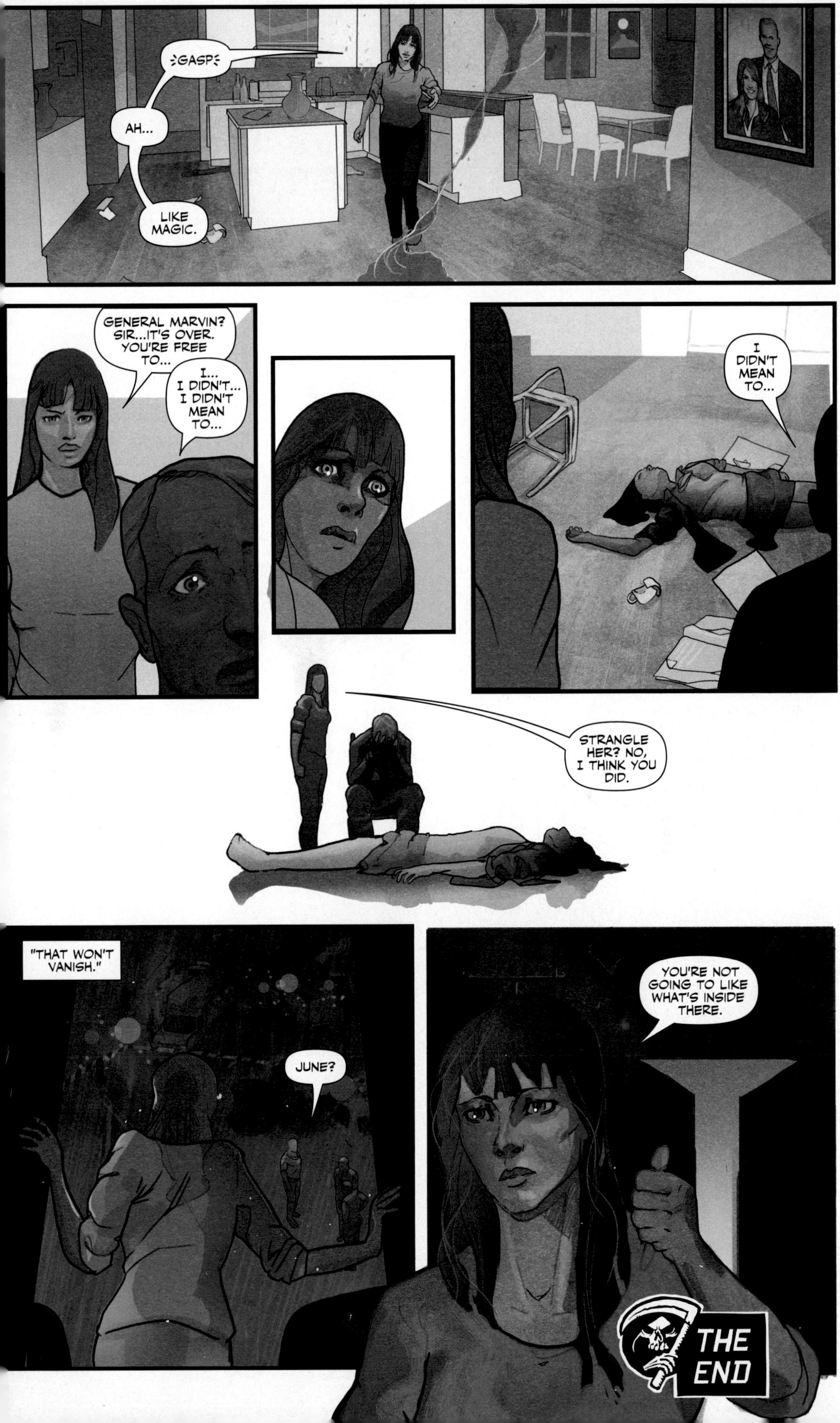

⁼GASP⁼
AH...
LIKE MAGIC.
GENERAL MARVIN? SIR...IT'S OVER. YOU'RE FREE TO...
I... I DIDN'T... I DIDN'T MEAN TO...
I DIDN'T MEAN TO...
STRANGLE HER? NO, I THINK YOU DID.
"THAT WON'T VANISH."
JUNE?
YOU'RE NOT GOING TO LIKE WHAT'S INSIDE THERE.
THE END

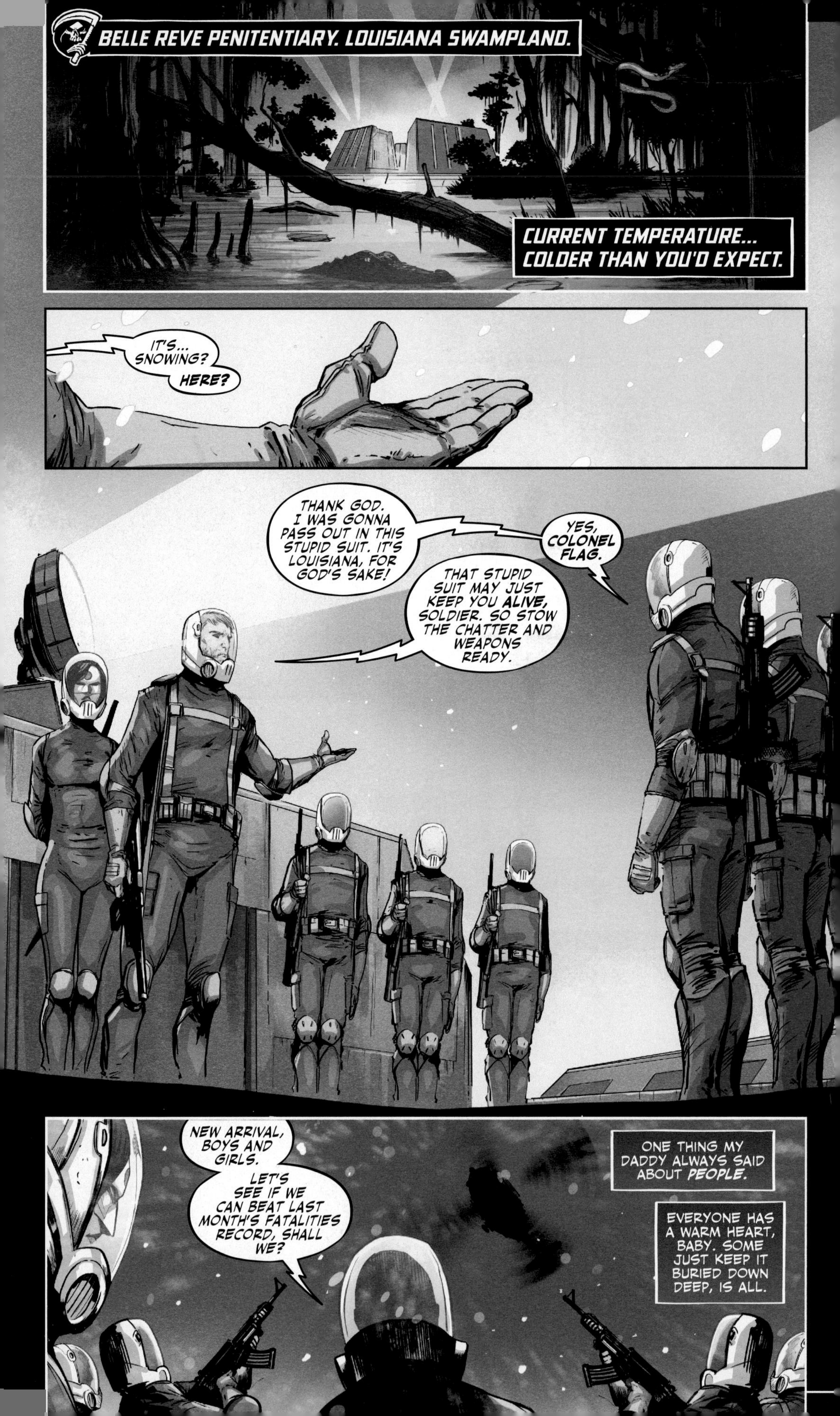
BELLE REVE PENITENTIARY. LOUISIANA SWAMPLAND.
CURRENT TEMPERATURE... COLDER THAN YOU'D EXPECT.
IT'S... SNOWING? HERE?
THANK GOD. I WAS GONNA PASS OUT IN THIS STUPID SUIT. IT'S LOUISIANA, FOR GOD'S SAKE!
THAT STUPID SUIT MAY JUST KEEP YOU ALIVE, SOLDIER. SO STOW THE CHATTER AND WEAPONS READY.
YES, COLONEL FLAG.
NEW ARRIVAL, BOYS AND GIRLS.
LET'S SEE IF WE CAN BEAT LAST MONTH'S FATALITIES RECORD, SHALL WE?
ONE THING MY DADDY ALWAYS SAID ABOUT PEOPLE.
EVERYONE HAS A WARM HEART, BABY. SOME JUST KEEP IT BURIED DOWN DEEP, IS ALL.

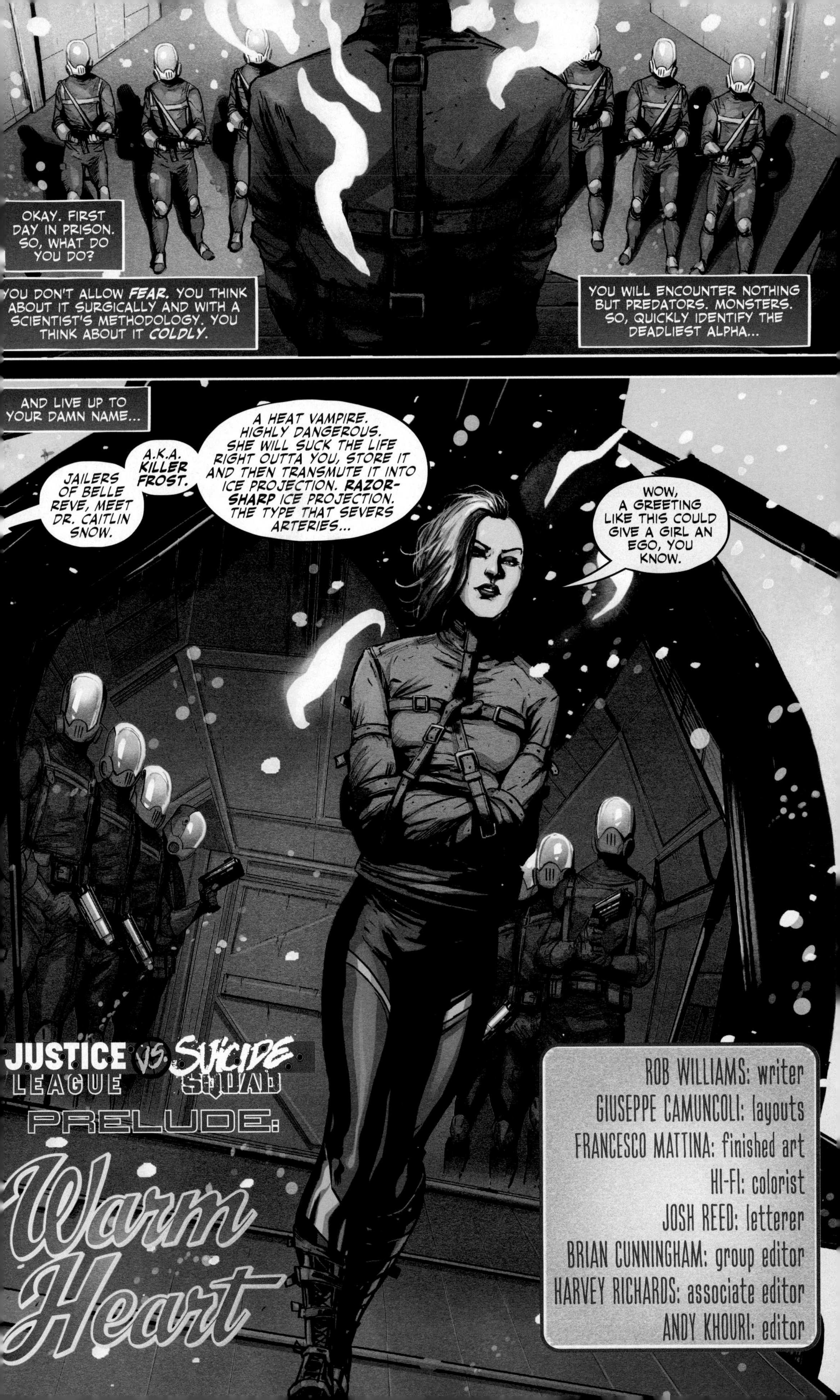
OKAY. FIRST DAY IN PRISON. SO, WHAT DO YOU DO?
YOU DON'T ALLOW FEAR. YOU THINK ABOUT IT SURGICALLY AND WITH A SCIENTIST'S METHODOLOGY. YOU THINK ABOUT IT COLDLY.
YOU WILL ENCOUNTER NOTHING BUT PREDATORS. MONSTERS. SO, QUICKLY IDENTIFY THE DEADLIEST ALPHA...
AND LIVE UP TO YOUR DAMN NAME...
JAILERS OF BELLE REVE, MEET DR. CAITLIN SNOW.
A.K.A. KILLER FROST.
A HEAT VAMPIRE. HIGHLY DANGEROUS. SHE WILL SUCK THE LIFE RIGHT OUTTA YOU, STORE IT AND THEN TRANSMUTE IT INTO ICE PROJECTION. RAZOR-SHARP ICE PROJECTION. THE TYPE THAT SEVERS ARTERIES...
WOW, A GREETING LIKE THIS COULD GIVE A GIRL AN EGO, YOU KNOW.
JUSTICE LEAGUE VS. SUICIDE SQUAD
PRELUDE:
Warm Heart
ROB WILLIAMS: writer
GIUSEPPE CAMUNCOLI: layouts
FRANCESCO MATTINA: finished art
HI-FI: colorist
JOSH REED: letterer
BRIAN CUNNINGHAM: group editor
HARVEY RICHARDS: associate editor
ANDY KHOURI: editor

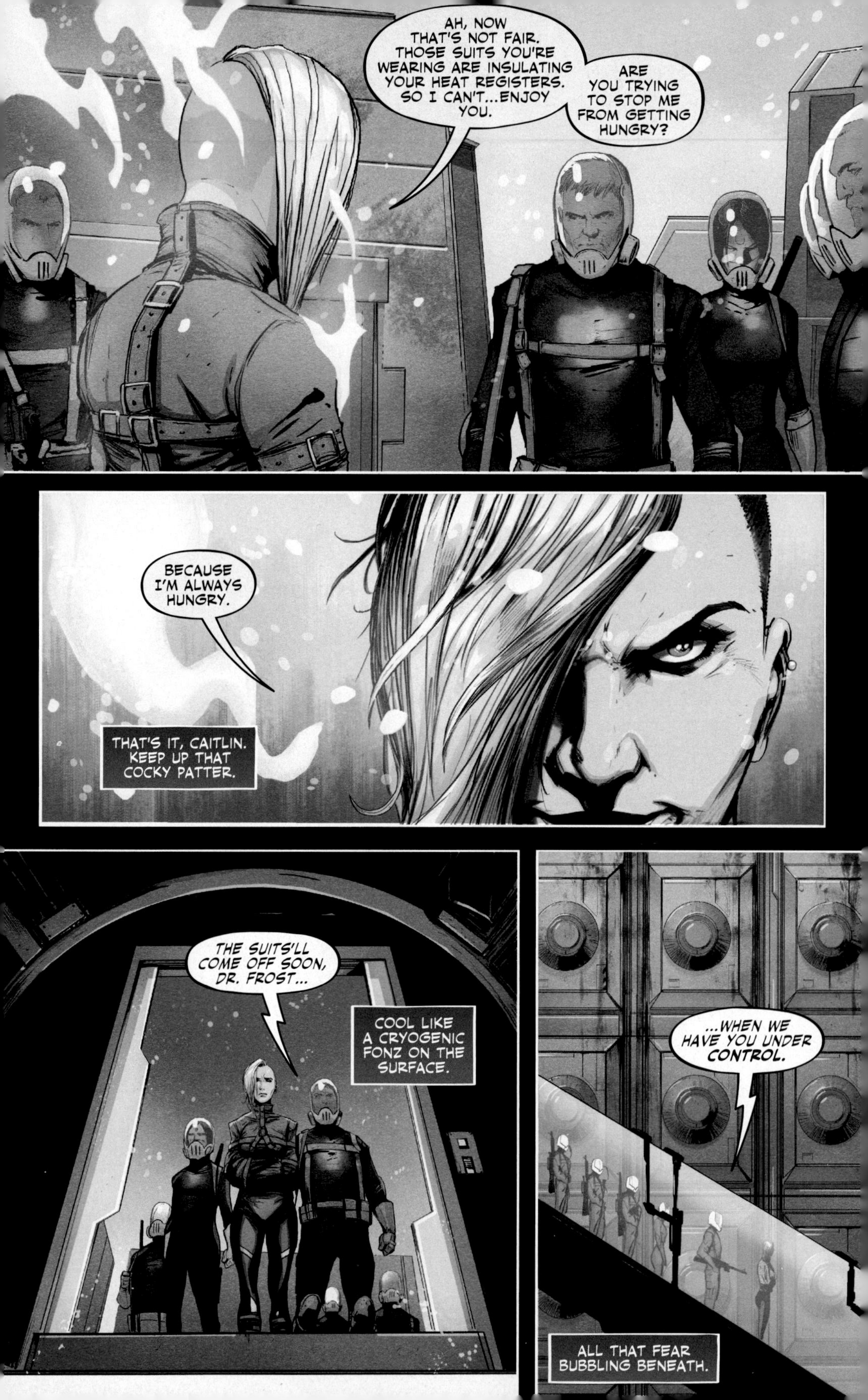
AH, NOW THAT'S NOT FAIR. THOSE SUITS YOU'RE WEARING ARE INSULATING YOUR HEAT REGISTERS. SO I CAN'T...ENJOY YOU.
ARE YOU TRYING TO STOP ME FROM GETTING HUNGRY?
BECAUSE I'M ALWAYS HUNGRY.
THAT'S IT, CAITLIN. KEEP UP THAT COCKY PATTER.
THE SUITS'LL COME OFF SOON, DR. FROST...
COOL LIKE A CRYOGENIC FONZ ON THE SURFACE.
...WHEN WE HAVE YOU UNDER CONTROL.
ALL THAT FEAR BUBBLING BENEATH.

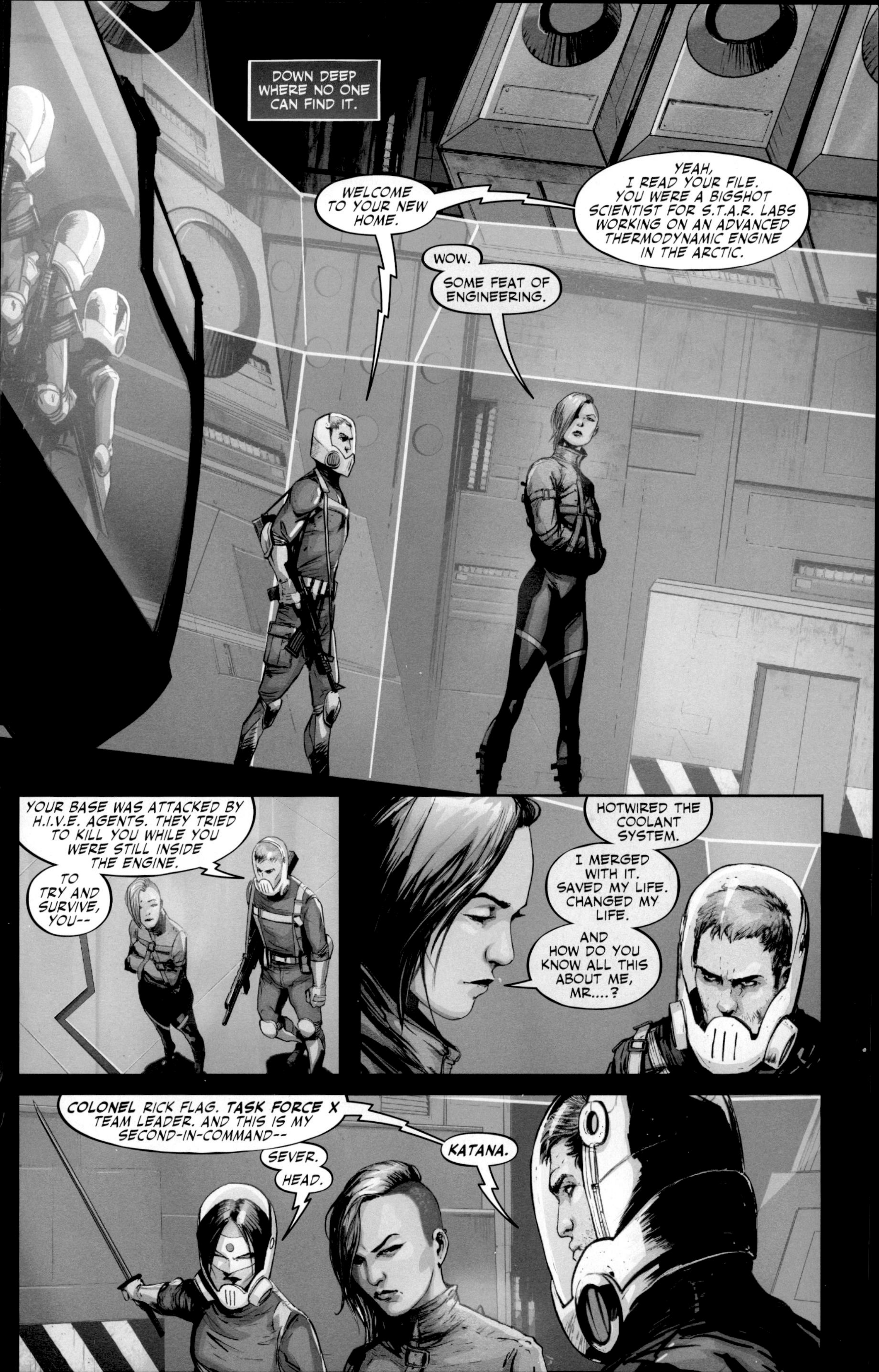
DOWN DEEP WHERE NO ONE CAN FIND IT.
WELCOME TO YOUR NEW HOME.
YEAH, I READ YOUR FILE. YOU WERE A BIGSHOT SCIENTIST FOR S.T.A.R. LABS WORKING ON AN ADVANCED THERMODYNAMIC ENGINE IN THE ARCTIC.
WOW.
SOME FEAT OF ENGINEERING.
YOUR BASE WAS ATTACKED BY H.I.V.E. AGENTS. THEY TRIED TO KILL YOU WHILE YOU WERE STILL INSIDE THE ENGINE.
TO TRY AND SURVIVE, YOU--
HOTWIRED THE COOLANT SYSTEM.
I MERGED WITH IT. SAVED MY LIFE. CHANGED MY LIFE.
AND HOW DO YOU KNOW ALL THIS ABOUT ME, MR....?
COLONEL RICK FLAG. TASK FORCE X TEAM LEADER. AND THIS IS MY SECOND-IN-COMMAND--
KATANA.
SEVER.
HEAD.

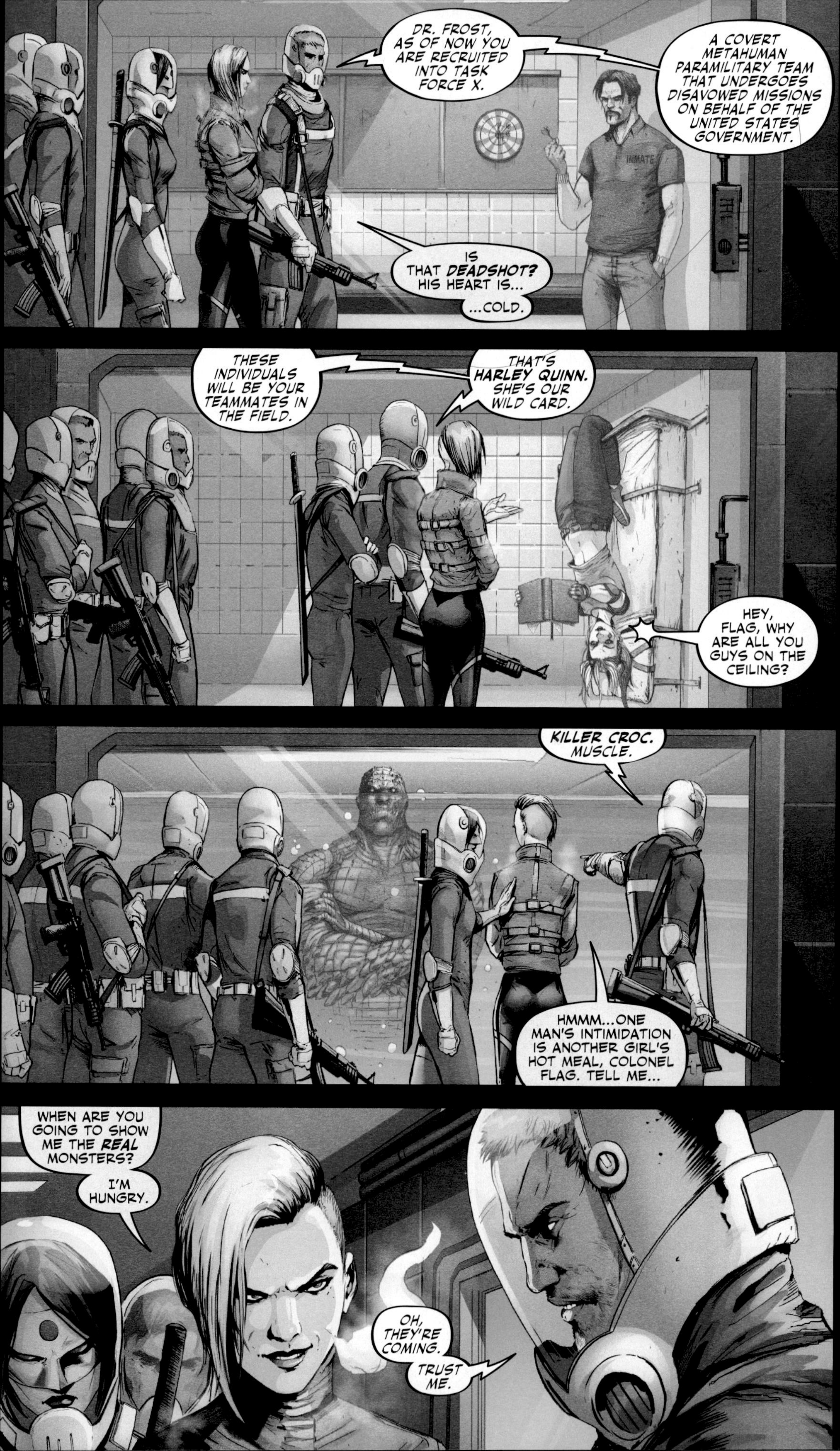
DR. FROST, AS OF NOW YOU ARE RECRUITED INTO TASK FORCE X.
A COVERT METAHUMAN PARAMILITARY TEAM THAT UNDERGOES DISAVOWED MISSIONS ON BEHALF OF THE UNITED STATES GOVERNMENT.
INMATE
IS THAT DEADSHOT? HIS HEART IS...
...COLD.
THESE INDIVIDUALS WILL BE YOUR TEAMMATES IN THE FIELD.
THAT'S HARLEY QUINN. SHE'S OUR WILD CARD.
HEY, FLAG, WHY ARE ALL YOU GUYS ON THE CEILING?
KILLER CROC. MUSCLE.
HMMM...ONE MAN'S INTIMIDATION IS ANOTHER GIRL'S HOT MEAL, COLONEL FLAG. TELL ME...
WHEN ARE YOU GOING TO SHOW ME THE REAL MONSTERS?
I'M HUNGRY.
OH, THEY'RE COMING.
TRUST ME.

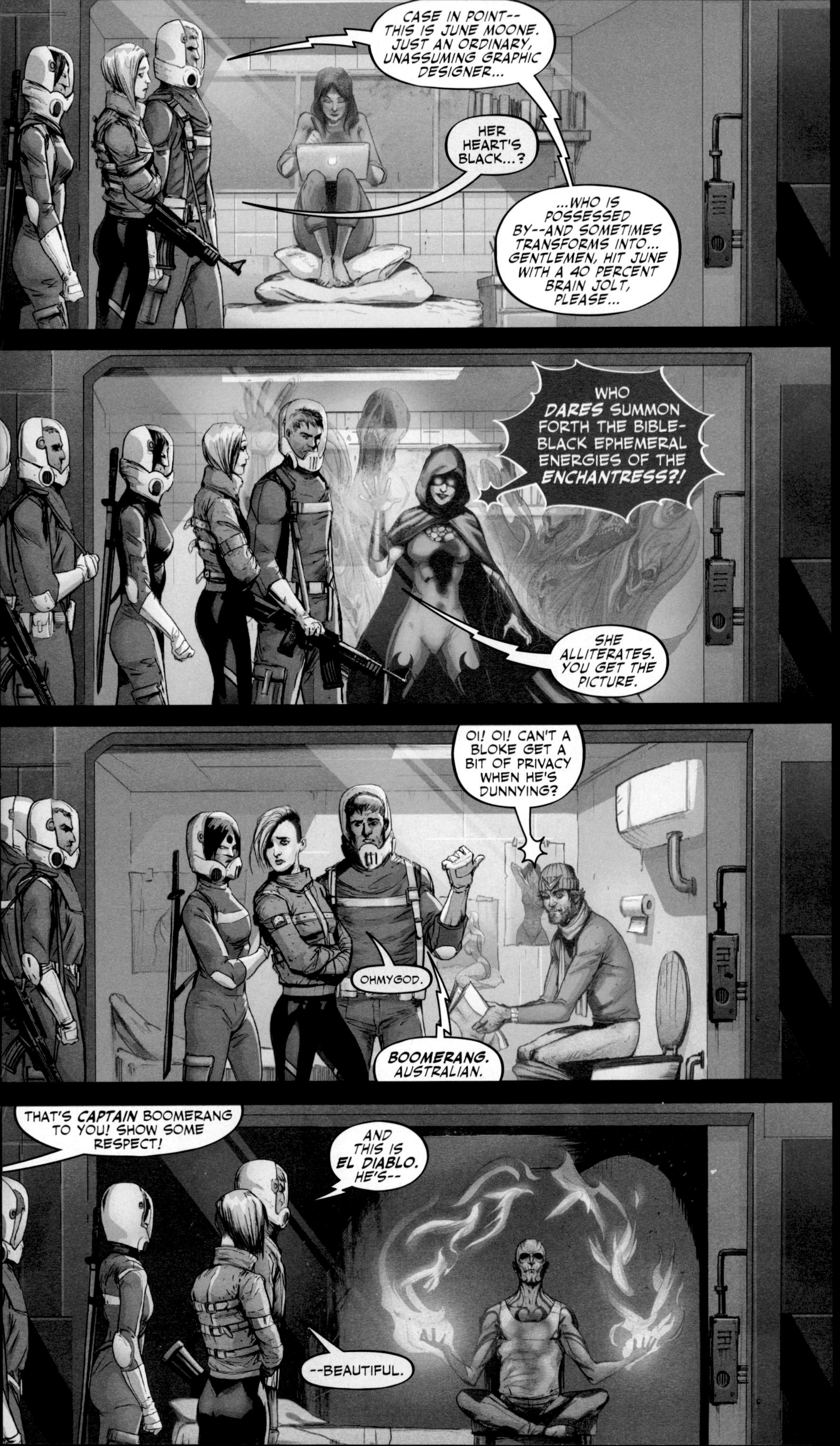
CASE IN POINT-- THIS IS JUNE MOONE. JUST AN ORDINARY, UNASSUMING GRAPHIC DESIGNER...
HER HEART'S BLACK...?
...WHO IS POSSESSED BY--AND SOMETIMES TRANSFORMS INTO... GENTLEMEN, HIT JUNE WITH A 40 PERCENT BRAIN JOLT, PLEASE...
WHO DARES SUMMON FORTH THE BIBLE-BLACK EPHEMERAL ENERGIES OF THE ENCHANTRESS?!
SHE ALLITERATES. YOU GET THE PICTURE.
OI! OI! CAN'T A BLOKE GET A BIT OF PRIVACY WHEN HE'S DUNNYING?
OHMYGOD.
BOOMERANG. AUSTRALIAN.
THAT'S CAPTAIN BOOMERANG TO YOU! SHOW SOME RESPECT!
AND THIS IS EL DIABLO. HE'S--
--BEAUTIFUL.

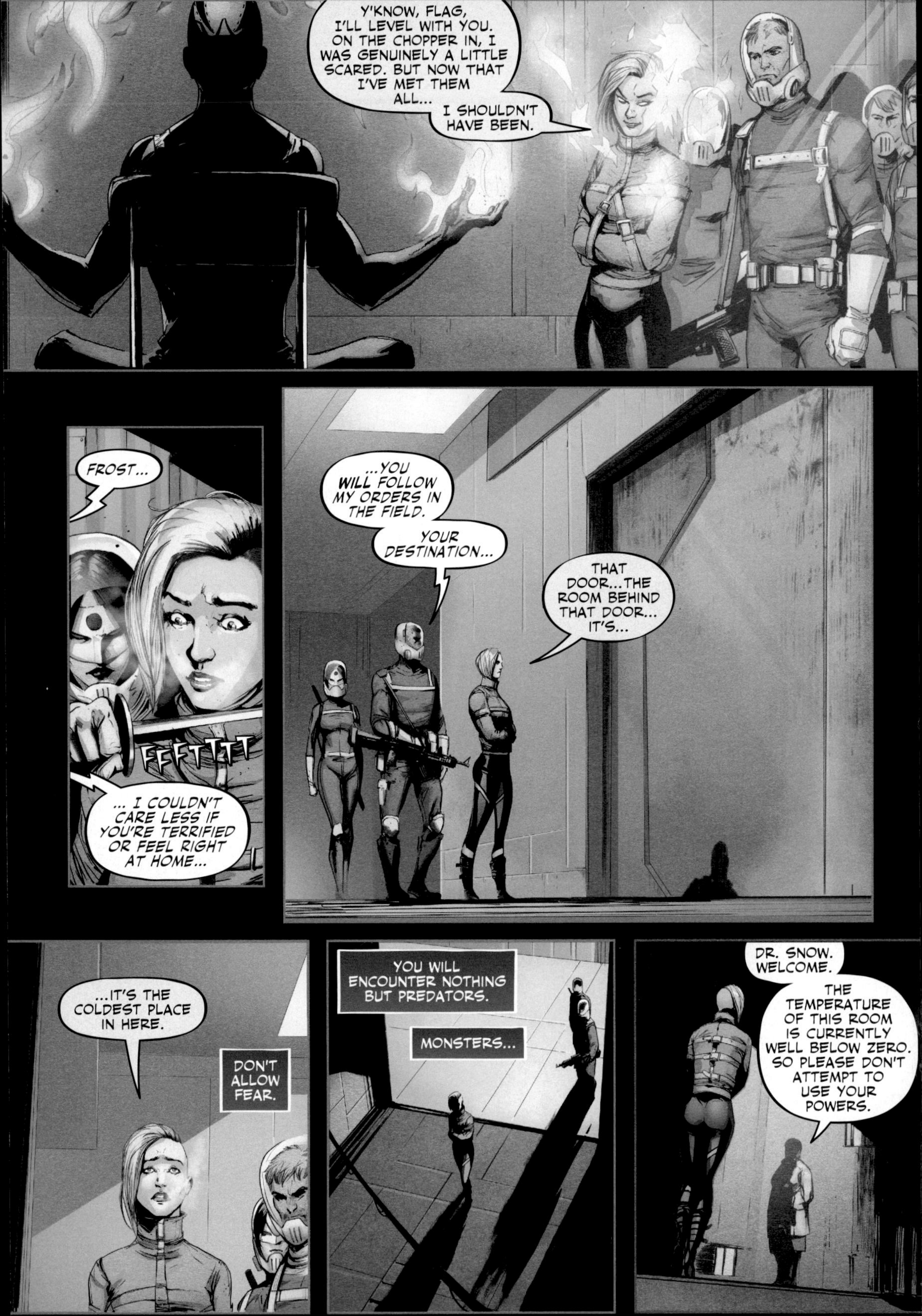
Y'KNOW, FLAG, I'LL LEVEL WITH YOU. ON THE CHOPPER IN, I WAS GENUINELY A LITTLE SCARED. BUT NOW THAT I'VE MET THEM ALL...
I SHOULDN'T HAVE BEEN.
FROST...
FFFTTTT
... I COULDN'T CARE LESS IF YOU'RE TERRIFIED OR FEEL RIGHT AT HOME...
...YOU WILL FOLLOW MY ORDERS IN THE FIELD.
YOUR DESTINATION...
THAT DOOR...THE ROOM BEHIND THAT DOOR... IT'S...
...IT'S THE COLDEST PLACE IN HERE.
DON'T ALLOW FEAR.
YOU WILL ENCOUNTER NOTHING BUT PREDATORS.
MONSTERS...
DR. SNOW. WELCOME.
THE TEMPERATURE OF THIS ROOM IS CURRENTLY WELL BELOW ZERO. SO PLEASE DON'T ATTEMPT TO USE YOUR POWERS.

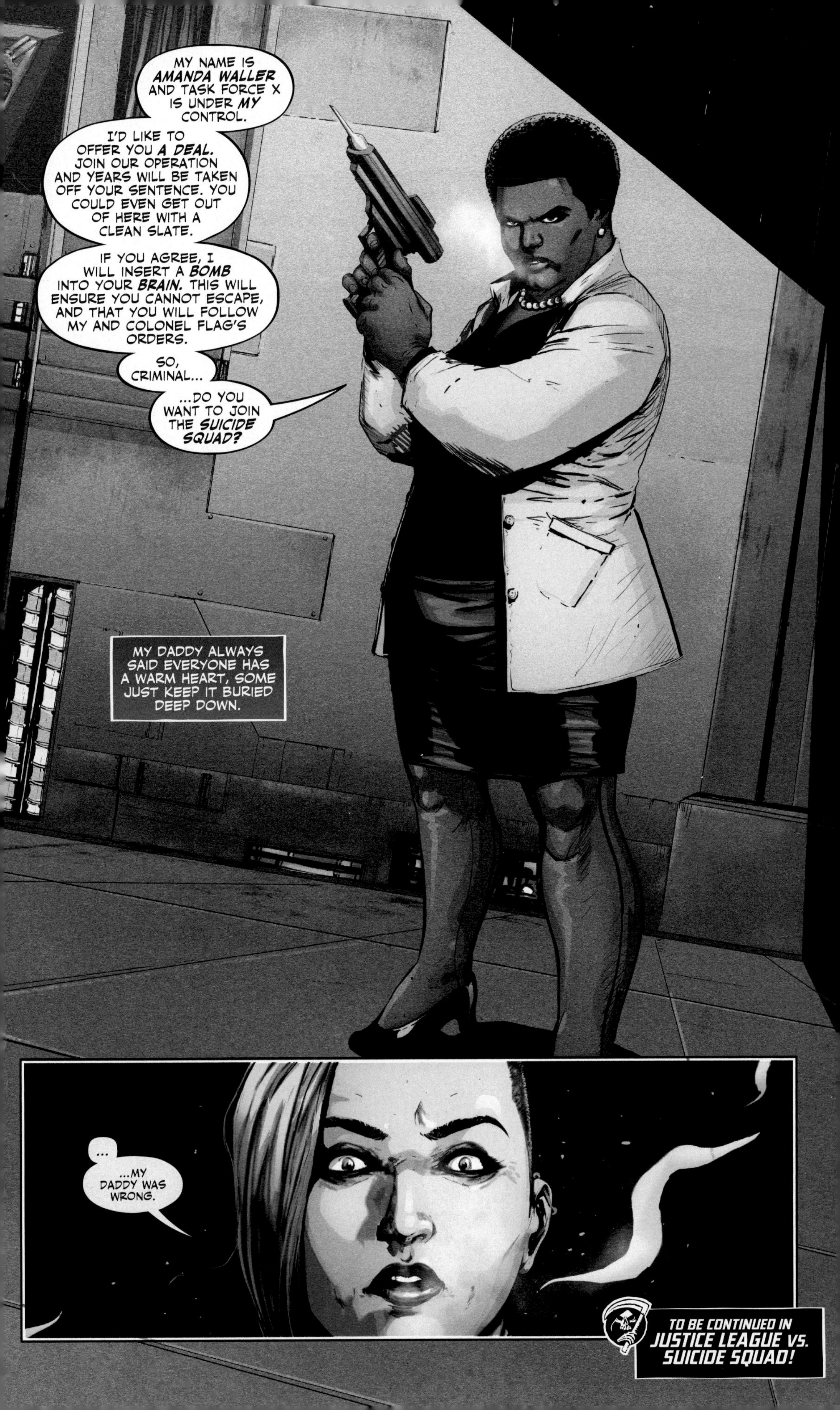
MY NAME IS AMANDA WALLER AND TASK FORCE X IS UNDER MY CONTROL.
I'D LIKE TO OFFER YOU A DEAL. JOIN OUR OPERATION AND YEARS WILL BE TAKEN OFF YOUR SENTENCE. YOU COULD EVEN GET OUT OF HERE WITH A CLEAN SLATE.
IF YOU AGREE, I WILL INSERT A BOMB INTO YOUR BRAIN. THIS WILL ENSURE YOU CANNOT ESCAPE, AND THAT YOU WILL FOLLOW MY AND COLONEL FLAG'S ORDERS.
SO, CRIMINAL...
...DO YOU WANT TO JOIN THE SUICIDE SQUAD?
MY DADDY ALWAYS SAID EVERYONE HAS A WARM HEART, SOME JUST KEEP IT BURIED DEEP DOWN.
...
...MY DADDY WAS WRONG.
TO BE CONTINUED IN JUSTICE LEAGUE VS. SUICIDE SQUAD!

FLASHBACK:
EVIL ANONYMOUS

ROB WILLIAMS
writer

JIM LEE
penciller (pages 98-107, 118-127)

SCOTT WILLIAMS * **SANDRA HOPE** * **RICHARD FRIEND**
inkers (pages 98-107, 118-127)

ALEX SINCLAIR
colorist (pages 98-107, 118-127)

SEAN "CHEEKS" GALLOWAY
artist (pages 108-117)

TRAVIS LANHAM
letterer

JIM LEE, SCOTT WILLIAMS and ALEX SINCLAIR
cover art

HARVEY RICHARDS
associate editor

ANDY KHOURI
editor

BRIAN CUNNINGHAM
group editor

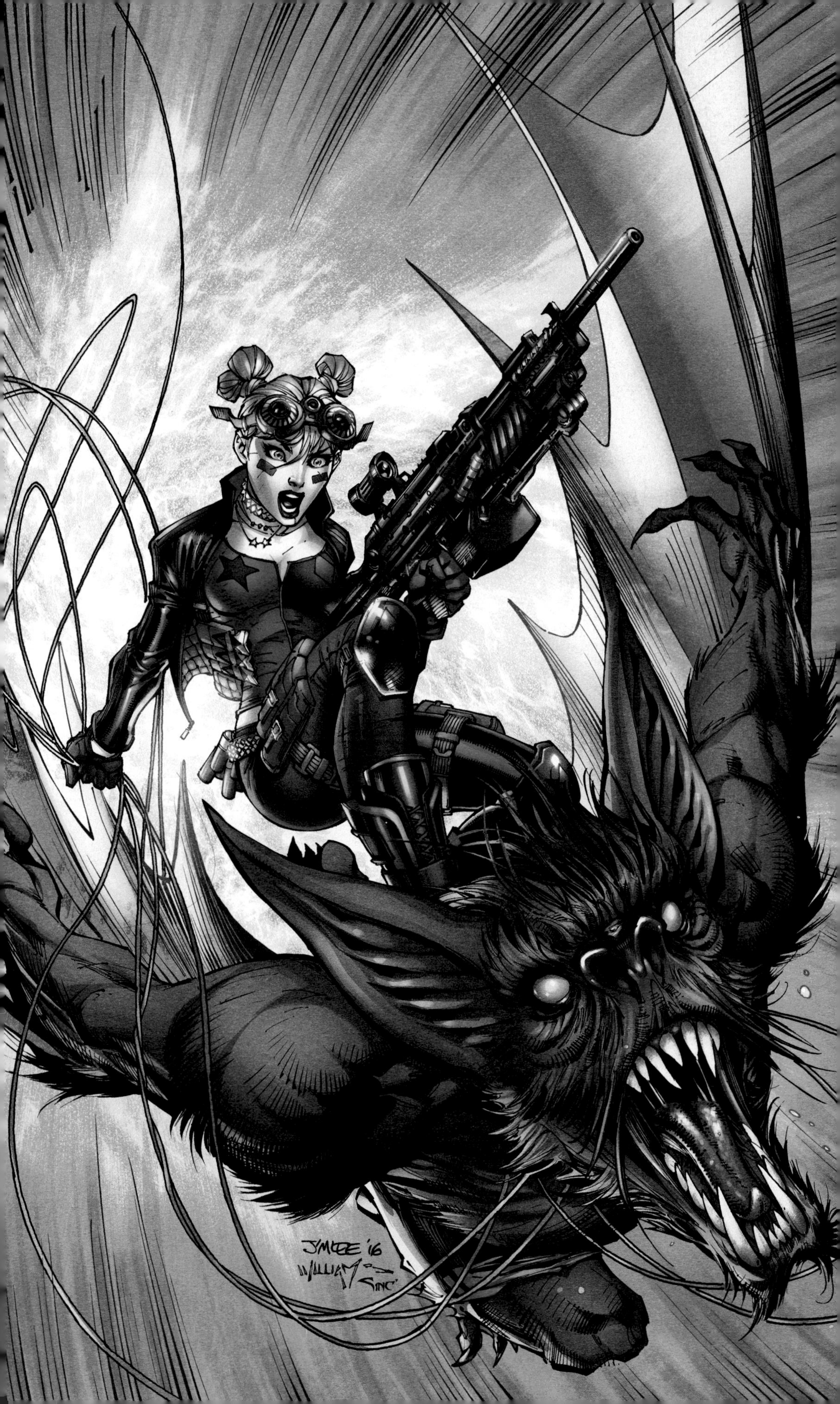

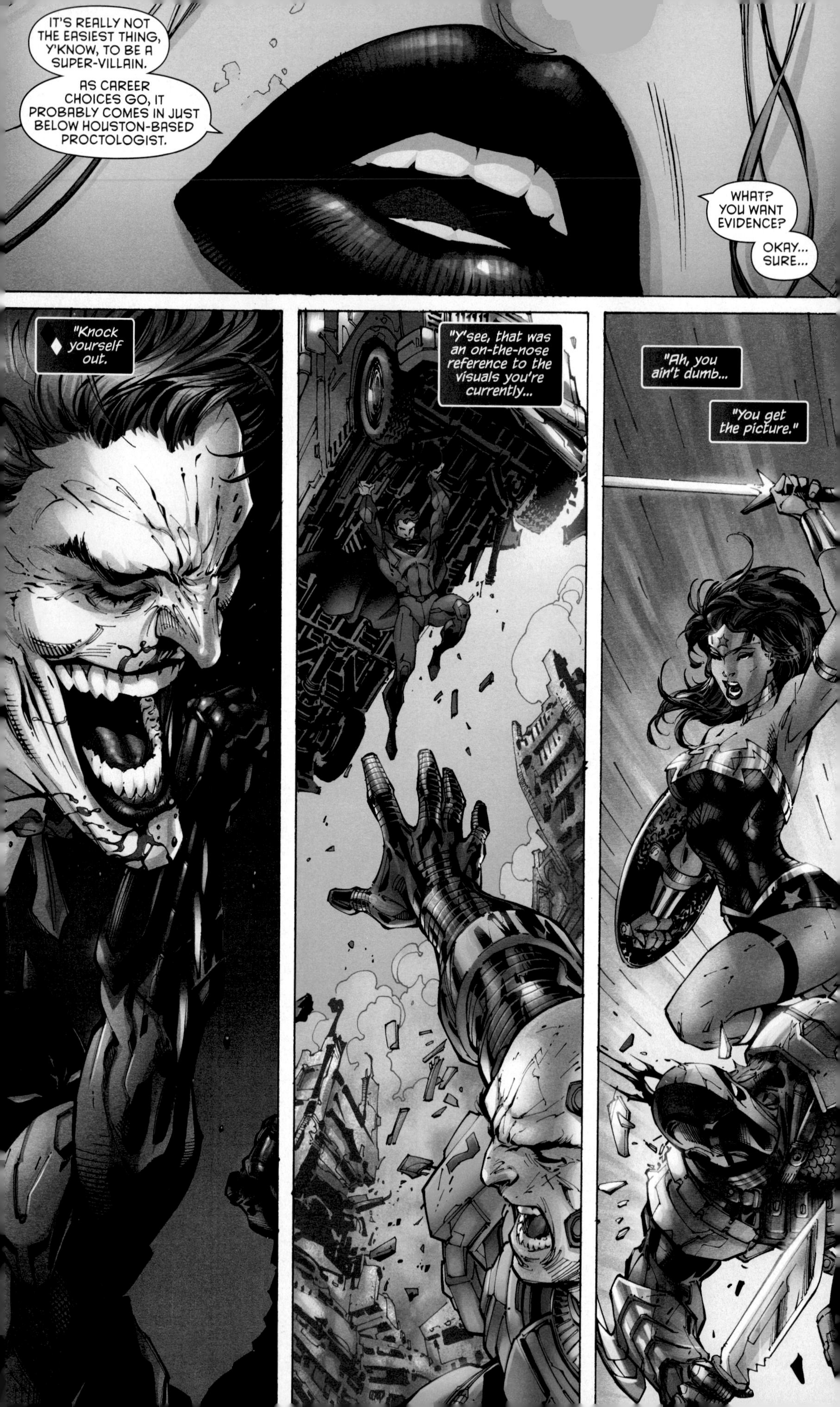

IT'S REALLY NOT THE EASIEST THING, Y'KNOW, TO BE A SUPER-VILLAIN.
AS CAREER CHOICES GO, IT PROBABLY COMES IN JUST BELOW HOUSTON-BASED PROCTOLOGIST.
WHAT? YOU WANT EVIDENCE?
OKAY... SURE...
"Knock yourself out.
"Y'see, that was an on-the-nose reference to the visuals you're currently...
"Ah, you ain't dumb...
"You get the picture."

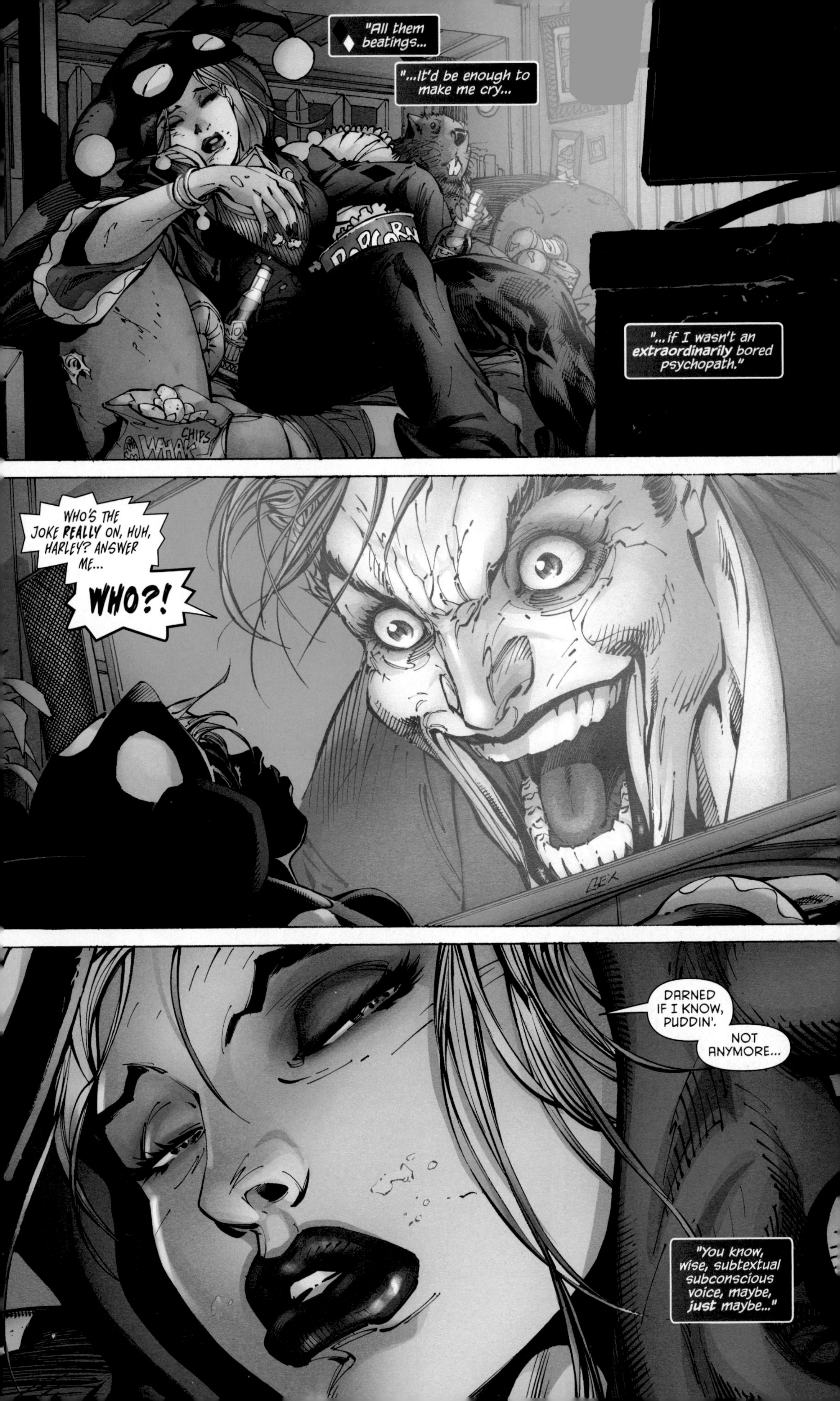

"All them beatings...
"...It'd be enough to make me cry...
"...if I wasn't an **extraordinarily** bored psychopath."
WHO'S THE JOKE **REALLY** ON, HUH, HARLEY? ANSWER ME...
WHO?!
DARNED IF I KNOW, PUDDIN'.
NOT ANYMORE...
"You know, wise, subtextual subconscious voice, maybe, *just* maybe..."

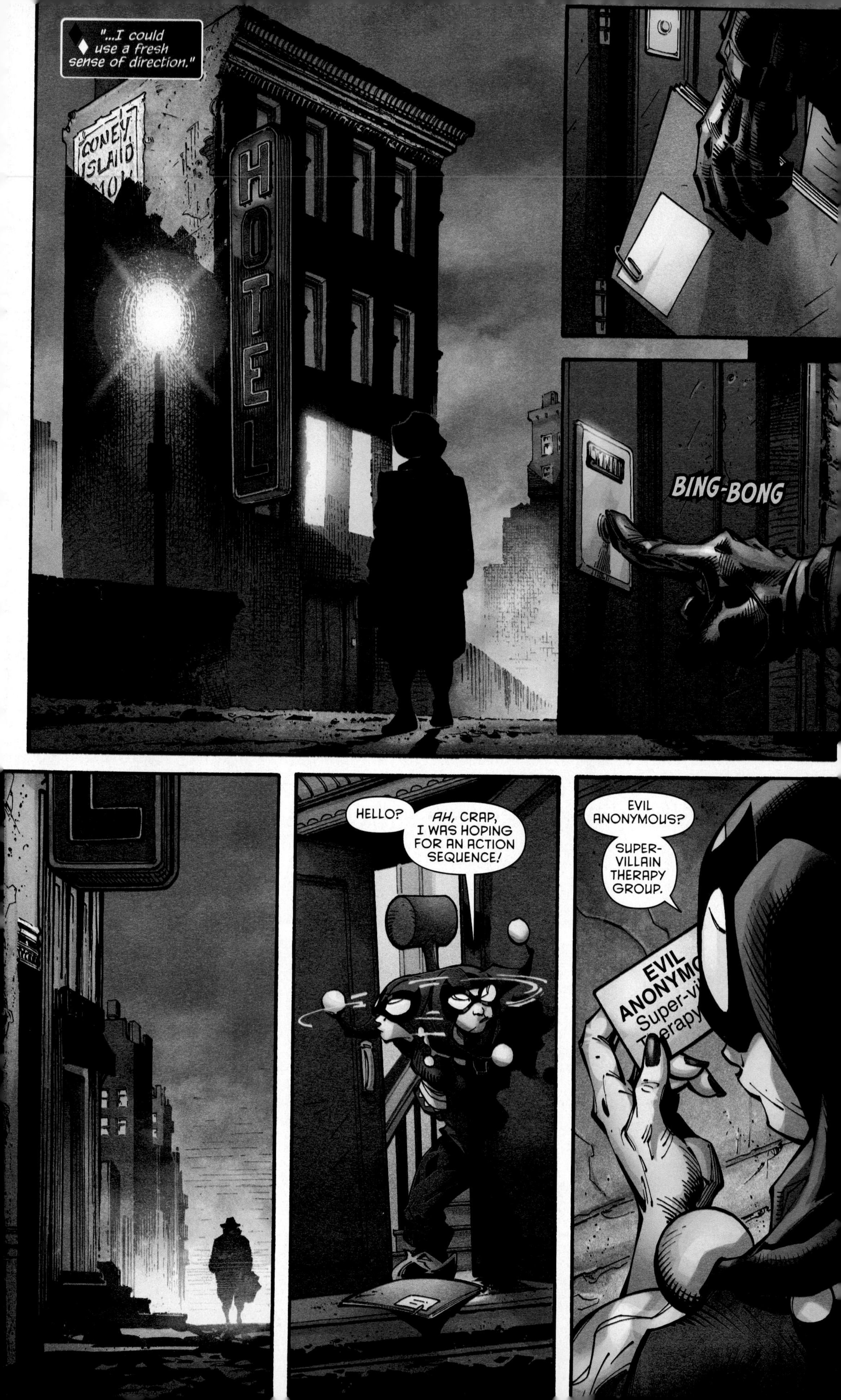
"...I could use a fresh sense of direction."
CONEY ISLAND
HOTEL
BING-BONG
HELLO?
AH, CRAP, I WAS HOPING FOR AN ACTION SEQUENCE!
EVIL ANONYMOUS?
SUPER-VILLAIN THERAPY GROUP.

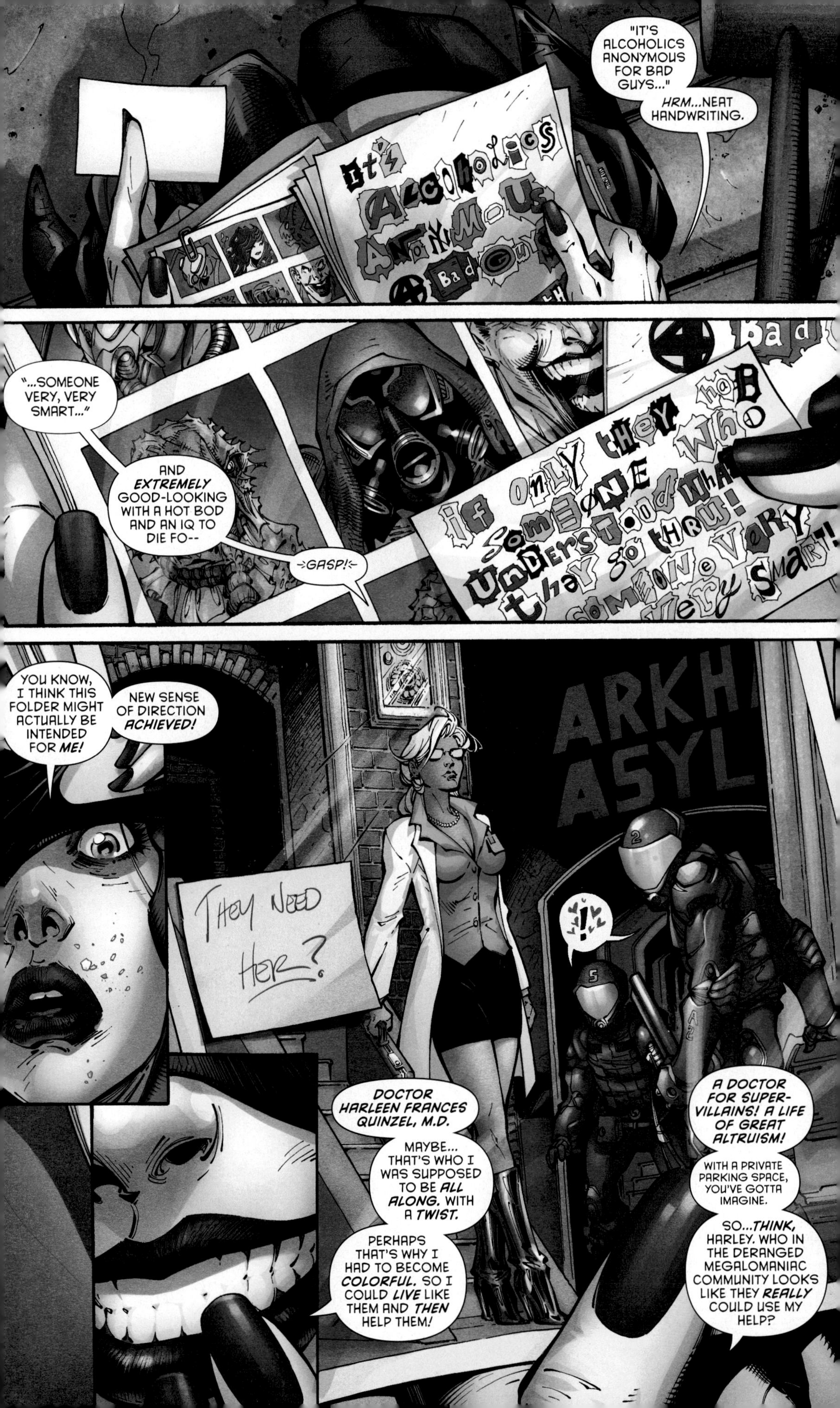

"IT'S ALCOHOLICS ANONYMOUS FOR BAD GUYS..."
HRM...NEAT HANDWRITING.
It's Alcoholics Anonymous 4 Bad Guys
"...SOMEONE VERY, VERY SMART..."
AND EXTREMELY GOOD-LOOKING WITH A HOT BOD AND AN IQ TO DIE FO--
GASP!
If only they had someone who understood what they go thru! Someone very very smart!
YOU KNOW, I THINK THIS FOLDER MIGHT ACTUALLY BE INTENDED FOR ME!
NEW SENSE OF DIRECTION ACHIEVED!
ARKH ASYL
THEY NEED HER?
!
DOCTOR HARLEEN FRANCES QUINZEL, M.D.
MAYBE... THAT'S WHO I WAS SUPPOSED TO BE ALL ALONG. WITH A TWIST.
PERHAPS THAT'S WHY I HAD TO BECOME COLORFUL. SO I COULD LIVE LIKE THEM AND THEN HELP THEM!
A DOCTOR FOR SUPER-VILLAINS! A LIFE OF GREAT ALTRUISM!
WITH A PRIVATE PARKING SPACE, YOU'VE GOTTA IMAGINE.
SO...THINK, HARLEY. WHO IN THE DERANGED MEGALOMANIAC COMMUNITY LOOKS LIKE THEY REALLY COULD USE MY HELP?

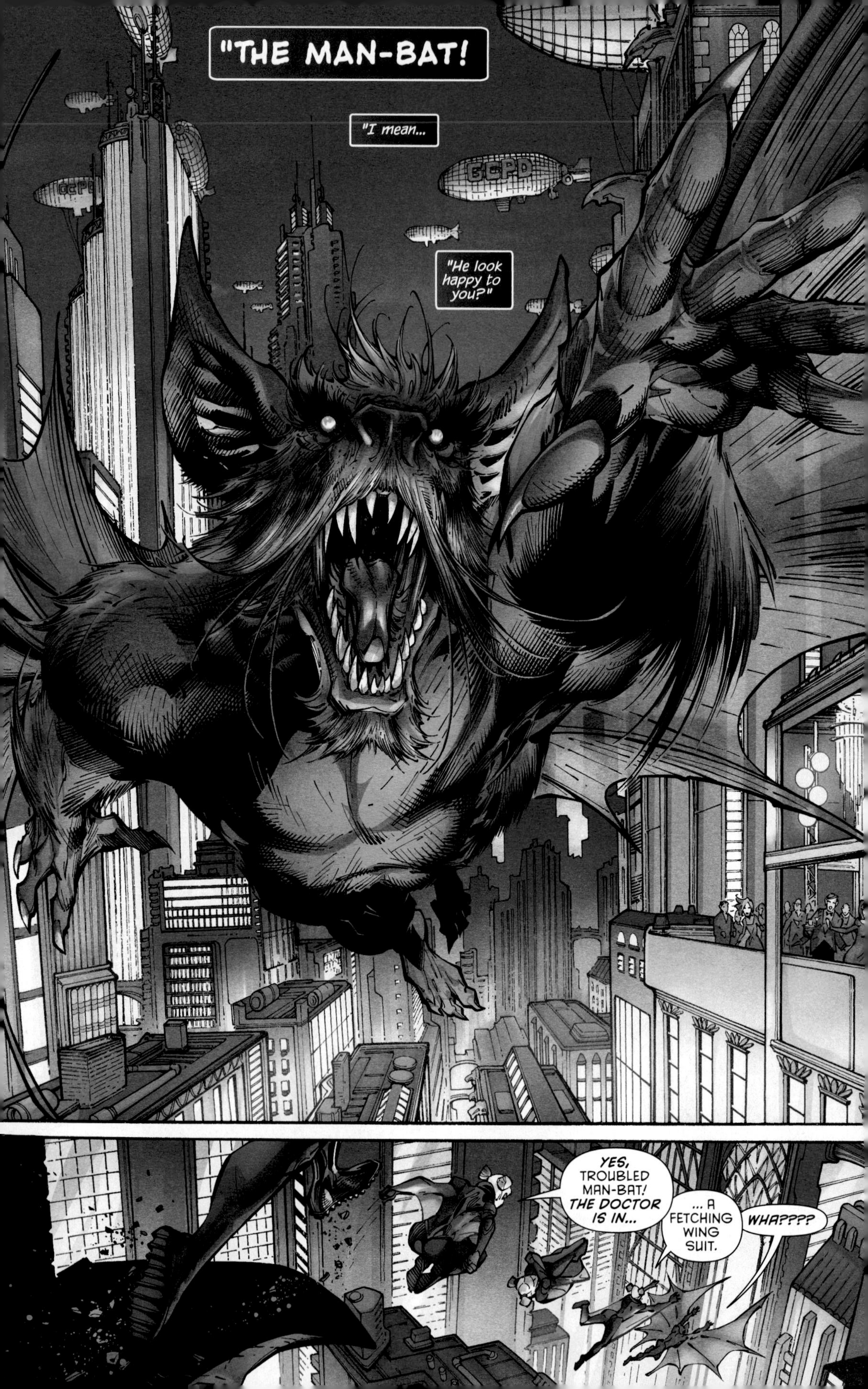
"THE MAN-BAT!
"I mean...
"He look happy to you?"
GCPD
YES, TROUBLED MAN-BAT! THE DOCTOR IS IN...
... A FETCHING WING SUIT.
WHA????

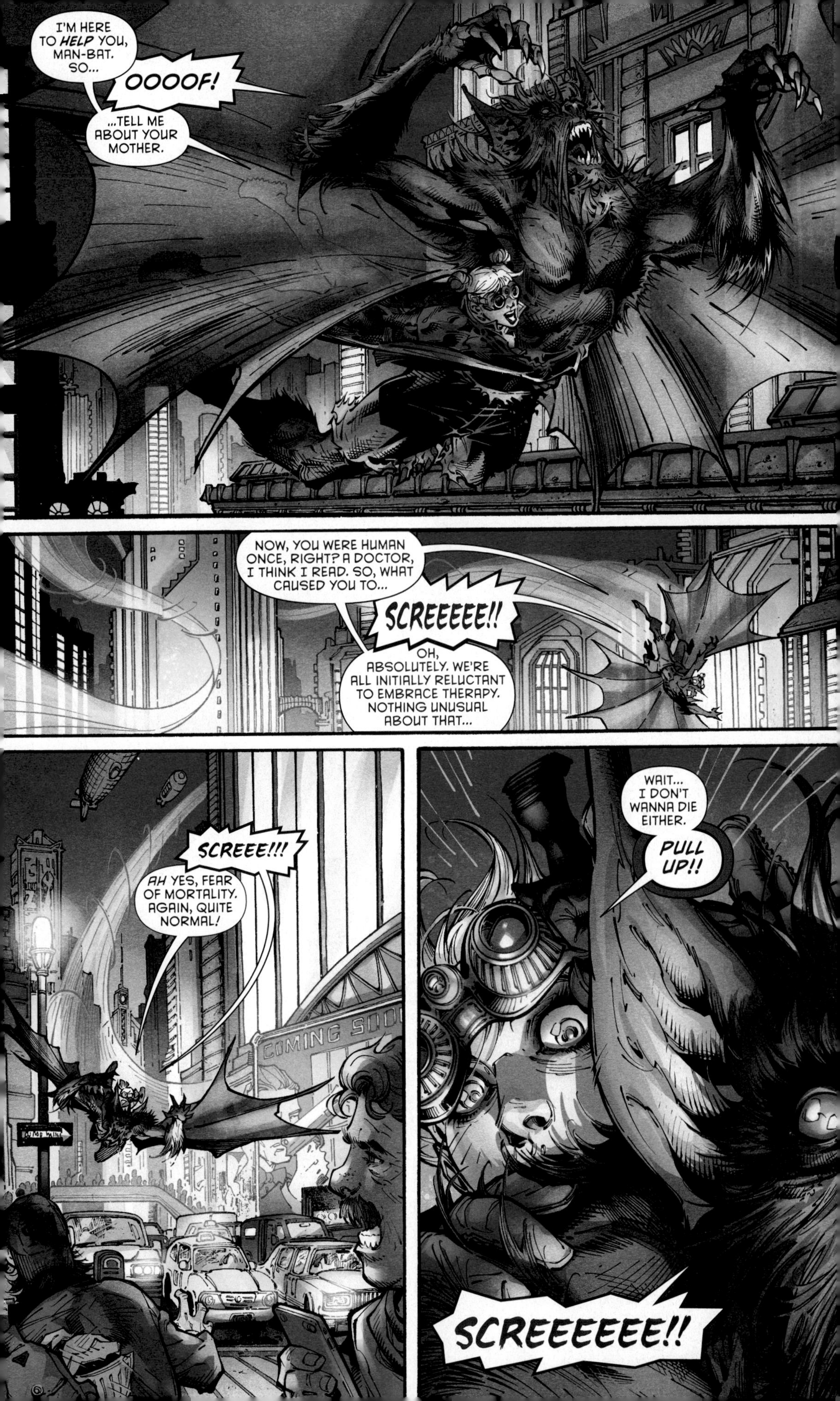
I'M HERE TO HELP YOU, MAN-BAT. SO...
OOOOF!
...TELL ME ABOUT YOUR MOTHER.
NOW, YOU WERE HUMAN ONCE, RIGHT? A DOCTOR, I THINK I READ. SO, WHAT CAUSED YOU TO...
SCREEEEE!!
OH, ABSOLUTELY. WE'RE ALL INITIALLY RELUCTANT TO EMBRACE THERAPY. NOTHING UNUSUAL ABOUT THAT...
SCREEE!!!
AH YES, FEAR OF MORTALITY. AGAIN, QUITE NORMAL!
WAIT... I DON'T WANNA DIE EITHER.
PULL UP!!
SCREEEEEEE!!

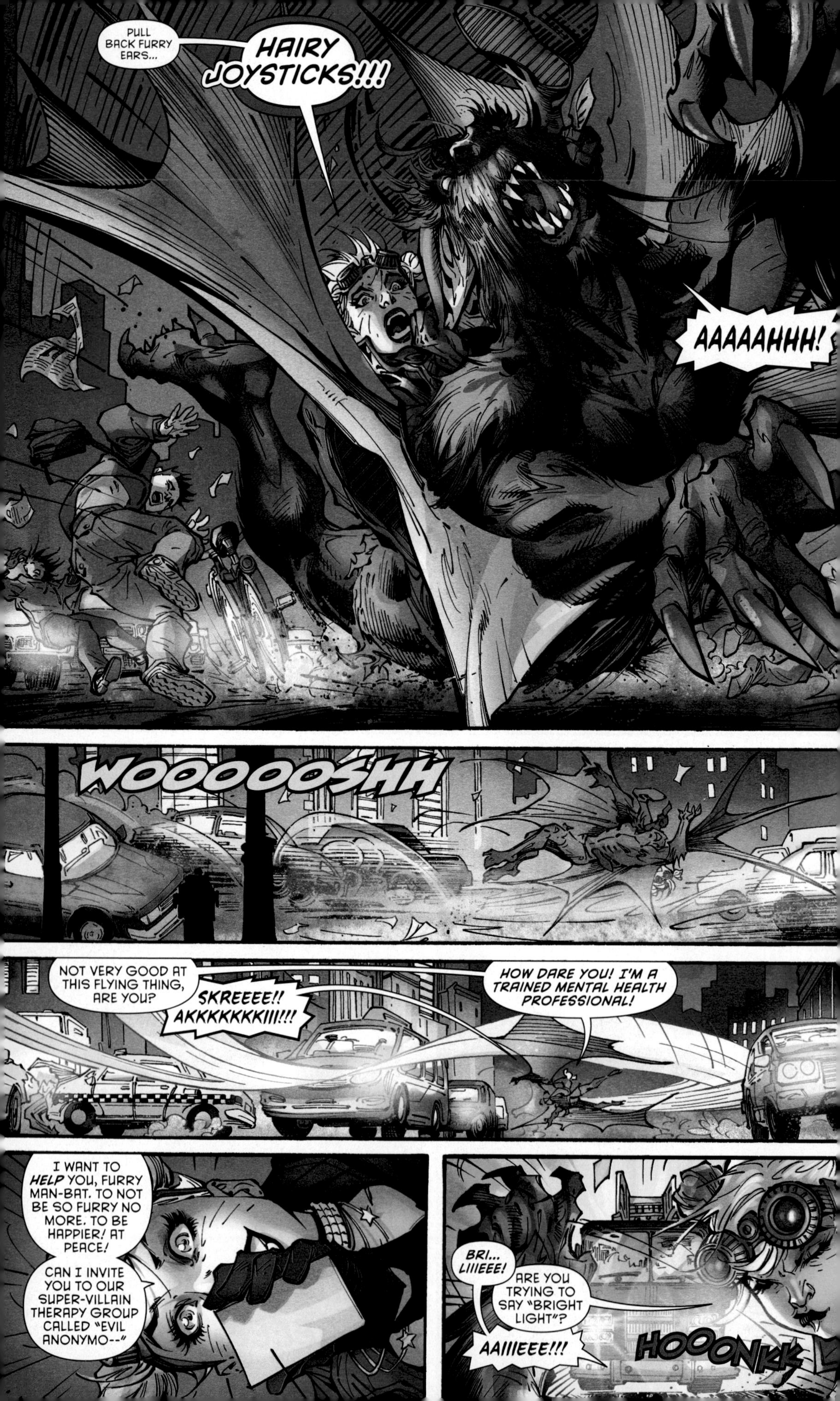

PULL BACK FURRY EARS...
HAIRY JOYSTICKS!!!
AAAAAHHH!
WOOOOOSHH
NOT VERY GOOD AT THIS FLYING THING, ARE YOU?
SKREEEE!! AKKKKKKIII!!!
HOW DARE YOU! I'M A TRAINED MENTAL HEALTH PROFESSIONAL!
I WANT TO HELP YOU, FURRY MAN-BAT. TO NOT BE SO FURRY NO MORE. TO BE HAPPIER! AT PEACE!
CAN I INVITE YOU TO OUR SUPER-VILLAIN THERAPY GROUP CALLED "EVIL ANONYMO--"
BRI... LIIIEEE!
ARE YOU TRYING TO SAY "BRIGHT LIGHT"?
AAIIIEEE!!!
HOOONKK

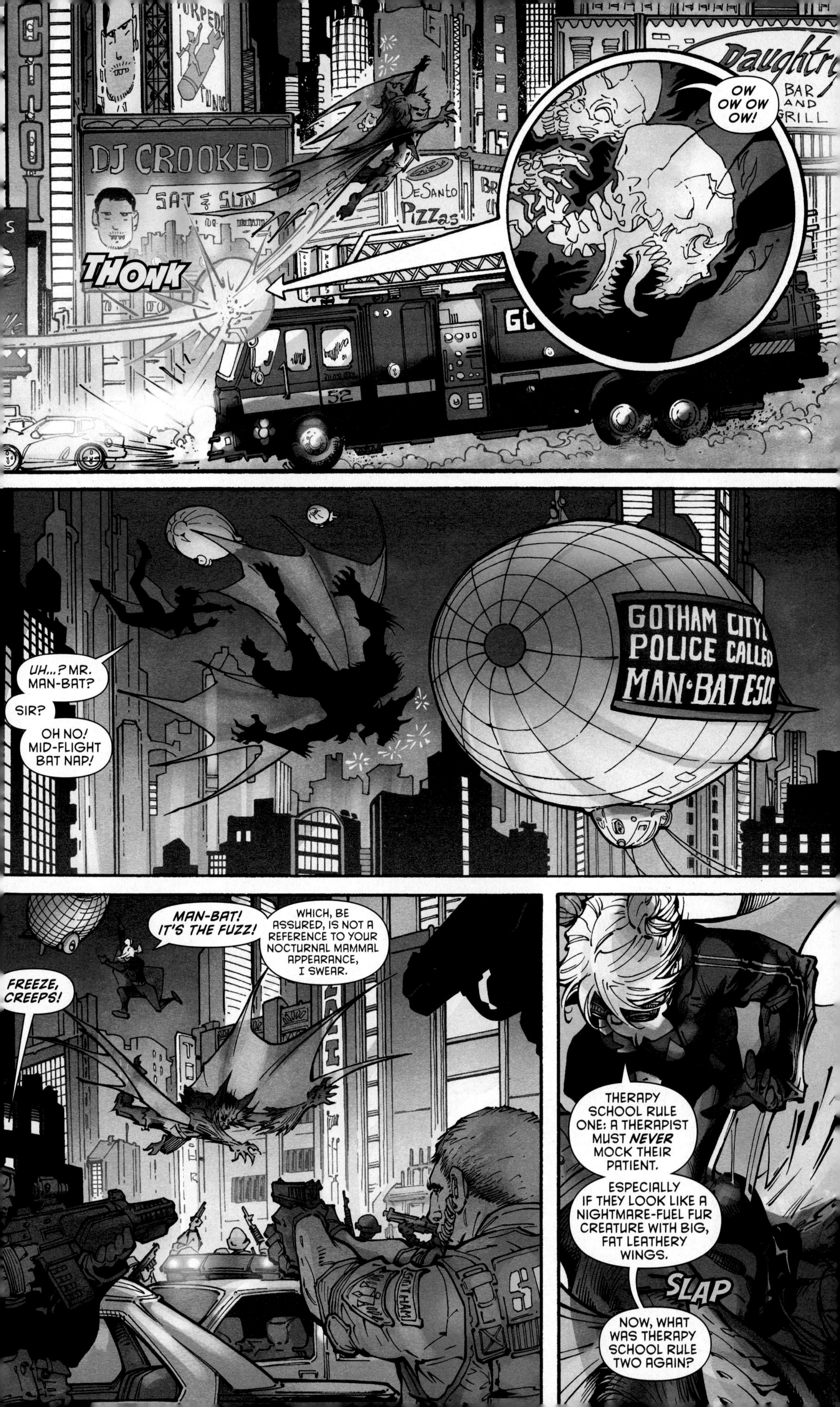

DJ CROOKED
SAT & SUN
DeSanto Pizzas
Daughtry BAR AND GRILL
THONK
OW OW OW OW!
52
GOTHAM CITY POLICE CALLED MAN-BAT ESC
UH...? MR. MAN-BAT?
SIR?
OH NO! MID-FLIGHT BAT NAP!
FREEZE, CREEPS!
MAN-BAT! IT'S THE FUZZ!
WHICH, BE ASSURED, IS NOT A REFERENCE TO YOUR NOCTURNAL MAMMAL APPEARANCE, I SWEAR.
THERAPY SCHOOL RULE ONE: A THERAPIST MUST NEVER MOCK THEIR PATIENT.
ESPECIALLY IF THEY LOOK LIKE A NIGHTMARE-FUEL FUR CREATURE WITH BIG, FAT LEATHERY WINGS.
SLAP
NOW, WHAT WAS THERAPY SCHOOL RULE TWO AGAIN?

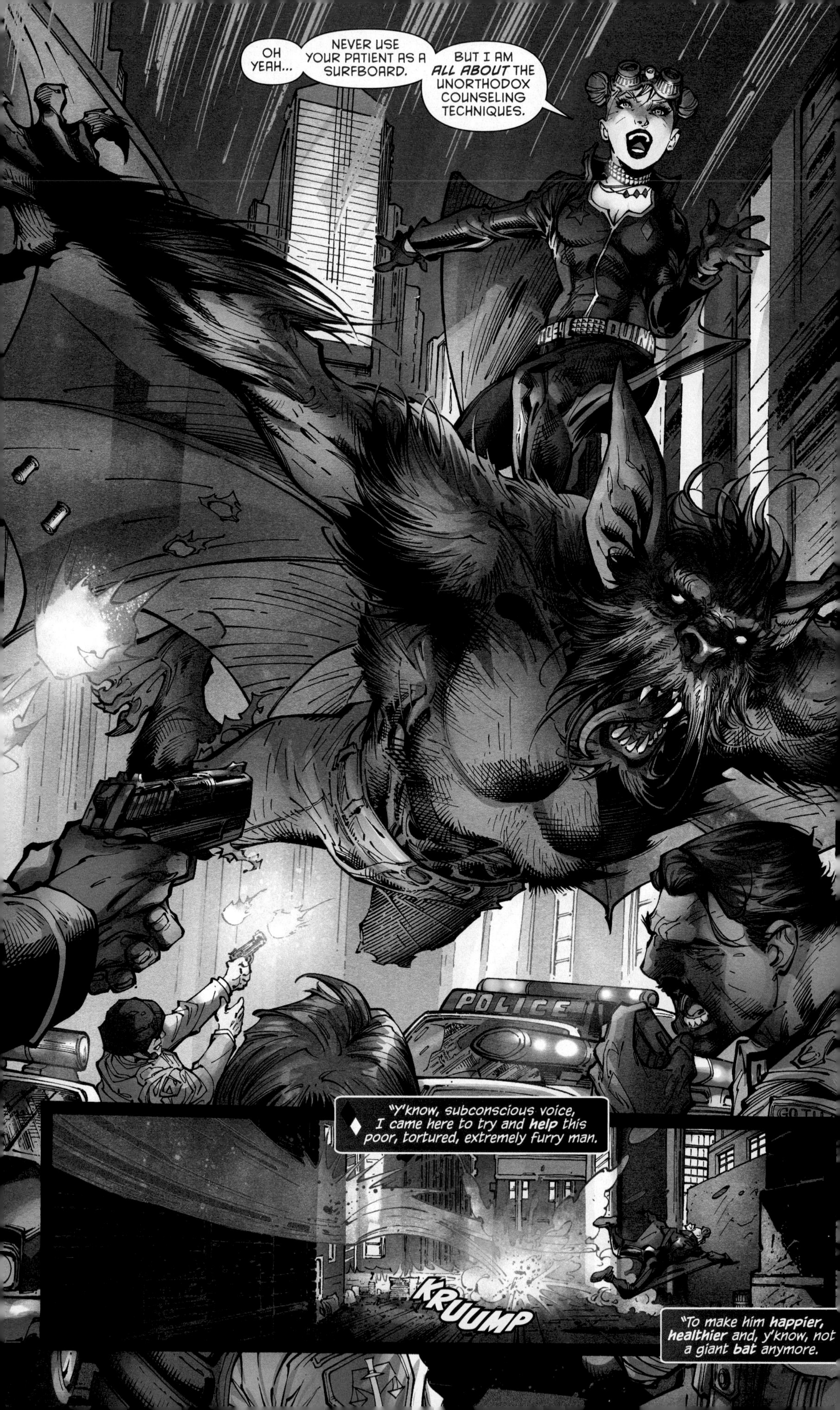
OH YEAH...
NEVER USE YOUR PATIENT AS A SURFBOARD.
BUT I AM ALL ABOUT THE UNORTHODOX COUNSELING TECHNIQUES.
POLICE
"Y'know, subconscious voice, I came here to try and help this poor, tortured, extremely furry man.
KRUUMP
"To make him happier, healthier and, y'know, not a giant bat anymore.

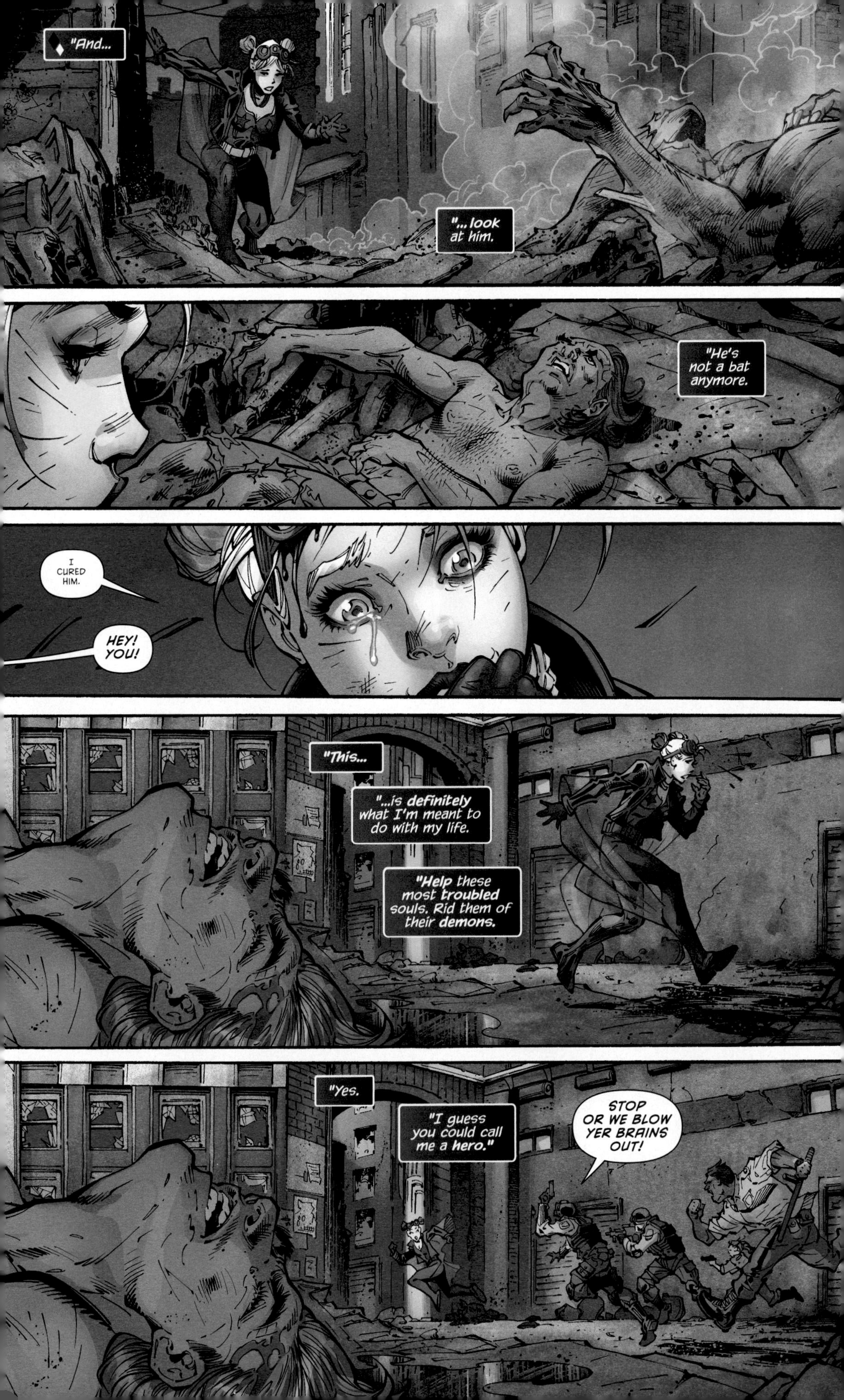
"And...
"...look at him.
"He's not a bat anymore.
I CURED HIM.
HEY! YOU!
"This...
"...is definitely what I'm meant to do with my life.
"Help these most troubled souls. Rid them of their demons.
"Yes.
"I guess you could call me a hero."
STOP OR WE BLOW YER BRAINS OUT!

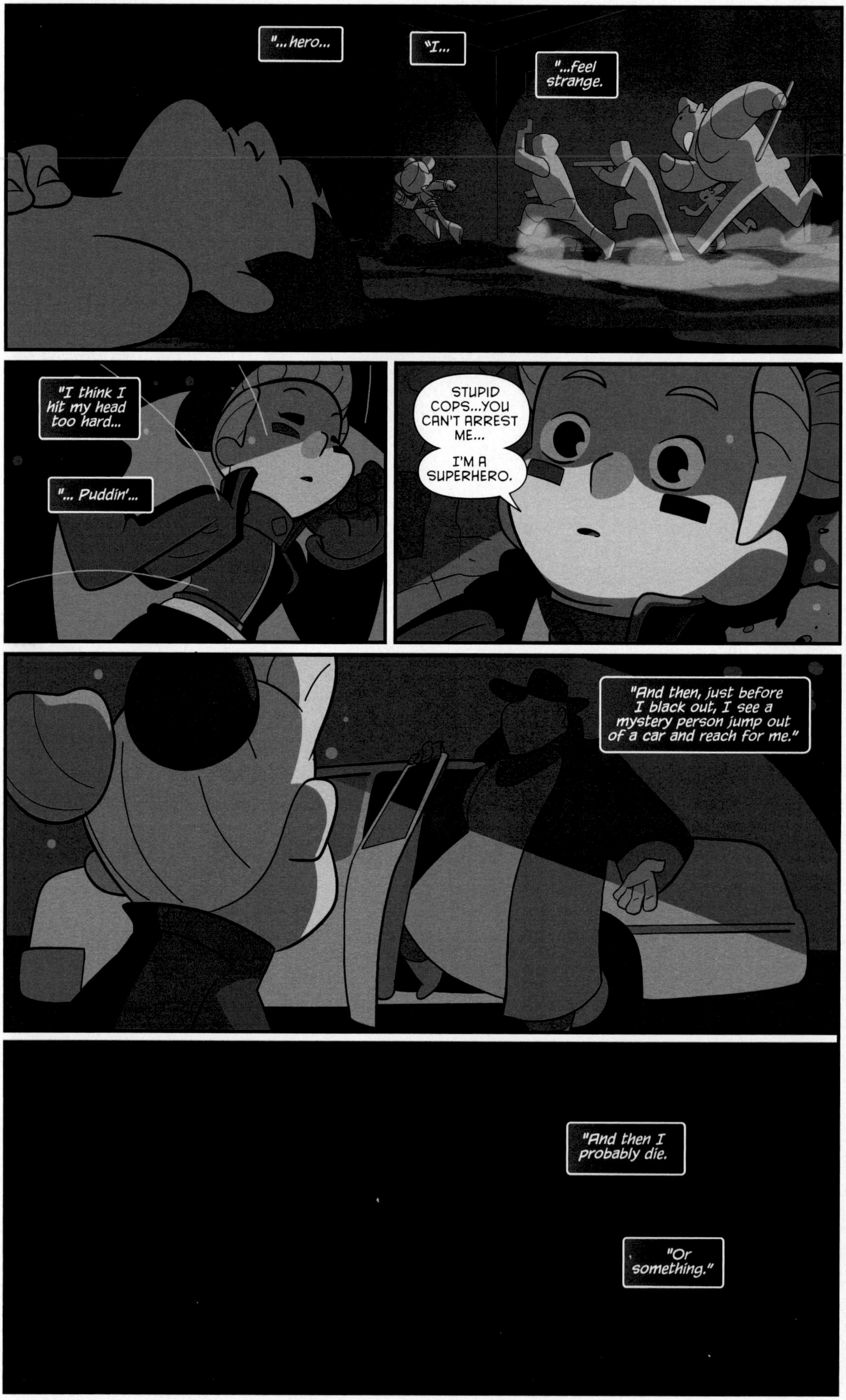
"...hero...
"I...
"...feel strange.
"I think I hit my head too hard...
"... Puddin'...
STUPID COPS...YOU CAN'T ARREST ME...
I'M A SUPERHERO.
"And then, just before I black out, I see a mystery person jump out of a car and reach for me."
"And then I probably die.
"Or something."

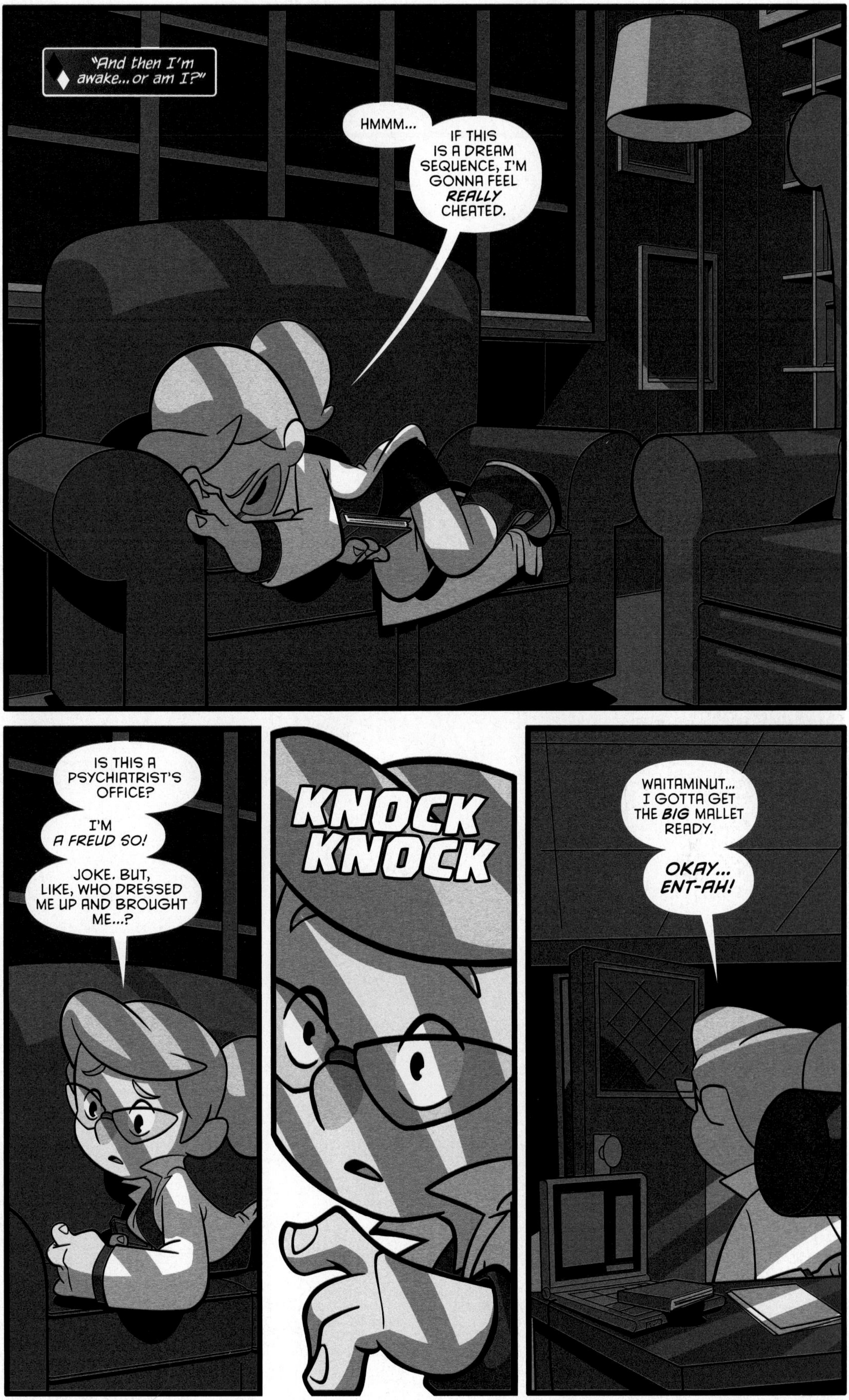
"And then I'm awake...or am I?"
HMMM...
IF THIS IS A DREAM SEQUENCE, I'M GONNA FEEL *REALLY* CHEATED.
IS THIS A PSYCHIATRIST'S OFFICE?
I'M *A FREUD SO!*
JOKE. BUT, LIKE, WHO DRESSED ME UP AND BROUGHT ME...?
KNOCK KNOCK
WAITAMINUT... I GOTTA GET THE *BIG* MALLET READY.
OKAY... ENT-AH!

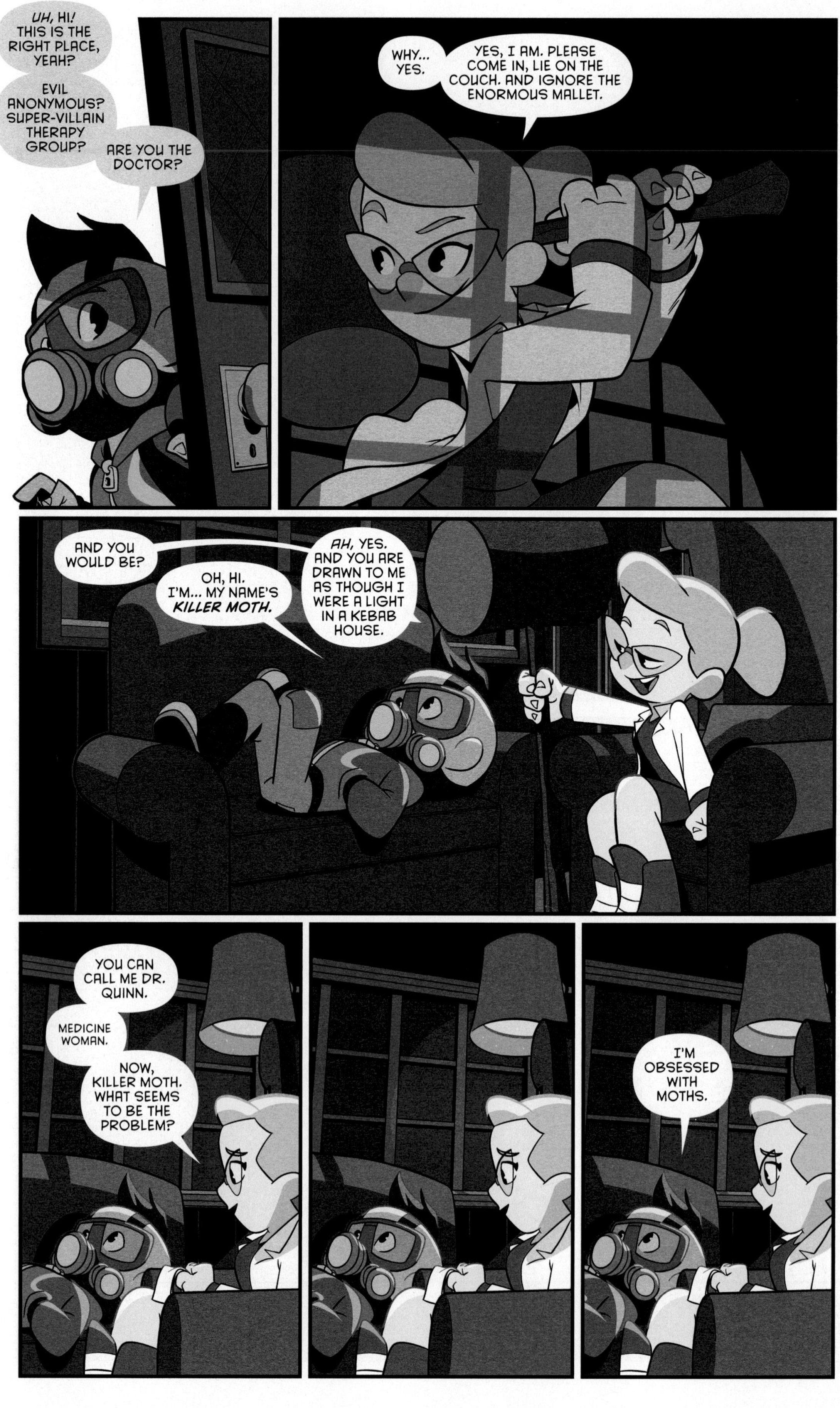

UH, HI! THIS IS THE RIGHT PLACE, YEAH?
EVIL ANONYMOUS? SUPER-VILLAIN THERAPY GROUP?
ARE YOU THE DOCTOR?
WHY... YES.
YES, I AM. PLEASE COME IN, LIE ON THE COUCH. AND IGNORE THE ENORMOUS MALLET.
AND YOU WOULD BE?
OH, HI. I'M... MY NAME'S *KILLER MOTH.*
AH, YES. AND YOU ARE DRAWN TO ME AS THOUGH I WERE A LIGHT IN A KEBAB HOUSE.
YOU CAN CALL ME DR. QUINN.
MEDICINE WOMAN.
NOW, KILLER MOTH. WHAT SEEMS TO BE THE PROBLEM?
I'M OBSESSED WITH MOTHS.

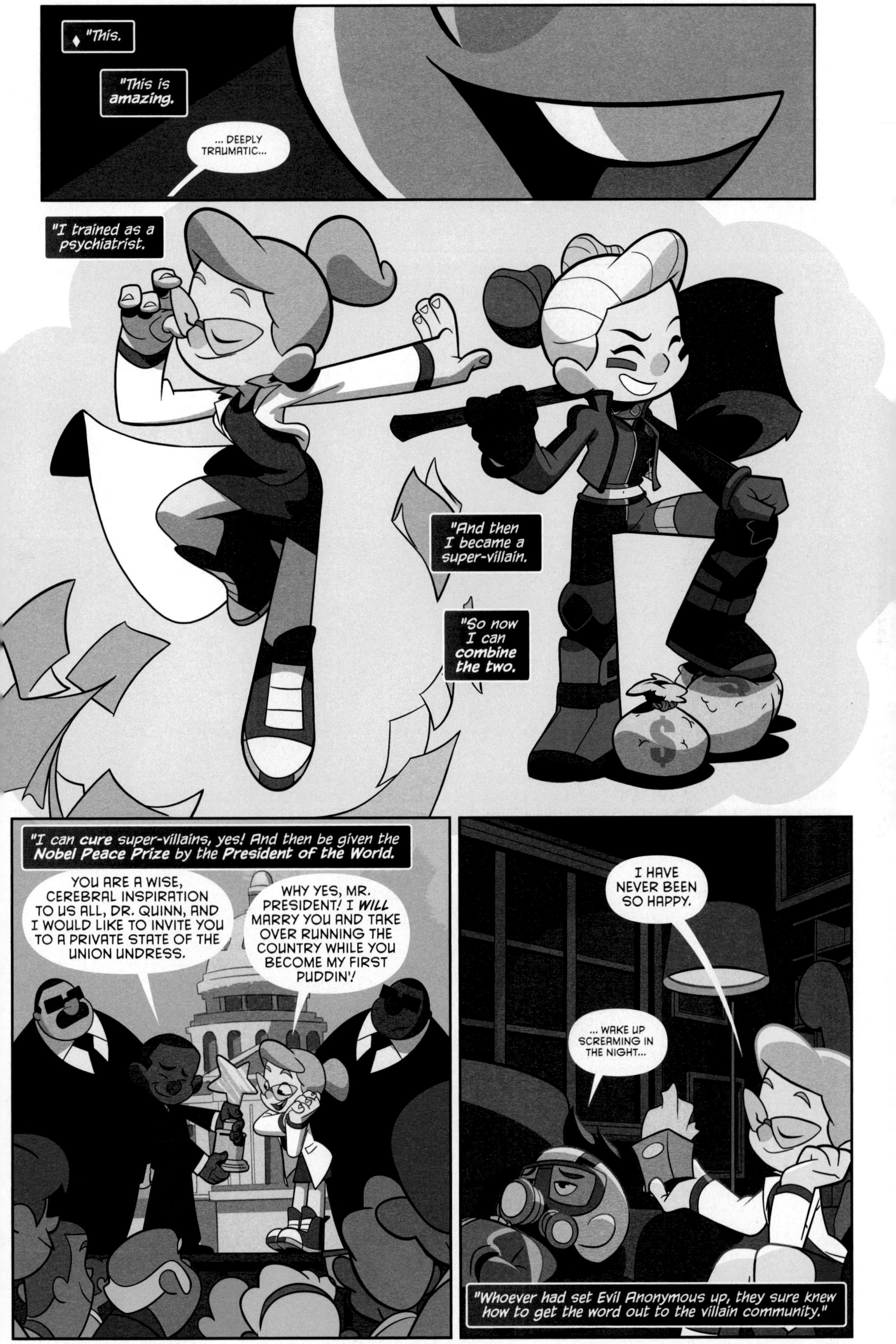
"This.
"This is amazing.
... DEEPLY TRAUMATIC...
"I trained as a psychiatrist.
"And then I became a super-villain.
"So now I can combine the two.
"I can cure super-villains, yes! And then be given the Nobel Peace Prize by the President of the World.
YOU ARE A WISE, CEREBRAL INSPIRATION TO US ALL, DR. QUINN, AND I WOULD LIKE TO INVITE YOU TO A PRIVATE STATE OF THE UNION UNDRESS.
WHY YES, MR. PRESIDENT! I WILL MARRY YOU AND TAKE OVER RUNNING THE COUNTRY WHILE YOU BECOME MY FIRST PUDDIN'!
I HAVE NEVER BEEN SO HAPPY.
... WAKE UP SCREAMING IN THE NIGHT...
"Whoever had set Evil Anonymous up, they sure knew how to get the word out to the villain community."

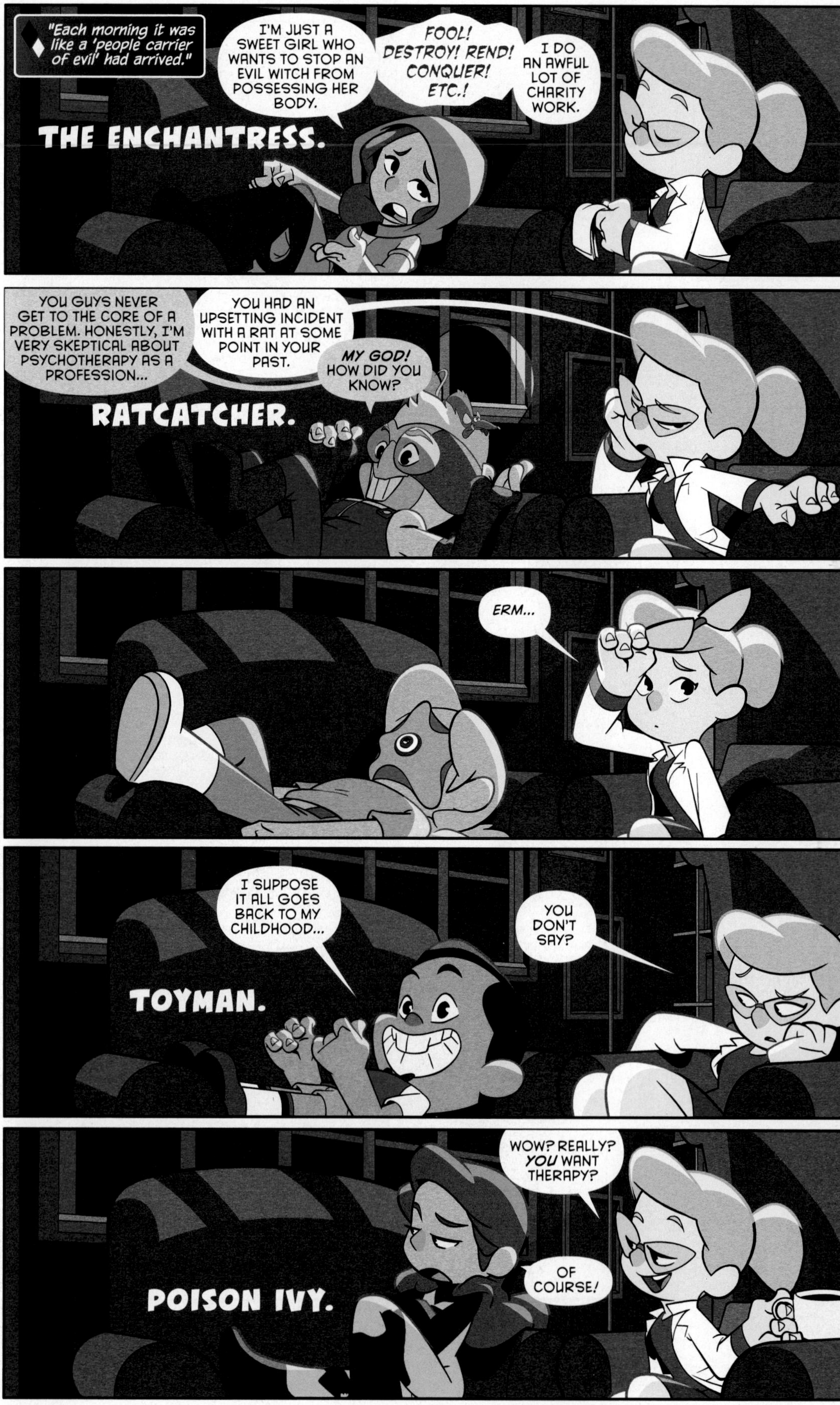
"Each morning it was like a 'people carrier of evil' had arrived."
I'M JUST A SWEET GIRL WHO WANTS TO STOP AN EVIL WITCH FROM POSSESSING HER BODY.
FOOL! DESTROY! REND! CONQUER! ETC.!
I DO AN AWFUL LOT OF CHARITY WORK.
THE ENCHANTRESS.
YOU GUYS NEVER GET TO THE CORE OF A PROBLEM. HONESTLY, I'M VERY SKEPTICAL ABOUT PSYCHOTHERAPY AS A PROFESSION...
YOU HAD AN UPSETTING INCIDENT WITH A RAT AT SOME POINT IN YOUR PAST.
MY GOD! HOW DID YOU KNOW?
RATCATCHER.
ERM...
I SUPPOSE IT ALL GOES BACK TO MY CHILDHOOD...
YOU DON'T SAY?
TOYMAN.
WOW? REALLY? YOU WANT THERAPY?
OF COURSE!
POISON IVY.

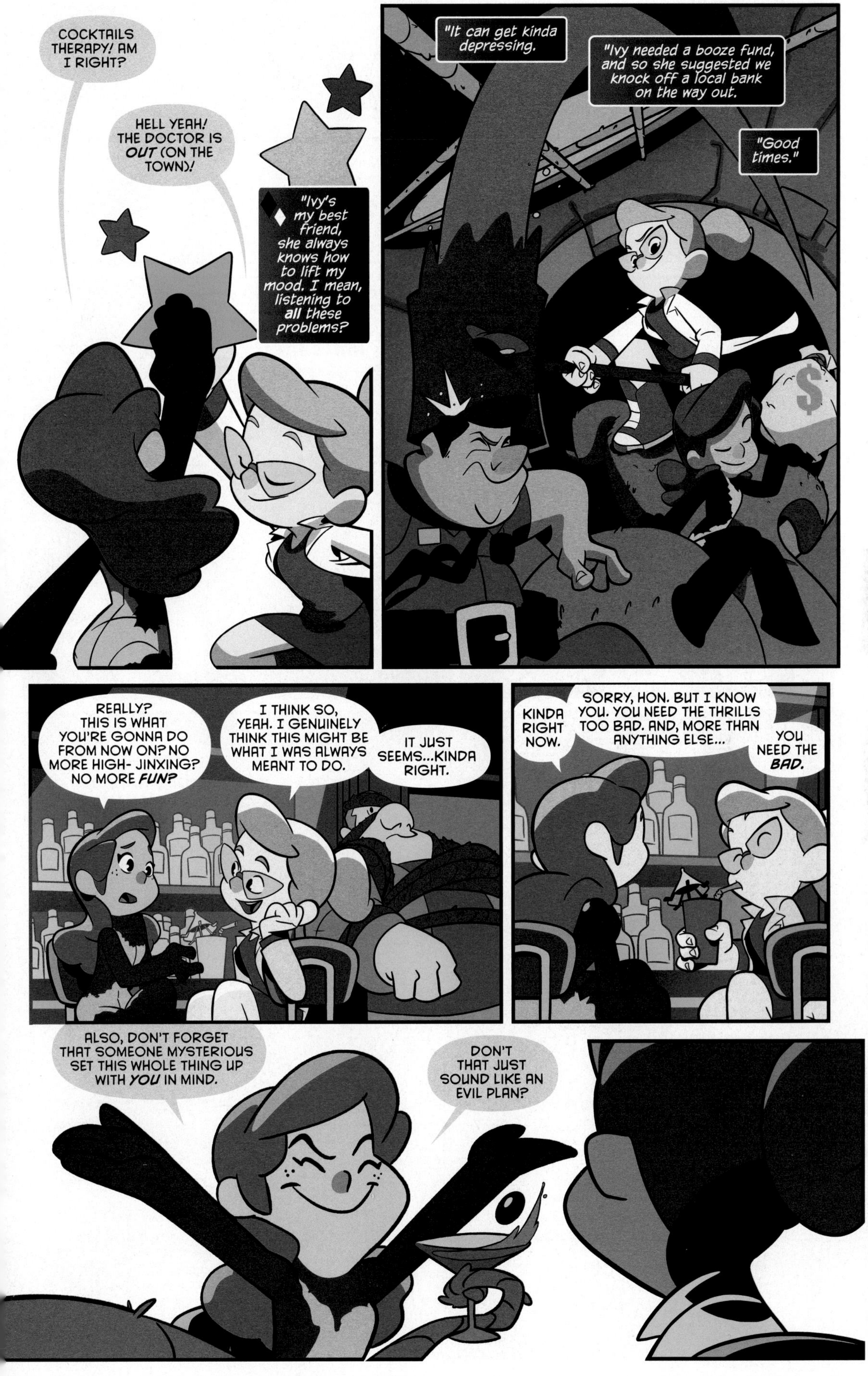
COCKTAILS THERAPY! AM I RIGHT?
HELL YEAH! THE DOCTOR IS *OUT* (ON THE TOWN)!
"Ivy's my best friend, she always knows how to lift my mood. I mean, listening to **all** these problems?
"It can get kinda depressing.
"Ivy needed a booze fund, and so she suggested we knock off a local bank on the way out.
"Good times."
REALLY? THIS IS WHAT YOU'RE GONNA DO FROM NOW ON? NO MORE HIGH- JINXING? NO MORE *FUN?*
I THINK SO, YEAH. I GENUINELY THINK THIS MIGHT BE WHAT I WAS ALWAYS MEANT TO DO.
IT JUST SEEMS...KINDA RIGHT.
KINDA RIGHT NOW.
SORRY, HON. BUT I KNOW YOU. YOU NEED THE THRILLS TOO BAD. AND, MORE THAN ANYTHING ELSE...
YOU NEED THE *BAD.*
ALSO, DON'T FORGET THAT SOMEONE MYSTERIOUS SET THIS WHOLE THING UP WITH *YOU* IN MIND.
DON'T THAT JUST SOUND LIKE AN EVIL PLAN?

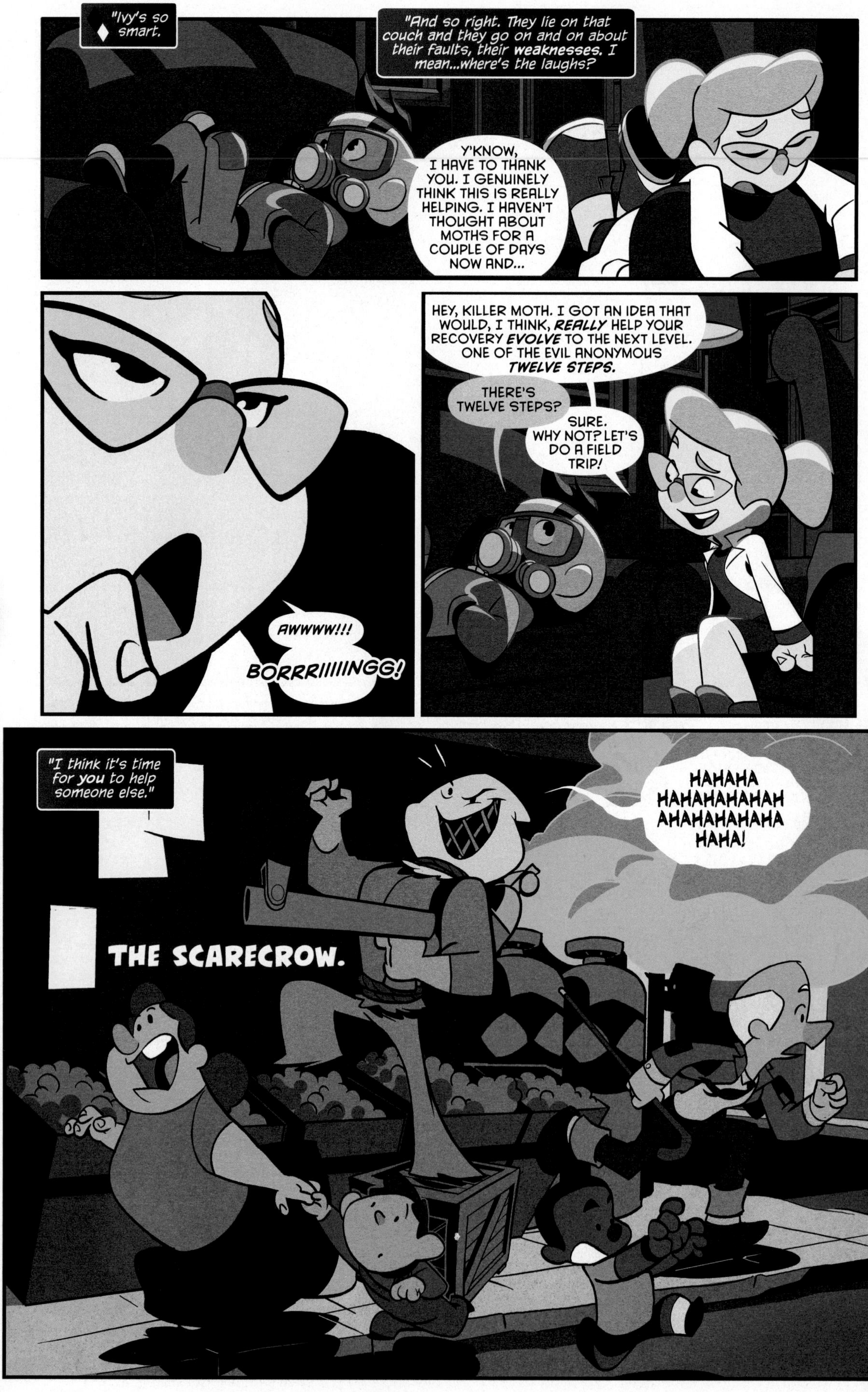
"Ivy's so smart.
"And so right. They lie on that couch and they go on and on about their faults, their **weaknesses.** I mean...where's the laughs?
Y'KNOW, I HAVE TO THANK YOU. I GENUINELY THINK THIS IS REALLY HELPING. I HAVEN'T THOUGHT ABOUT MOTHS FOR A COUPLE OF DAYS NOW AND...
AWWWW!!!
BORRRIIIIINGG!
HEY, KILLER MOTH. I GOT AN IDEA THAT WOULD, I THINK, *REALLY* HELP YOUR RECOVERY *EVOLVE* TO THE NEXT LEVEL. ONE OF THE EVIL ANONYMOUS *TWELVE STEPS.*
THERE'S TWELVE STEPS?
SURE. WHY NOT? LET'S DO A FIELD TRIP!
"I think it's time for **you** to help someone else."
HAHAHA HAHAHAHAHAH AHAHAHAHAHA HAHA!
THE SCARECROW.

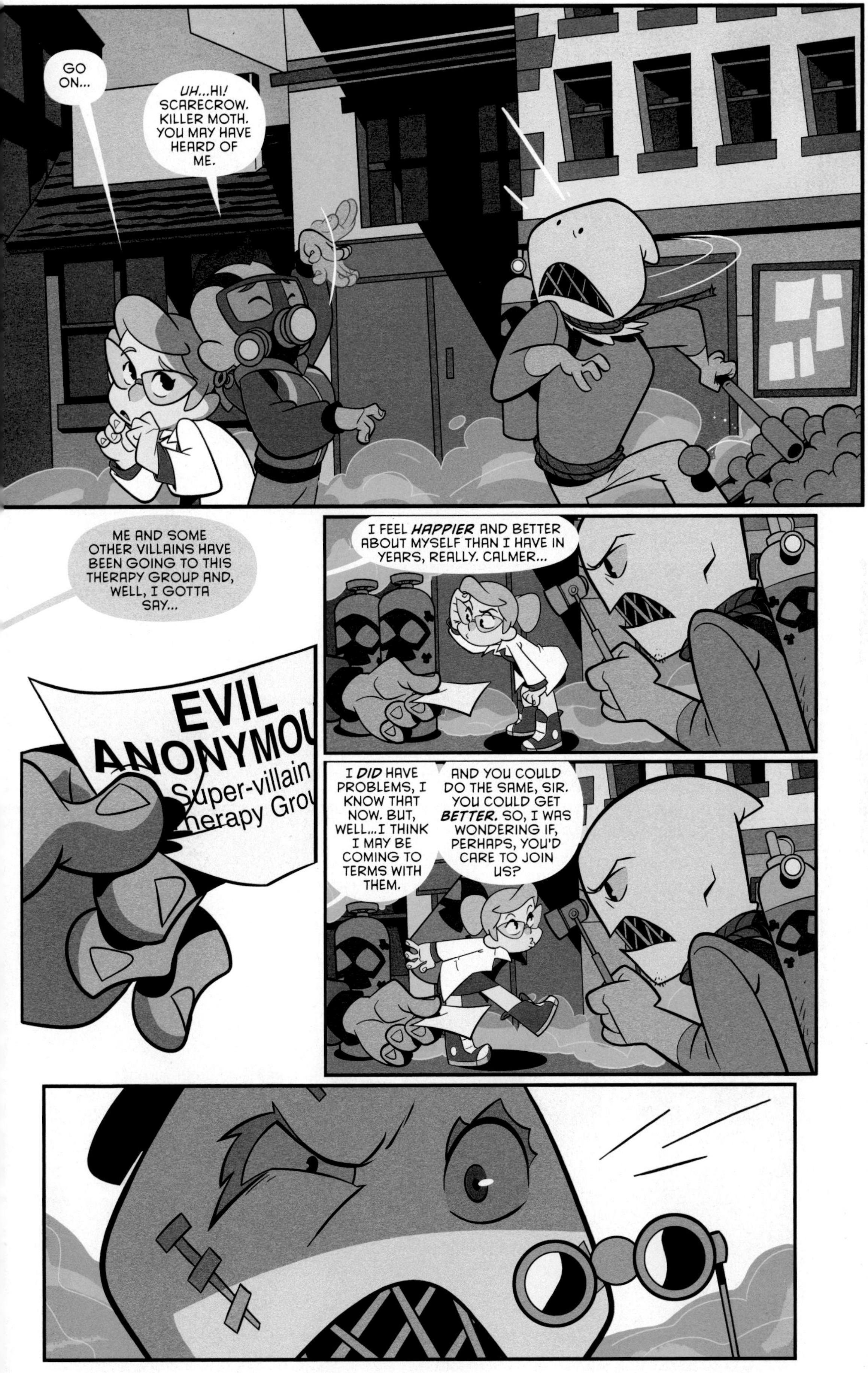
GO ON...
UH...HI! SCARECROW. KILLER MOTH. YOU MAY HAVE HEARD OF ME.
ME AND SOME OTHER VILLAINS HAVE BEEN GOING TO THIS THERAPY GROUP AND, WELL, I GOTTA SAY...
EVIL ANONYMOU
Super-villain Therapy Grou
I FEEL HAPPIER AND BETTER ABOUT MYSELF THAN I HAVE IN YEARS, REALLY. CALMER...
I DID HAVE PROBLEMS, I KNOW THAT NOW. BUT, WELL...I THINK I MAY BE COMING TO TERMS WITH THEM.
AND YOU COULD DO THE SAME, SIR. YOU COULD GET BETTER. SO, I WAS WONDERING IF, PERHAPS, YOU'D CARE TO JOIN US?

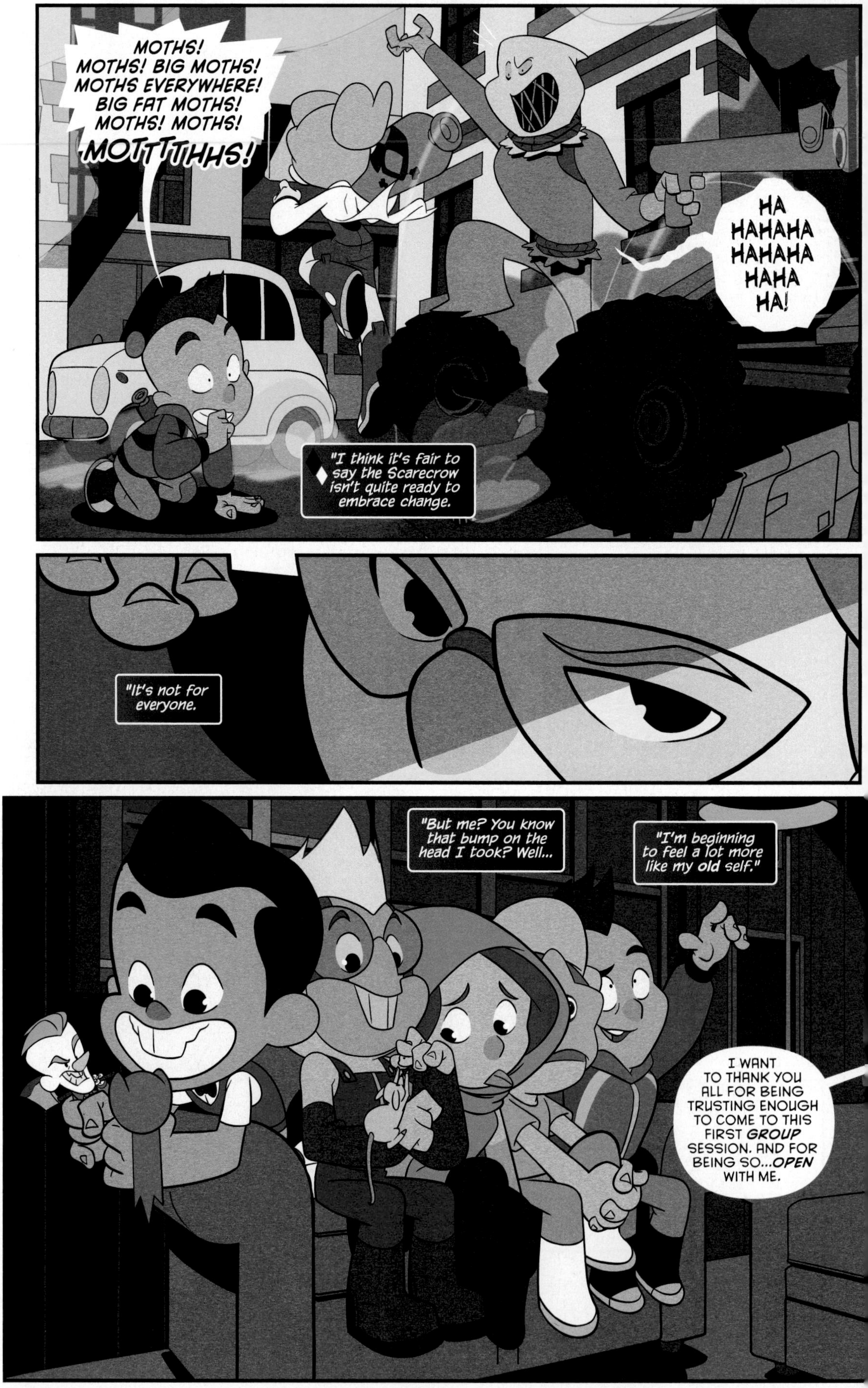
MOTHS! MOTHS! BIG MOTHS! MOTHS EVERYWHERE! BIG FAT MOTHS! MOTHS! MOTHS! MOTTTTHHS!
HA HAHAHA HAHAHA HAHA HA!
"I think it's fair to say the Scarecrow isn't quite ready to embrace change.
"It's not for everyone.
"But me? You know that bump on the head I took? Well...
"I'm beginning to feel a lot more like my old self."
I WANT TO THANK YOU ALL FOR BEING TRUSTING ENOUGH TO COME TO THIS FIRST GROUP SESSION. AND FOR BEING SO...OPEN WITH ME.

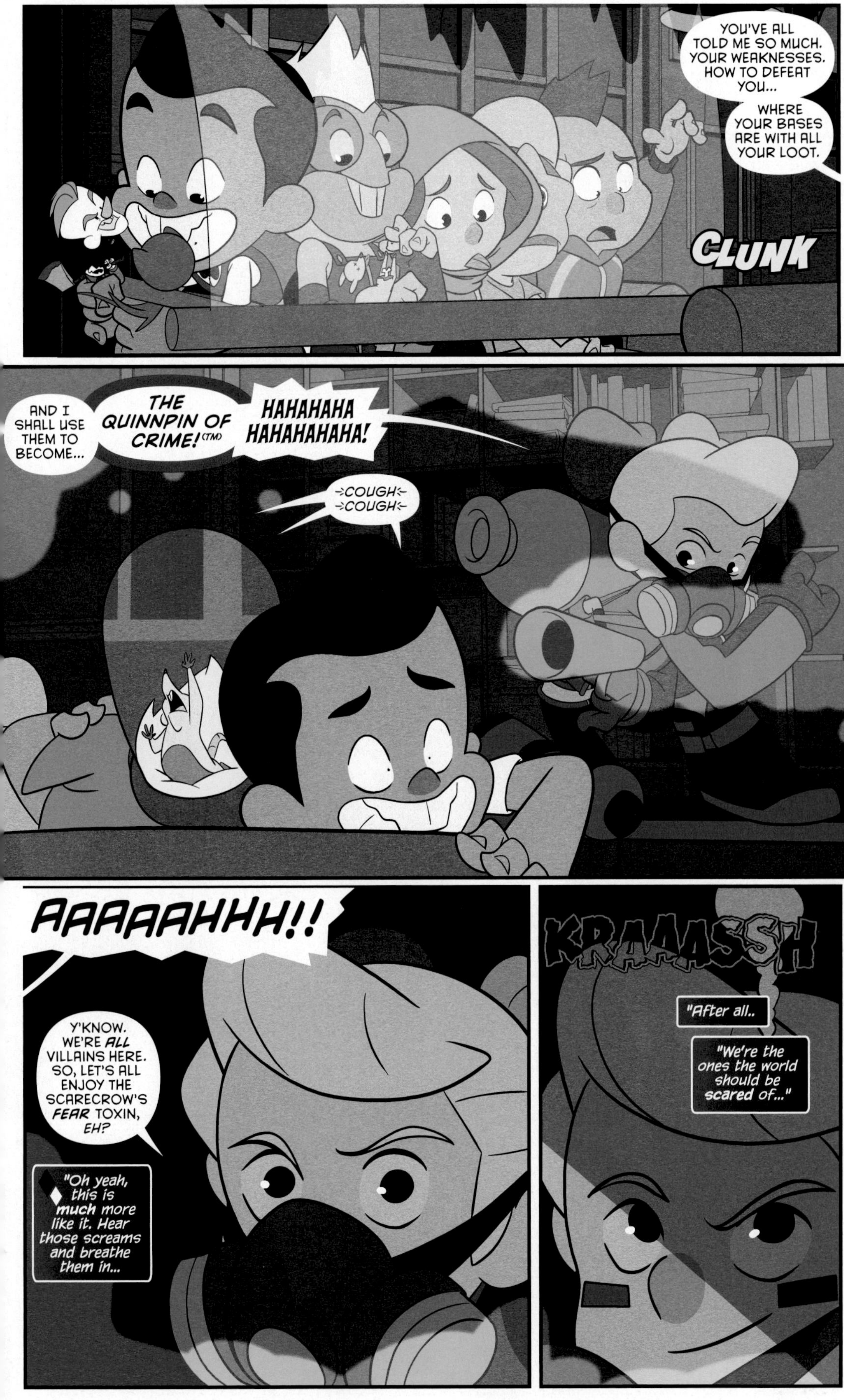

YOU'VE ALL TOLD ME SO MUCH. YOUR WEAKNESSES. HOW TO DEFEAT YOU...
WHERE YOUR BASES ARE WITH ALL YOUR LOOT.
CLUNK
AND I SHALL USE THEM TO BECOME...
THE QUINNPIN OF CRIME!(TM)
HAHAHAHA HAHAHAHAHA!
COUGH COUGH
AAAAAHHH!!
Y'KNOW. WE'RE ALL VILLAINS HERE. SO, LET'S ALL ENJOY THE SCARECROW'S FEAR TOXIN, EH?
"Oh yeah, this is much more like it. Hear those screams and breathe them in...
KRAAASSH
"After all..
"We're the ones the world should be scared of..."

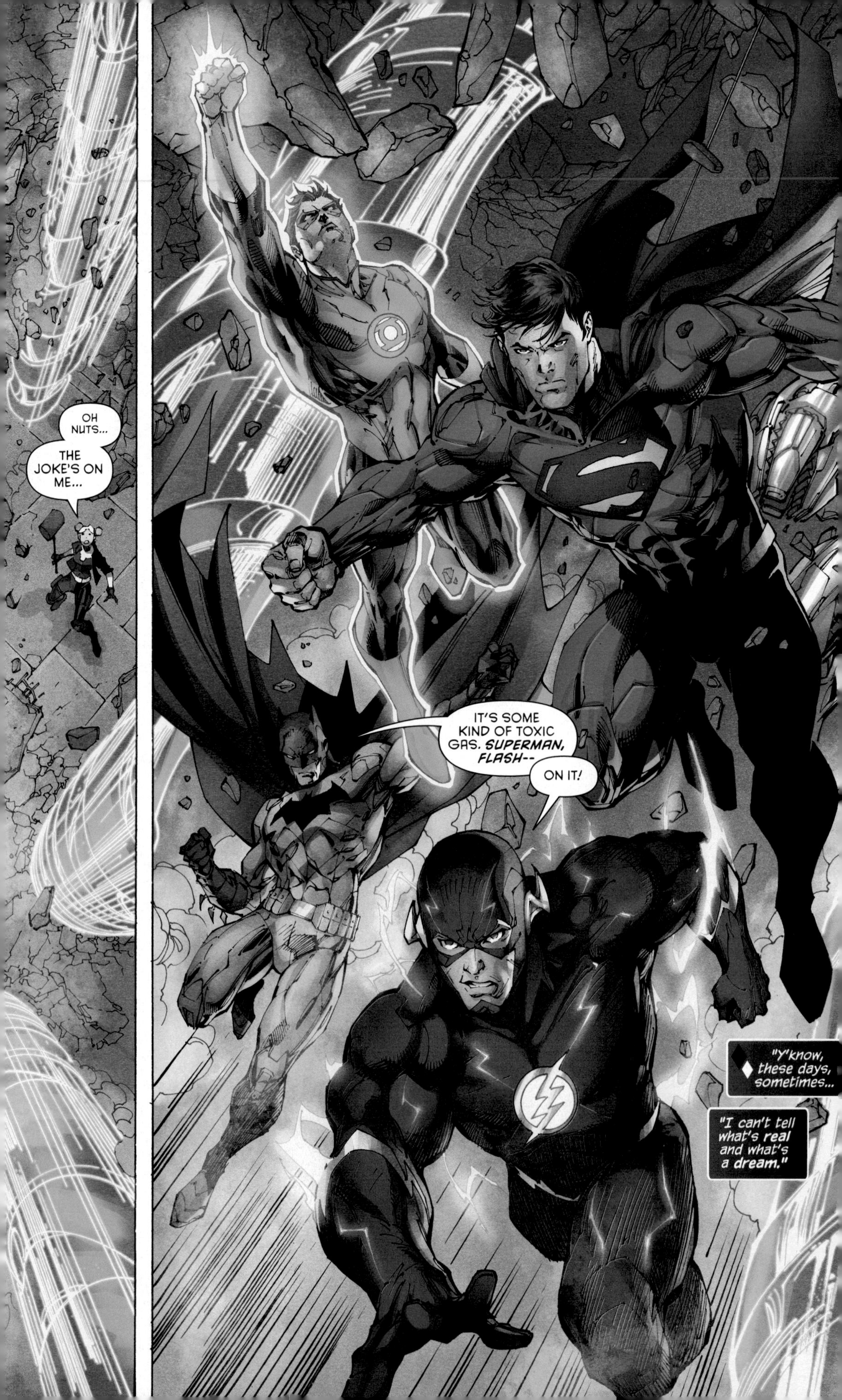
OH NUTS...
THE JOKE'S ON ME...
IT'S SOME KIND OF TOXIC GAS. SUPERMAN, FLASH--
ON IT!
"Y'know, these days, sometimes...
"I can't tell what's real and what's a dream."

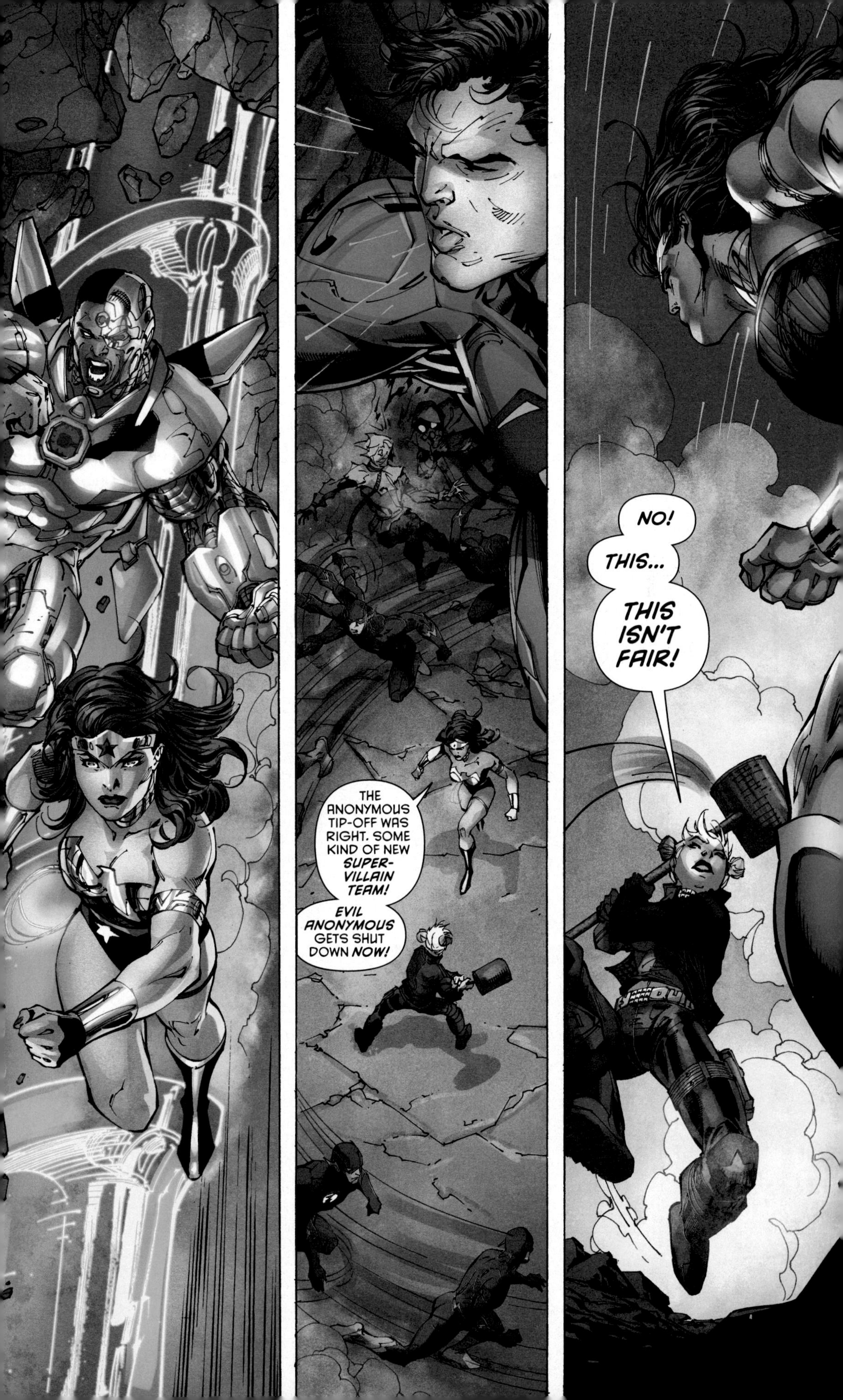
THE ANONYMOUS TIP-OFF WAS RIGHT. SOME KIND OF NEW SUPER-VILLAIN TEAM!
EVIL ANONYMOUS GETS SHUT DOWN NOW!
NO!
THIS...
THIS ISN'T FAIR!

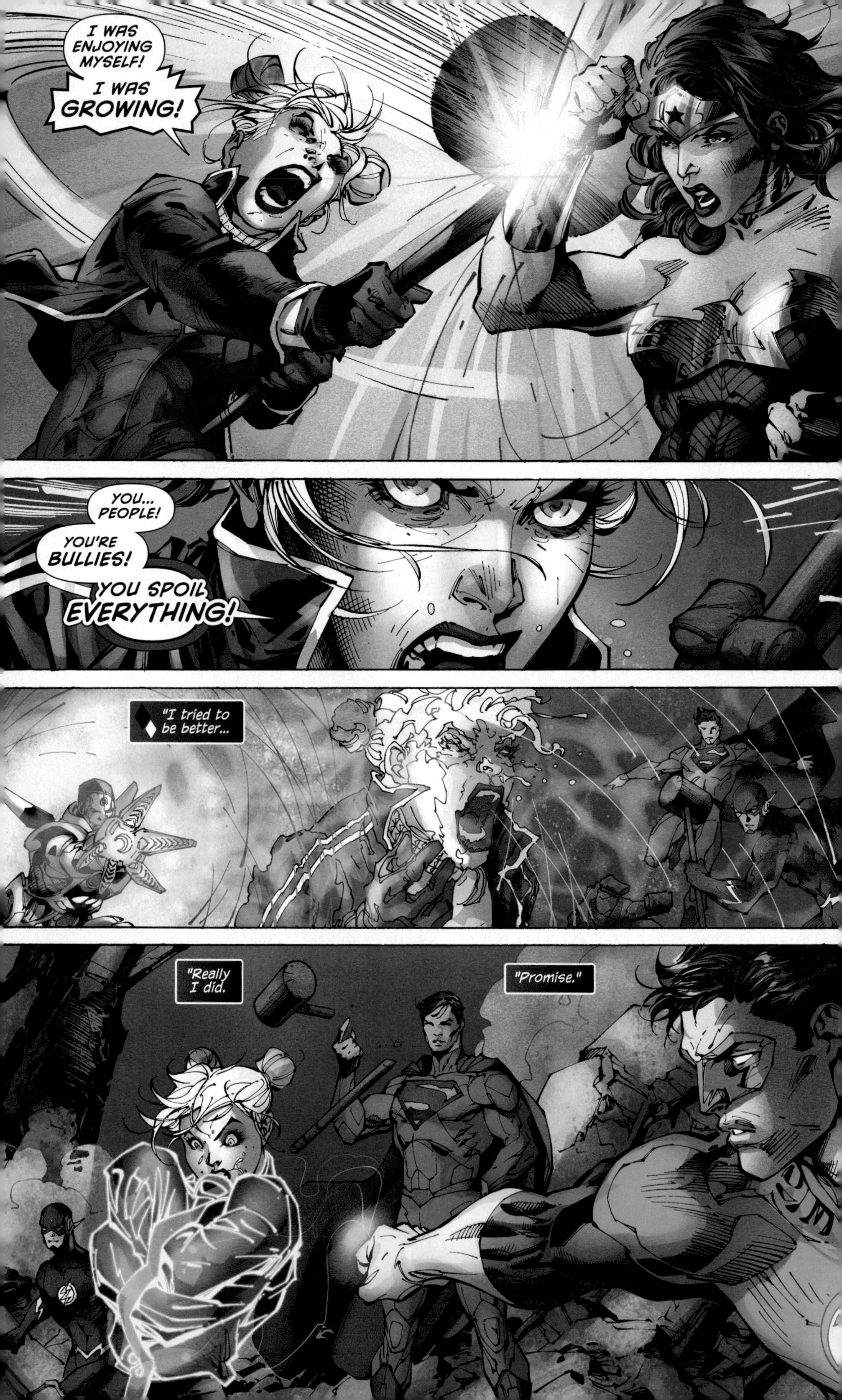

I WAS ENJOYING MYSELF!
I WAS GROWING!
YOU... PEOPLE!
YOU'RE BULLIES!
YOU SPOIL EVERYTHING!
"I tried to be better...
"Really I did.
"Promise."

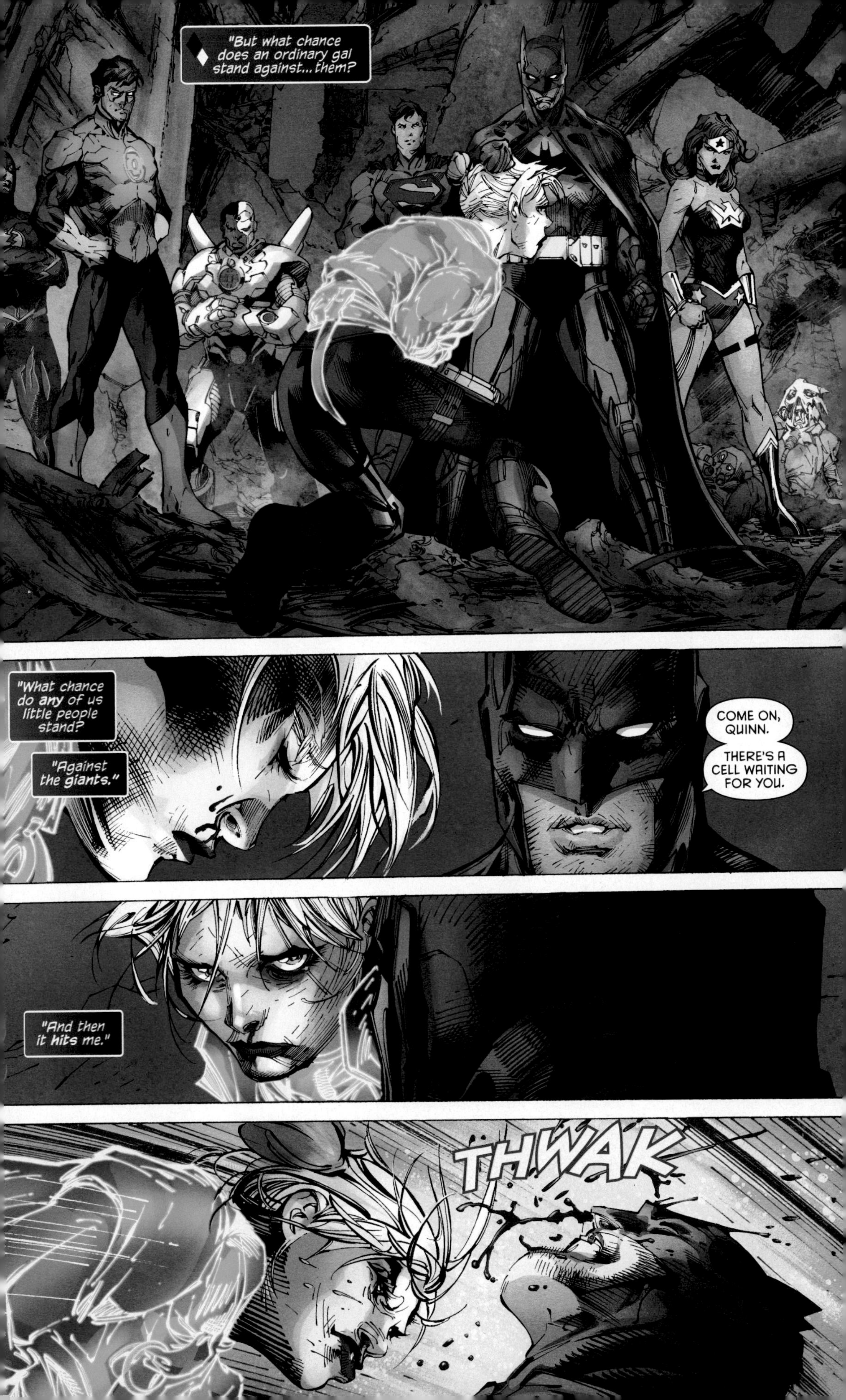
"But what chance does an ordinary gal stand against...them?
"What chance do any of us little people stand?
"Against the giants."
COME ON, QUINN.
THERE'S A CELL WAITING FOR YOU.
"And then it hits me."
THWAK

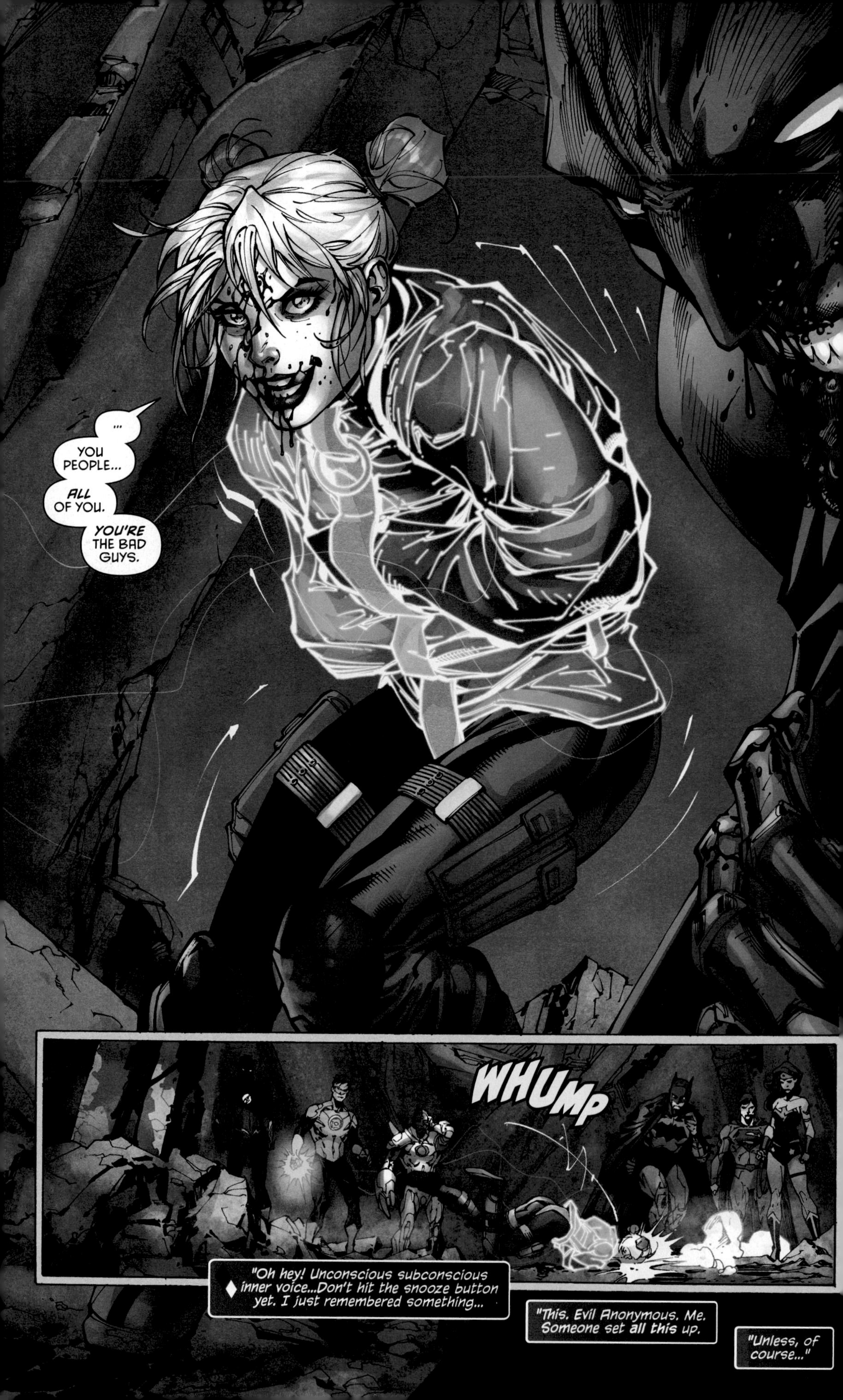
...
YOU PEOPLE...
ALL OF YOU.
YOU'RE THE BAD GUYS.
WHUMP
"Oh hey! Unconscious subconscious inner voice...Don't hit the snooze button yet. I just remembered something...
"This. Evil Anonymous. Me. Someone set all this up.
"Unless, of course..."

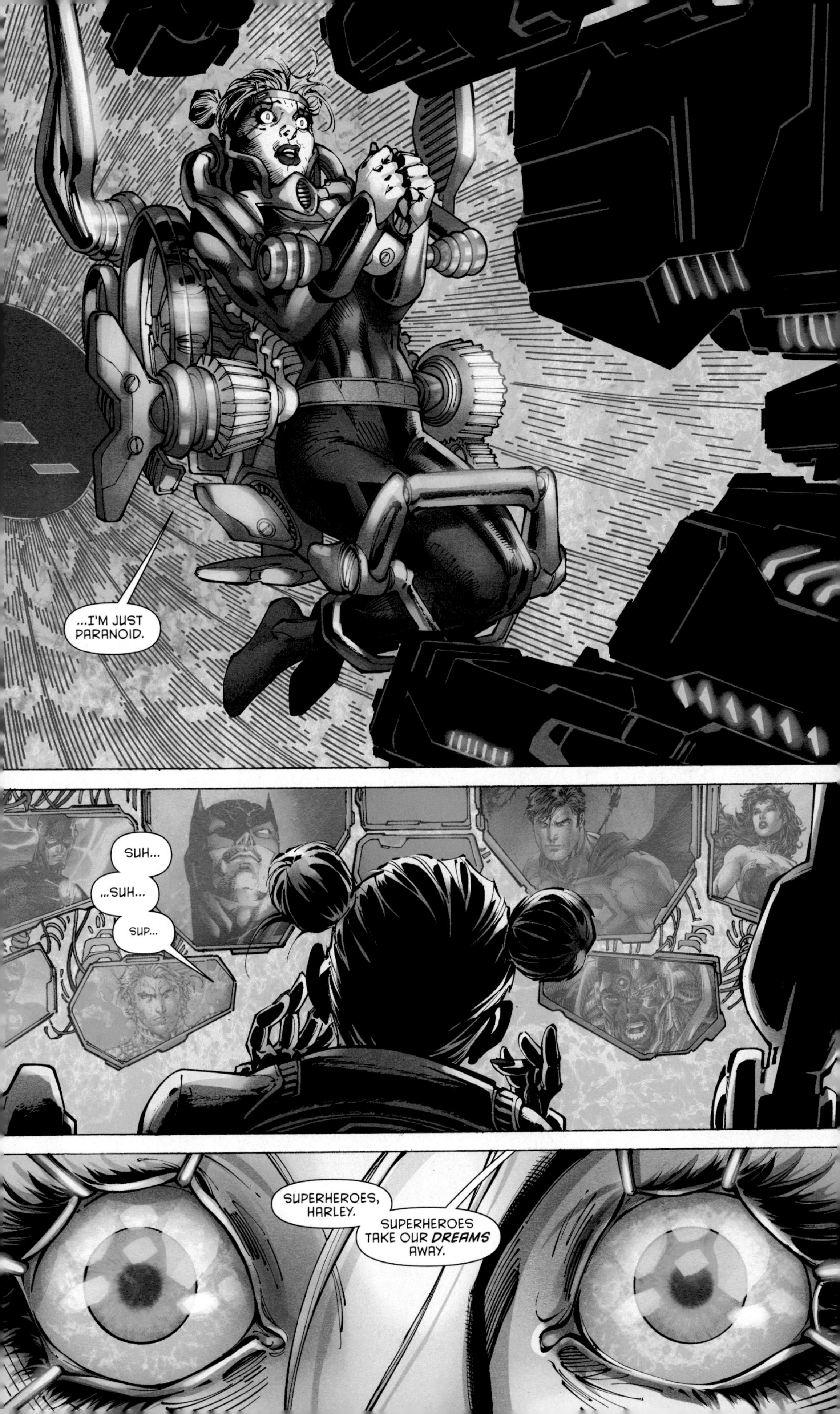
...I'M JUST PARANOID.
SUH...
...SUH...
SUP...
SUPERHEROES, HARLEY.
SUPERHEROES TAKE OUR *DREAMS* AWAY.

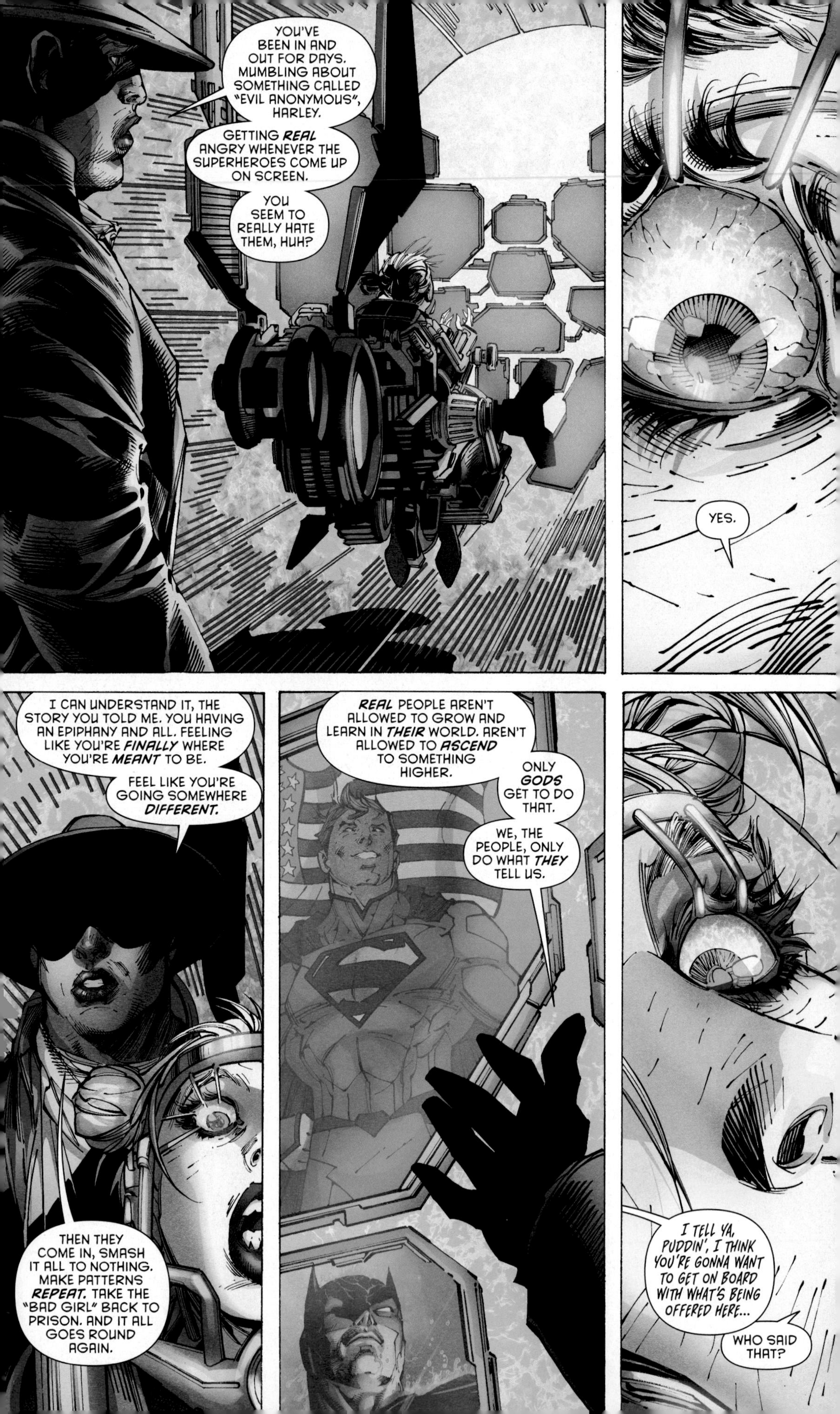
YOU'VE BEEN IN AND OUT FOR DAYS. MUMBLING ABOUT SOMETHING CALLED "EVIL ANONYMOUS", HARLEY.
GETTING REAL ANGRY WHENEVER THE SUPERHEROES COME UP ON SCREEN.
YOU SEEM TO REALLY HATE THEM, HUH?
YES.
I CAN UNDERSTAND IT, THE STORY YOU TOLD ME. YOU HAVING AN EPIPHANY AND ALL. FEELING LIKE YOU'RE FINALLY WHERE YOU'RE MEANT TO BE.
FEEL LIKE YOU'RE GOING SOMEWHERE DIFFERENT.
THEN THEY COME IN, SMASH IT ALL TO NOTHING. MAKE PATTERNS REPEAT. TAKE THE "BAD GIRL" BACK TO PRISON. AND IT ALL GOES ROUND AGAIN.
REAL PEOPLE AREN'T ALLOWED TO GROW AND LEARN IN THEIR WORLD. AREN'T ALLOWED TO ASCEND TO SOMETHING HIGHER.
ONLY GODS GET TO DO THAT.
WE, THE PEOPLE, ONLY DO WHAT THEY TELL US.
I TELL YA, PUDDIN', I THINK YOU'RE GONNA WANT TO GET ON BOARD WITH WHAT'S BEING OFFERED HERE...
WHO SAID THAT?

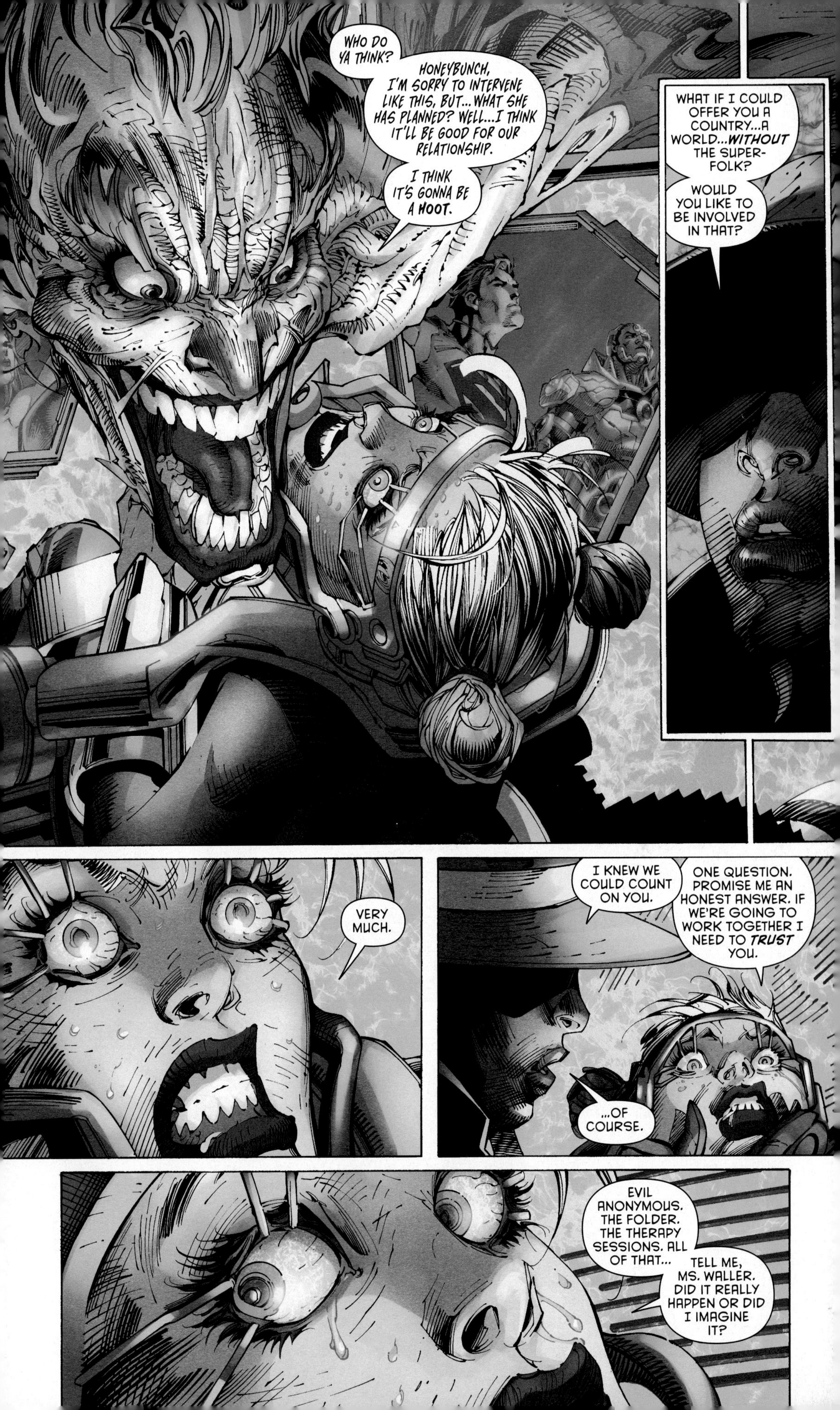
WHO DO YA THINK?
HONEYBUNCH, I'M SORRY TO INTERVENE LIKE THIS, BUT... WHAT SHE HAS PLANNED? WELL... I THINK IT'LL BE GOOD FOR OUR RELATIONSHIP.
I THINK IT'S GONNA BE A **HOOT**.
WHAT IF I COULD OFFER YOU A COUNTRY...A WORLD...***WITHOUT*** THE SUPER-FOLK?
WOULD YOU LIKE TO BE INVOLVED IN THAT?
VERY MUCH.
I KNEW WE COULD COUNT ON YOU.
ONE QUESTION. PROMISE ME AN HONEST ANSWER. IF WE'RE GOING TO WORK TOGETHER I NEED TO ***TRUST*** YOU.
...OF COURSE.
EVIL ANONYMOUS. THE FOLDER. THE THERAPY SESSIONS. ALL OF THAT...
TELL ME, MS. WALLER. DID IT REALLY HAPPEN OR DID I IMAGINE IT?

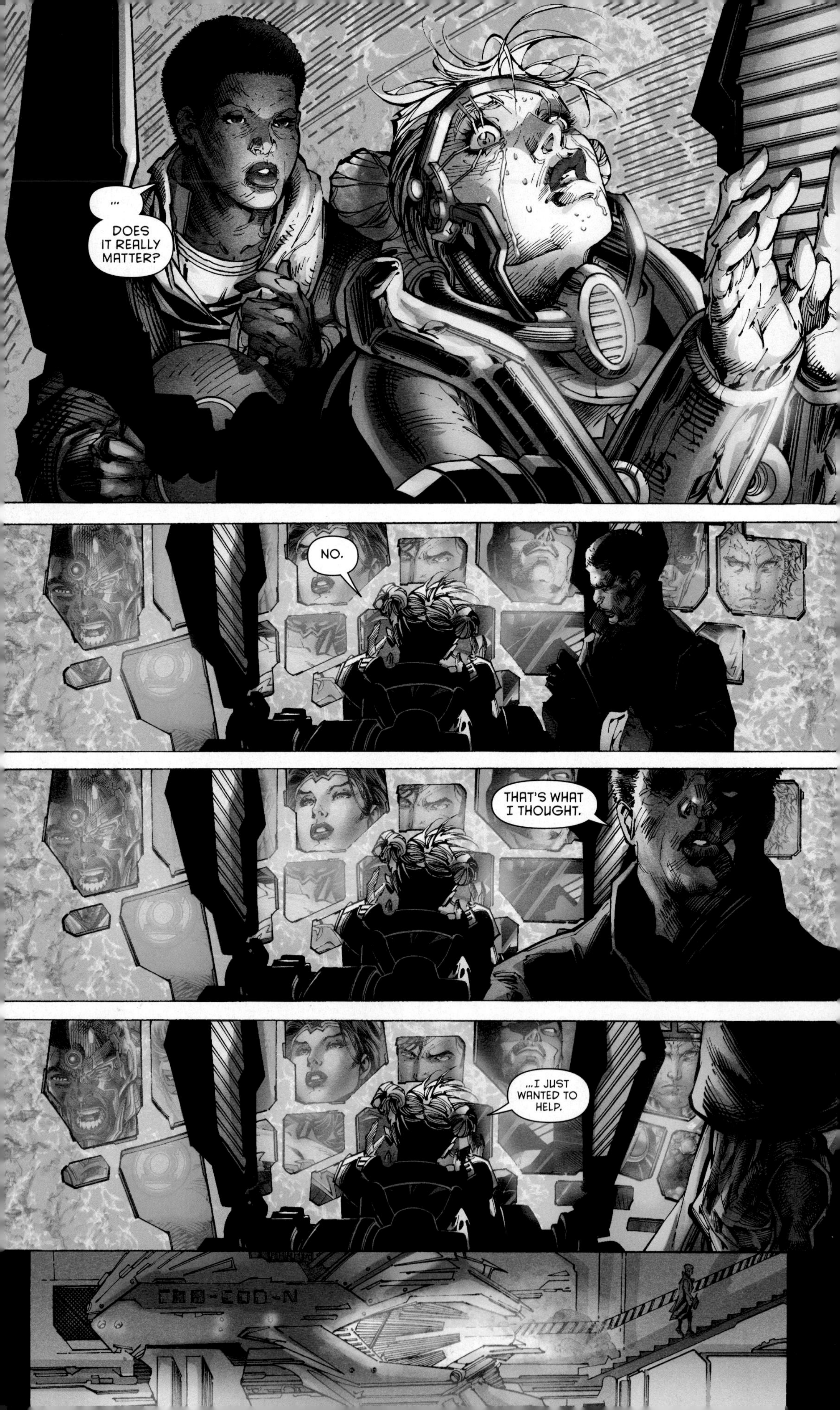

...
DOES IT REALLY MATTER?
NO.
THAT'S WHAT I THOUGHT.
...I JUST WANTED TO HELP.

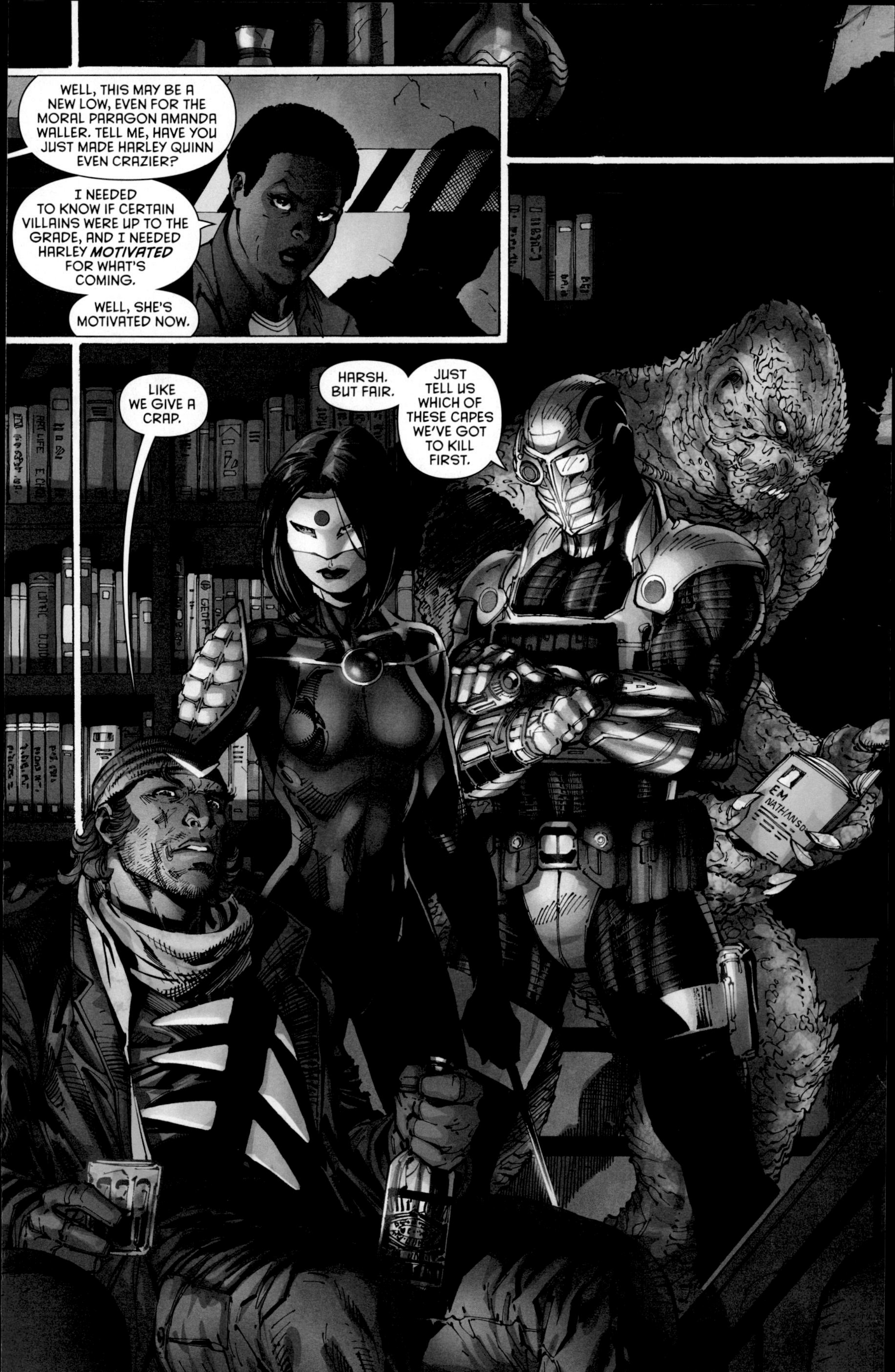
WELL, THIS MAY BE A NEW LOW, EVEN FOR THE MORAL PARAGON AMANDA WALLER. TELL ME, HAVE YOU JUST MADE HARLEY QUINN EVEN CRAZIER?
I NEEDED TO KNOW IF CERTAIN VILLAINS WERE UP TO THE GRADE, AND I NEEDED HARLEY *MOTIVATED* FOR WHAT'S COMING.
WELL, SHE'S MOTIVATED NOW.
LIKE WE GIVE A CRAP.
HARSH. BUT FAIR.
JUST TELL US WHICH OF THESE CAPES WE'VE GOT TO KILL FIRST.

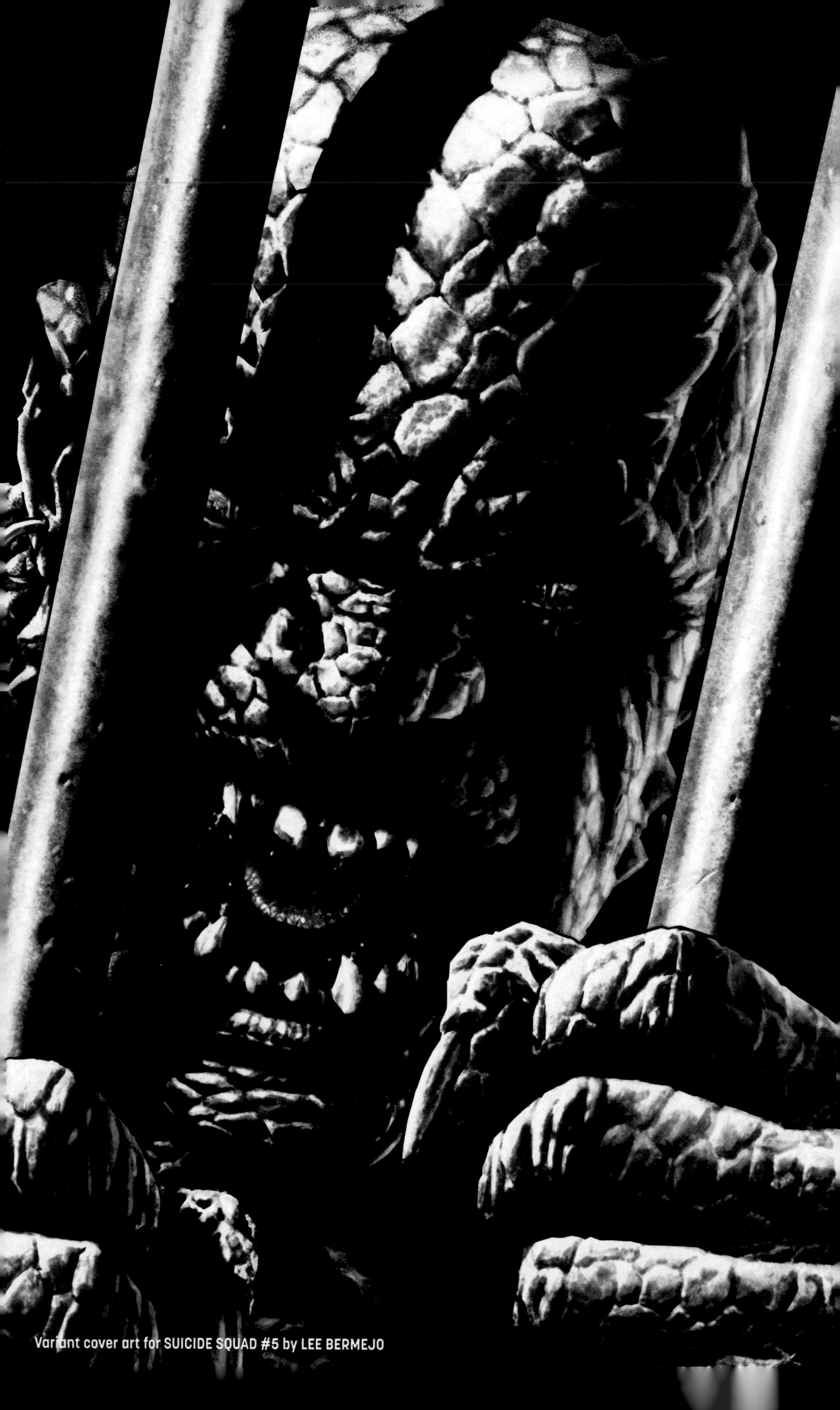

Variant cover art for SUICIDE SQUAD #5 by LEE BERMEJO

Variant cover art for SUICIDE SQUAD #6 by LEE BERMEJO

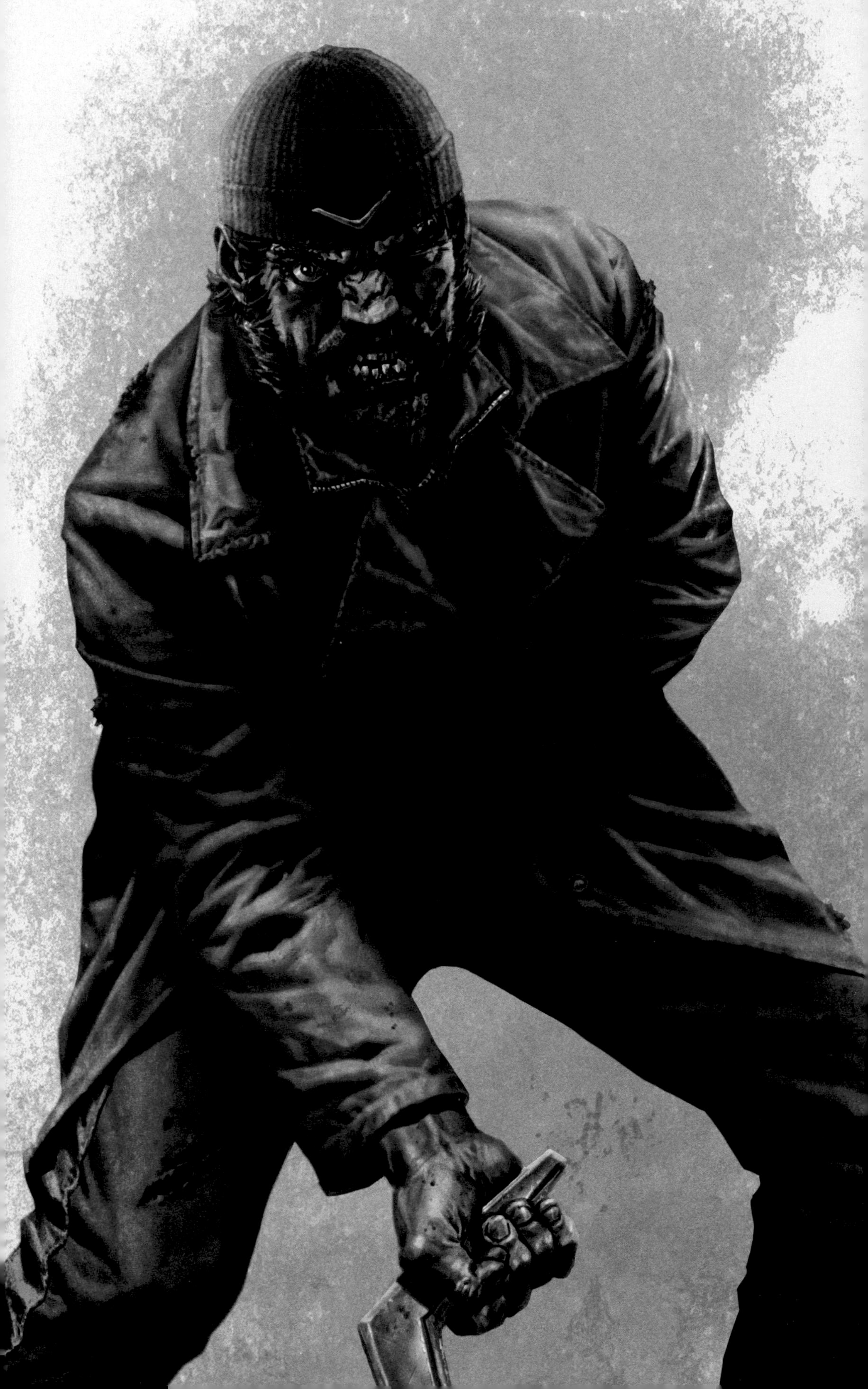

Variant cover art for SUICIDE SQUAD #7 by LEE BERMEJO

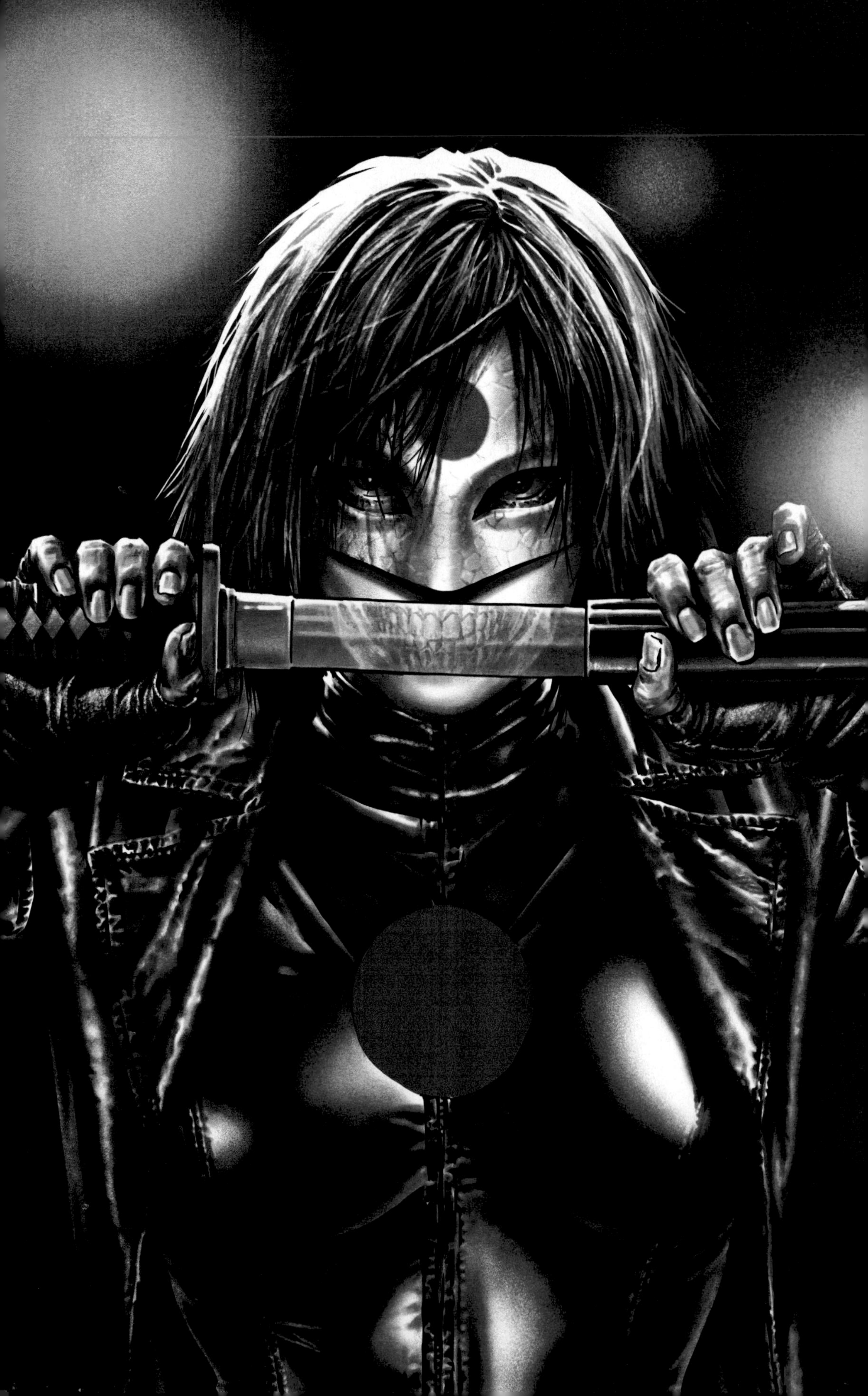

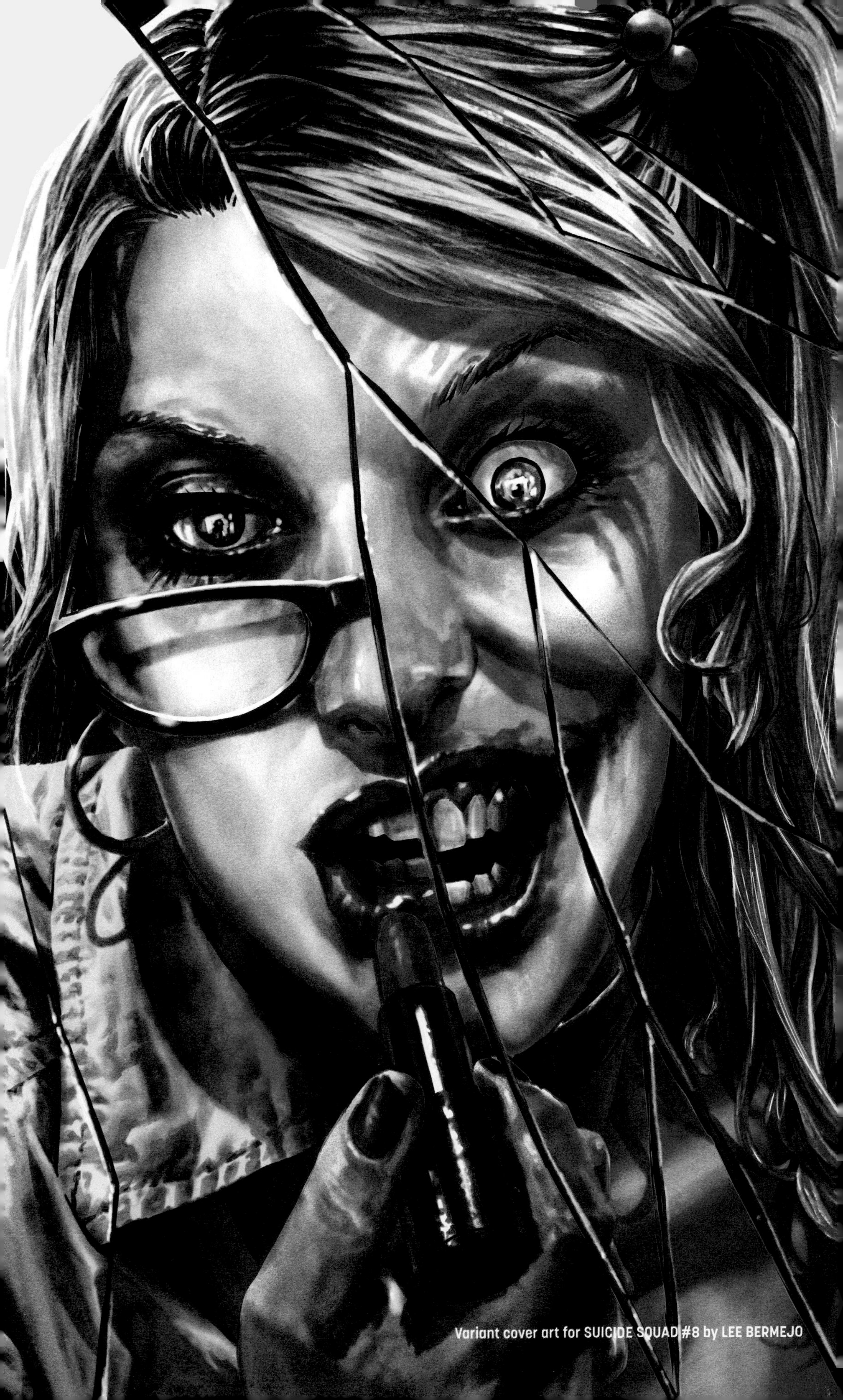

Variant cover art for SUICIDE SQUAD #8 by LEE BERMEJO

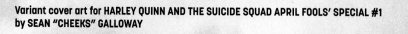

**Variant cover art for HARLEY QUINN AND THE SUICIDE SQUAD APRIL FOOLS' SPECIAL #1
by SEAN "CHEEKS" GALLOWAY**

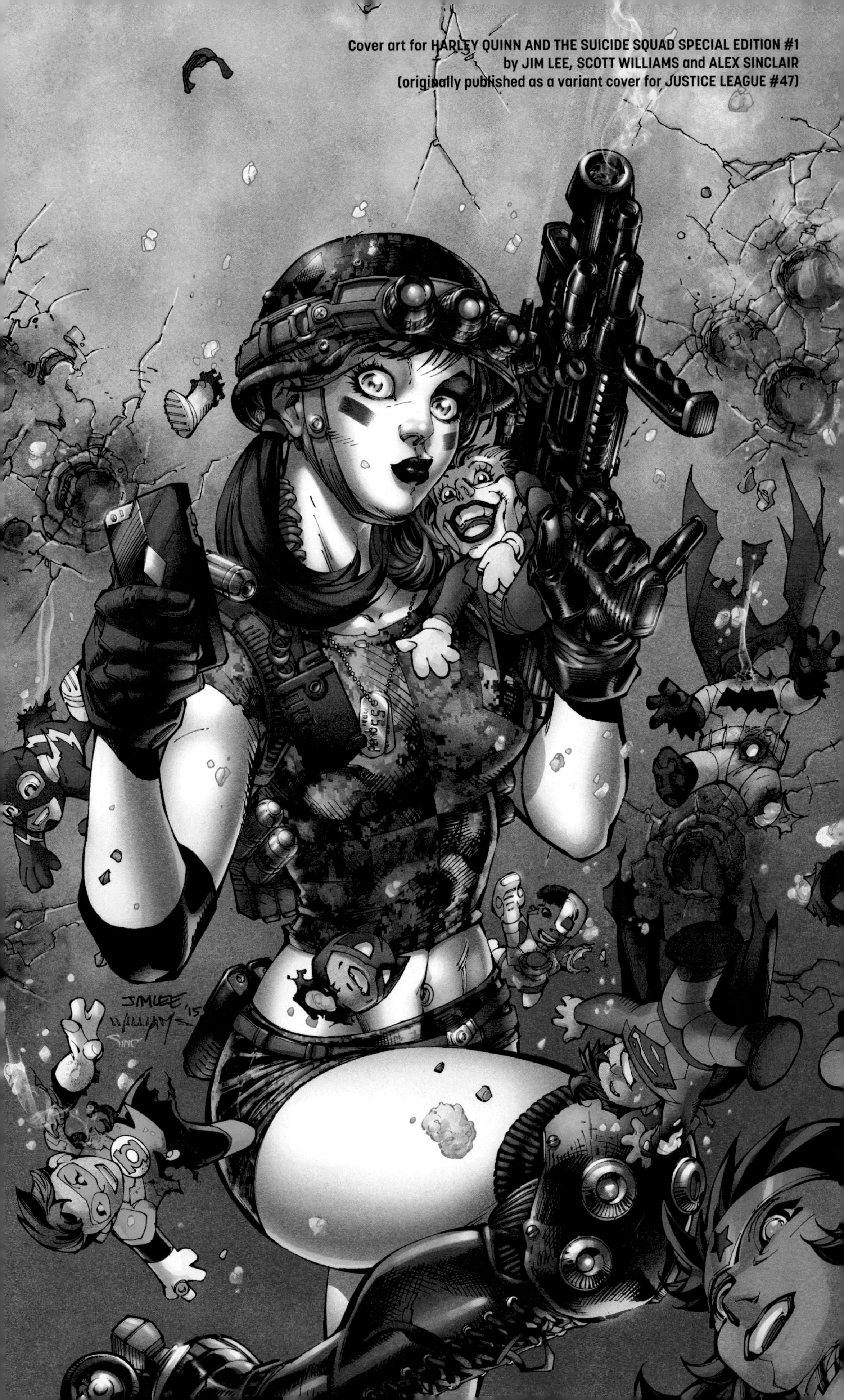

Cover art for HARLEY QUINN AND THE SUICIDE SQUAD SPECIAL EDITION #1
by JIM LEE, SCOTT WILLIAMS and ALEX SINCLAIR
(originally published as a variant cover for JUSTICE LEAGUE #47)

COUCH TRIP

Preliminary layouts by Sean "Cheeks" Galloway for HARLEY QUINN AND THE SUICIDE SQUAD APRIL FOOLS' SPECIAL

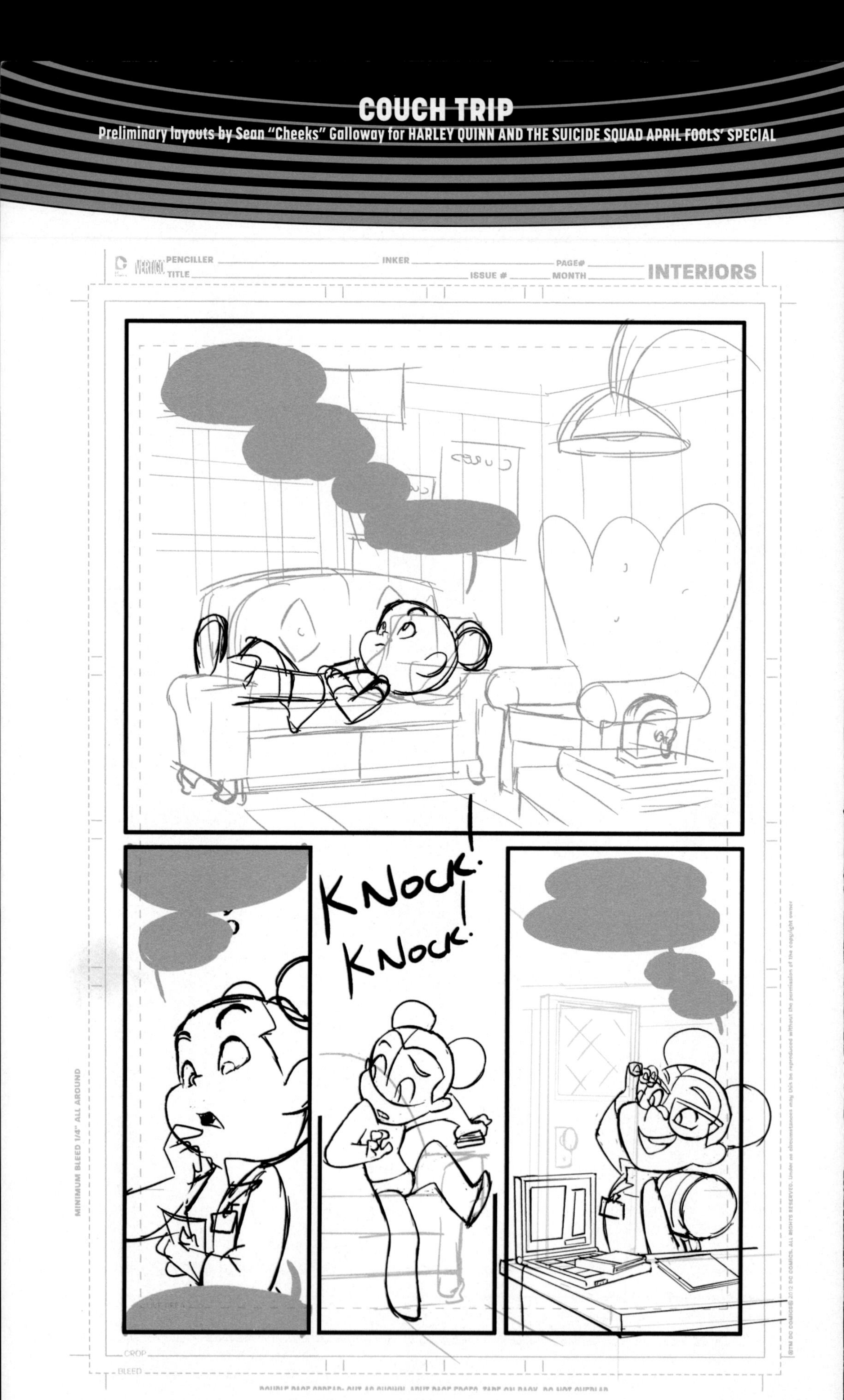
PENCILLER
INKER
PAGE#
TITLE
ISSUE #
MONTH
INTERIORS
KNOCK!
KNOCK!
MINIMUM BLEED 1/4" ALL AROUND
CROP
BLEED

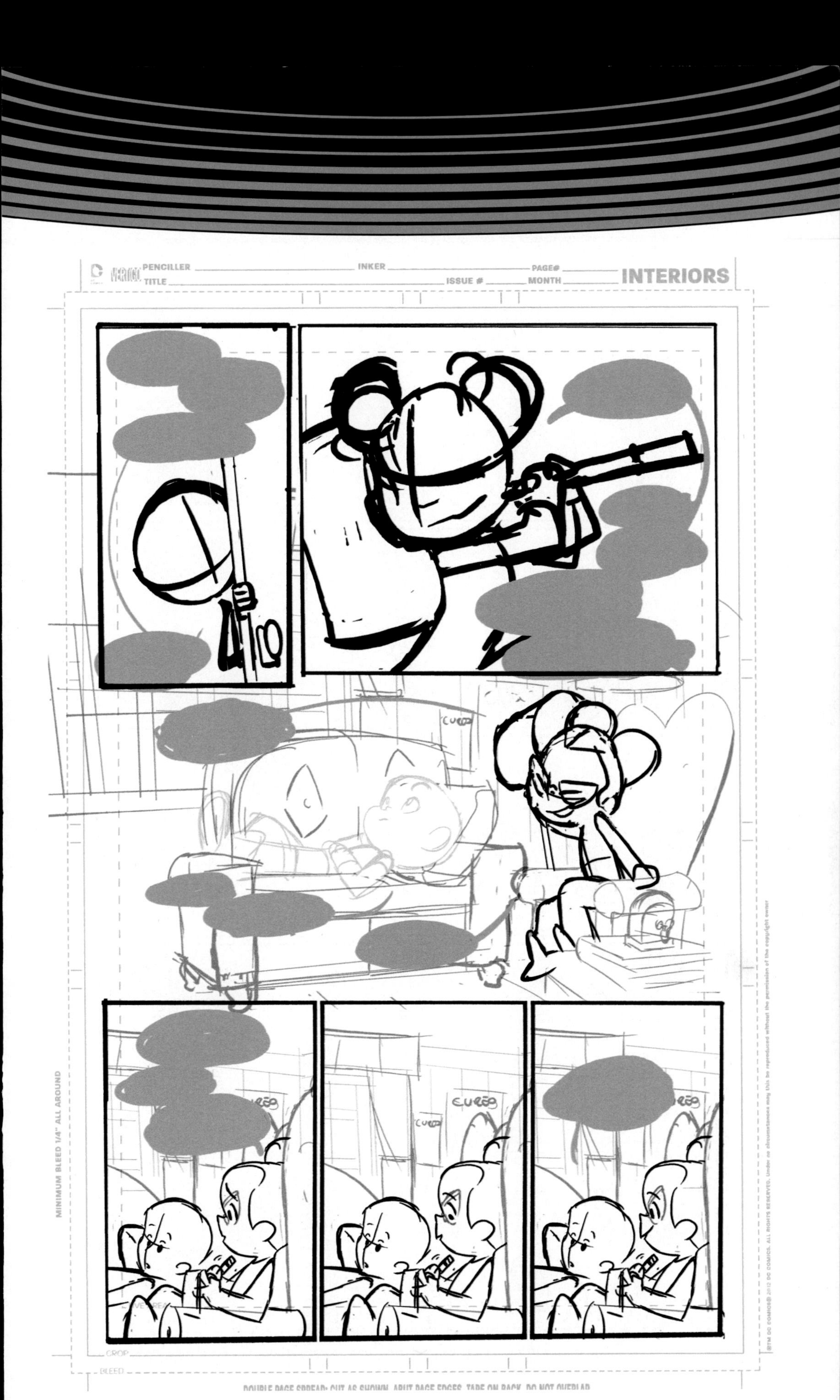
PENCILLER
INKER
PAGE#
TITLE
ISSUE #
MONTH
INTERIORS
MINIMUM BLEED 1/4" ALL AROUND
CROP
BLEED
DOUBLE PAGE SPREAD: CUT AS SHOWN. ABUT PAGE EDGES. TAPE ON BACK. DO NOT OVERLAP

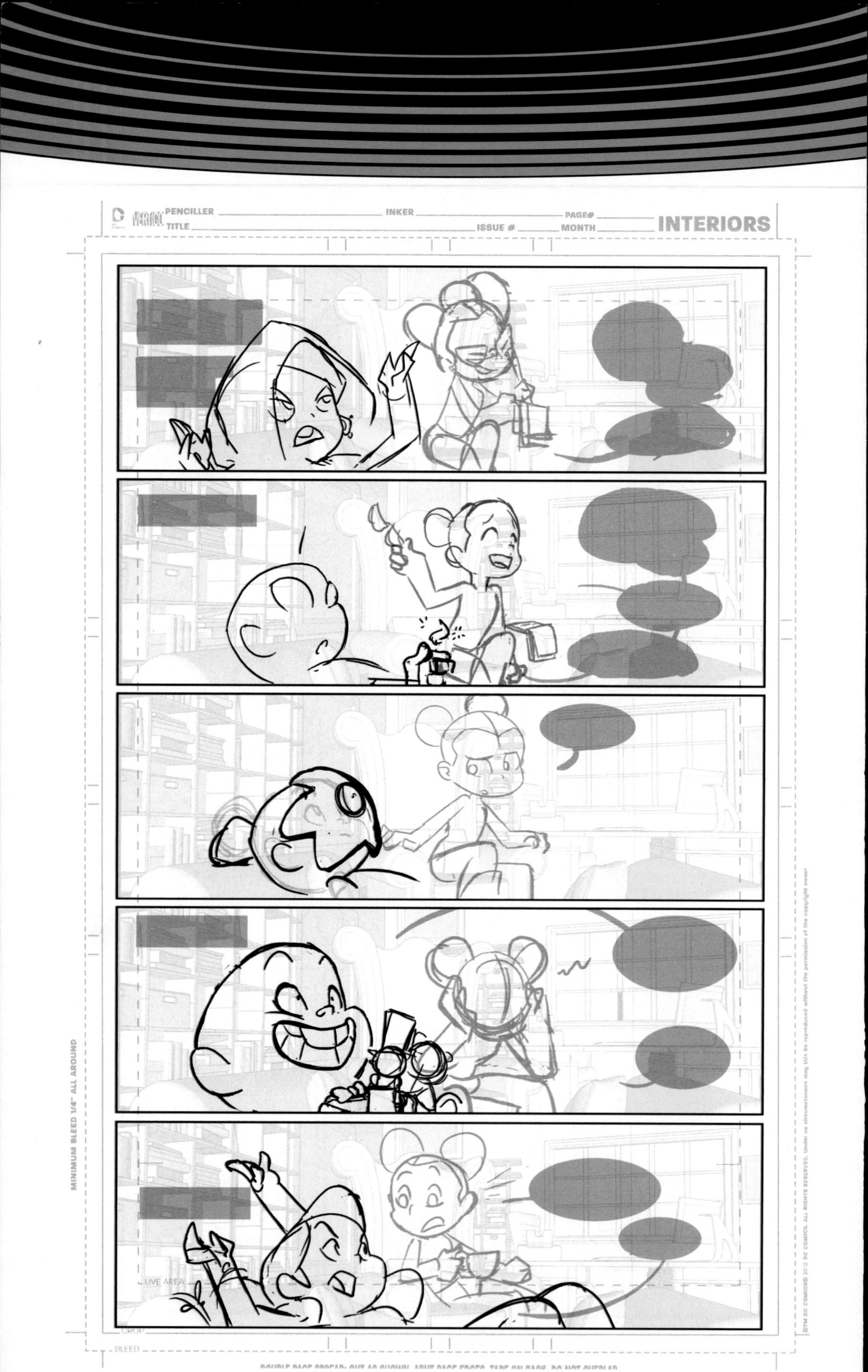
PENCILLER
INKER
PAGE#
TITLE
ISSUE #
MONTH
INTERIORS
LIVE AREA
CROP
BLEED
MINIMUM BLEED 1/4" ALL AROUND
©TM DC COMICS© 2012 DC COMICS. ALL RIGHTS RESERVED. Under no circumstances may this be reproduced without the permission of the copyright owner

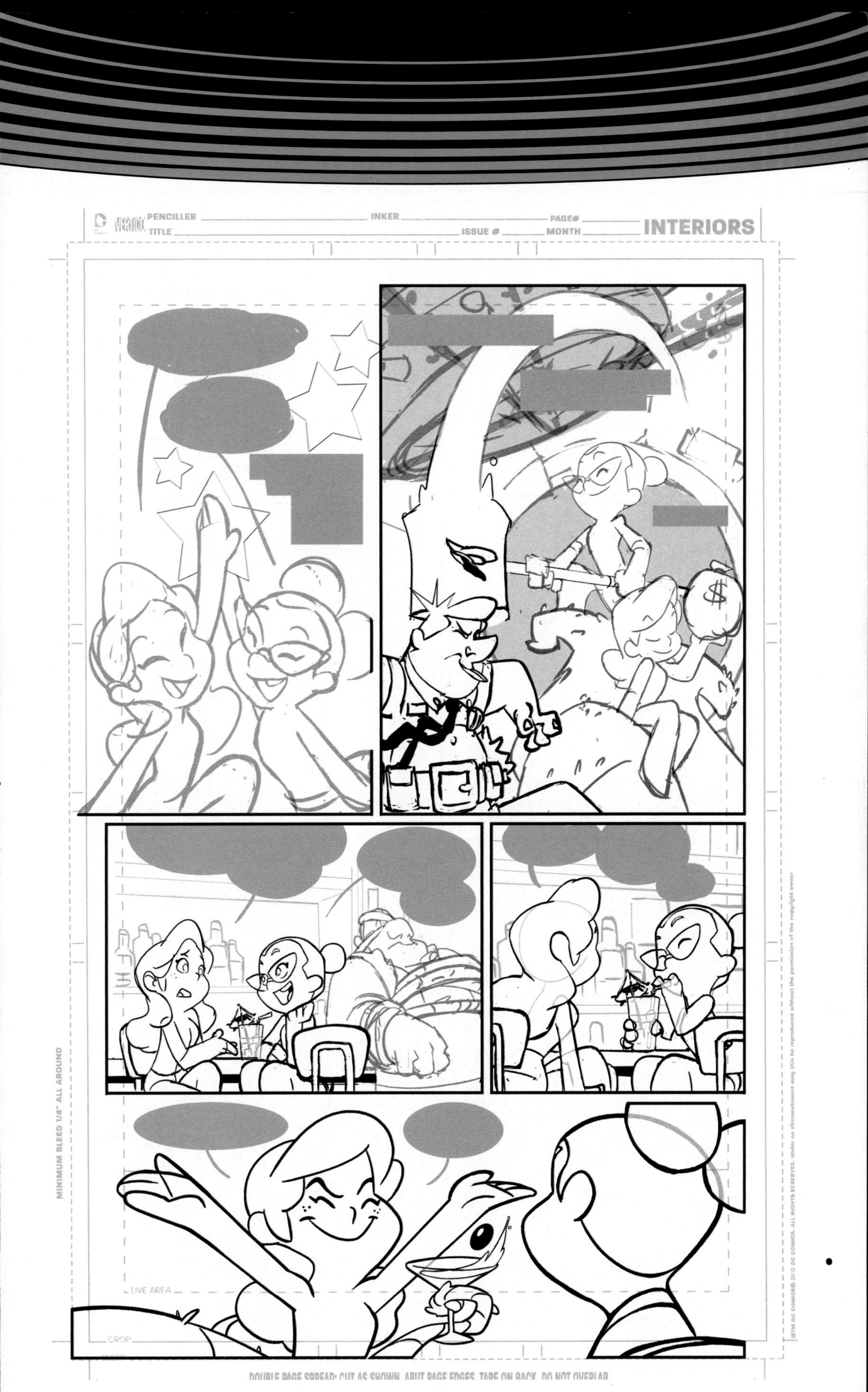

PENCILLER
INKER
PAGE#
TITLE
ISSUE #
MONTH
INTERIORS
MINIMUM BLEED 1/4" ALL AROUND
LIVE AREA
CROP
©TM DC COMICS© 2012 DC COMICS. ALL RIGHTS RESERVED. Under no circumstances may this be reproduced without the permission of the copyright owner
DOUBLE PAGE SPREAD: CUT AS SHOWN. ABUT PAGE EDGES. TAPE ON BACK. DO NOT OVERLAP

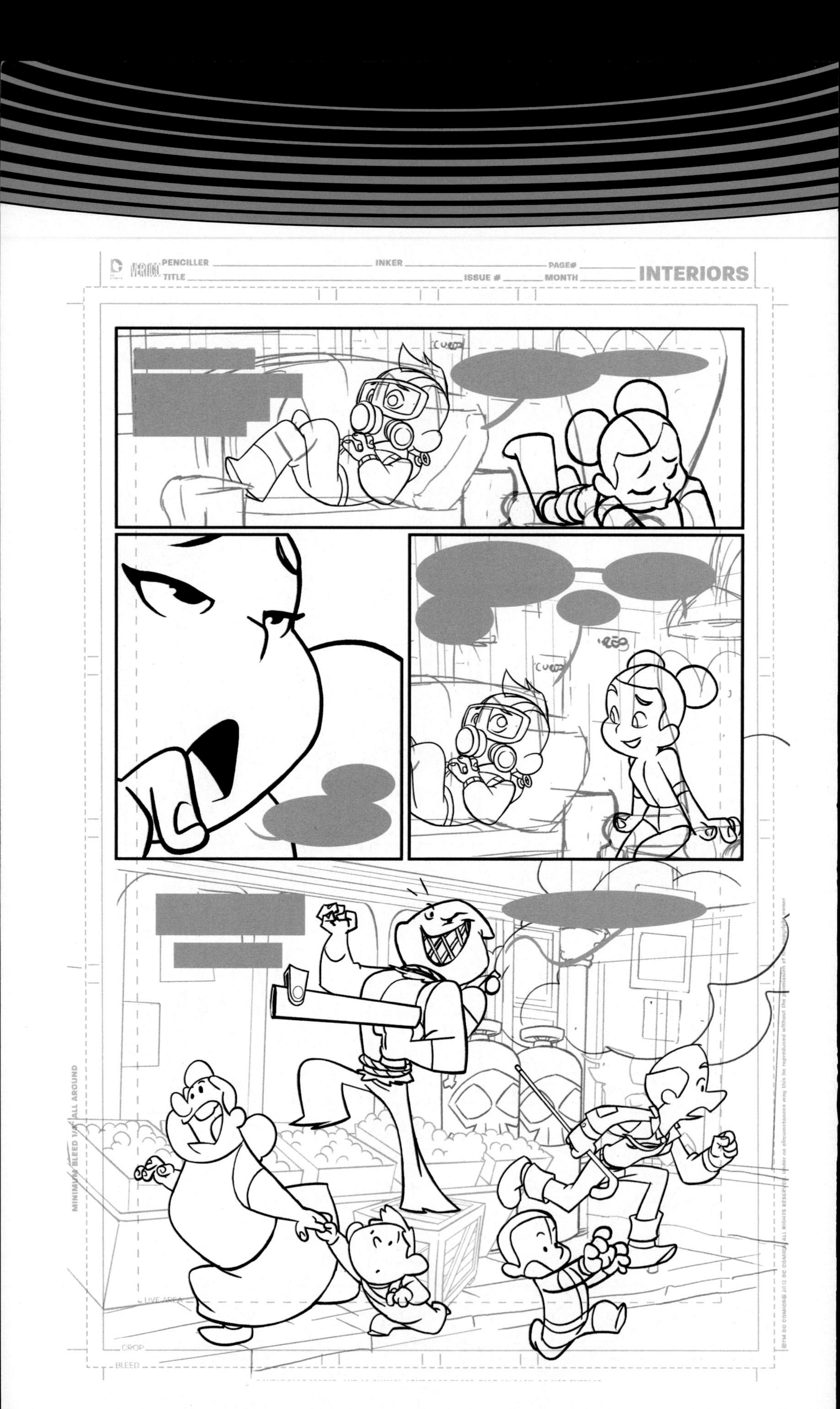
PENCILLER
INKER
PAGE#
TITLE
ISSUE #
MONTH
INTERIORS
MINIMUM BLEED 1/4" ALL AROUND
LIVE AREA
CROP
BLEED

PENCILLER ________ INKER ________ PAGE# ________

TITLE ________ ISSUE # ________ MONTH ________ **INTERIORS**

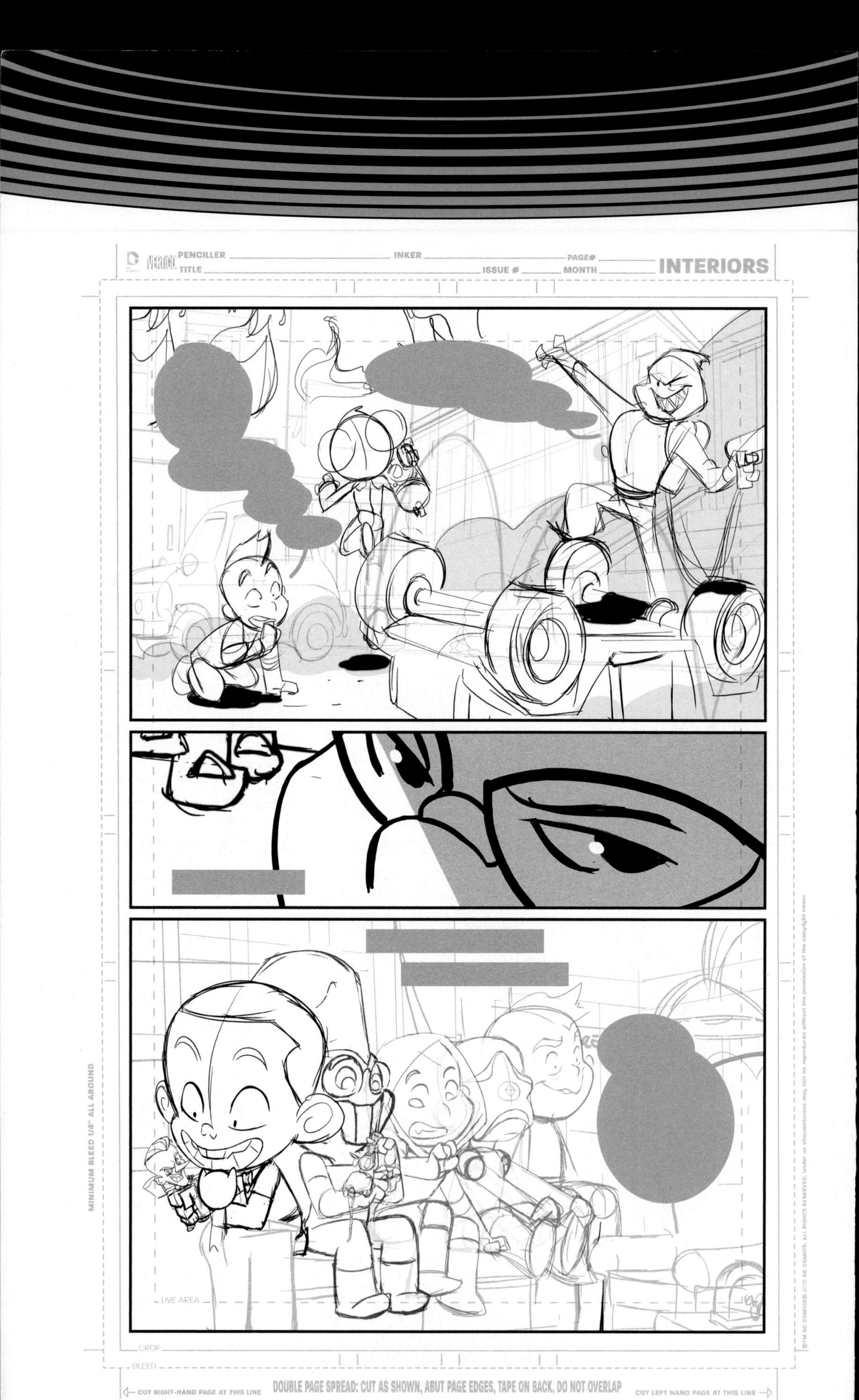

LIVE AREA

CROP

BLEED

MINIMUM BLEED 1/4" ALL AROUND

CUT RIGHT-HAND PAGE AT THIS LINE — DOUBLE PAGE SPREAD: CUT AS SHOWN, ABUT PAGE EDGES, TAPE ON BACK, DO NOT OVERLAP — CUT LEFT HAND PAGE AT THIS LINE

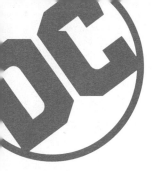

"It's nice to see one of the best comics of the late '80s return so strongly."
– Comic Book Resources

"It's high energy from page one through to the last page." **– BATMAN NEWS**

DC UNIVERSE REBIRTH

SUICIDE SQUAD

VOL. 1: THE BLACK VAULT

ROB WILLIAMS
with JIM LEE and others

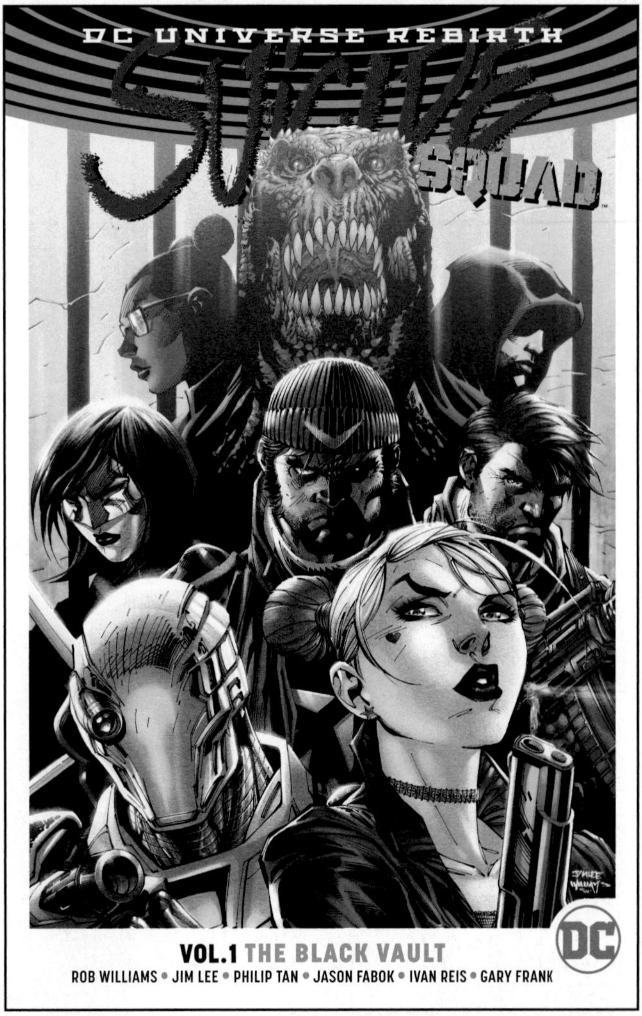
DC UNIVERSE REBIRTH
SUICIDE SQUAD
VOL.1 THE BLACK VAULT
ROB WILLIAMS • JIM LEE • PHILIP TAN • JASON FABOK • IVAN REIS • GARY FRANK

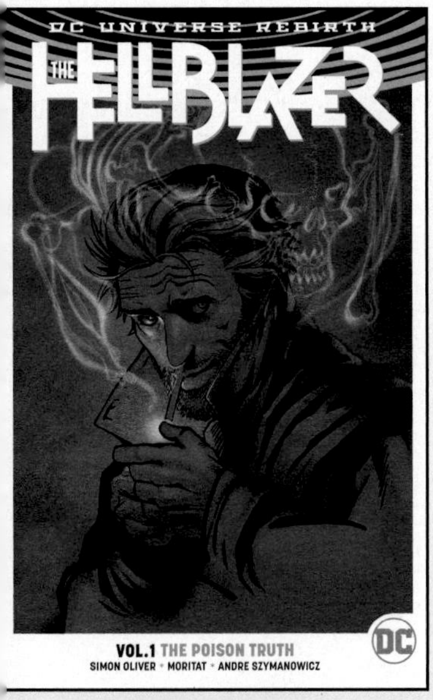
DC UNIVERSE REBIRTH
THE HELLBLAZER
VOL.1 THE POISON TRUTH
SIMON OLIVER • MORITAT • ANDRE SZYMANOWICZ

THE HELLBLAZER VOL. 1: THE POISON TRUTH

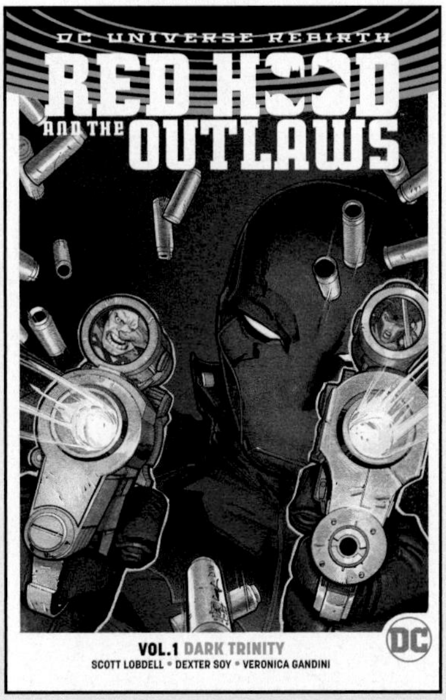
DC UNIVERSE REBIRTH
RED HOOD AND THE OUTLAWS
VOL.1 DARK TRINITY
SCOTT LOBDELL • DEXTER SOY • VERONICA GANDINI

RED HOOD AND THE OUTLAWS VOL. 1: DARK TRINITY

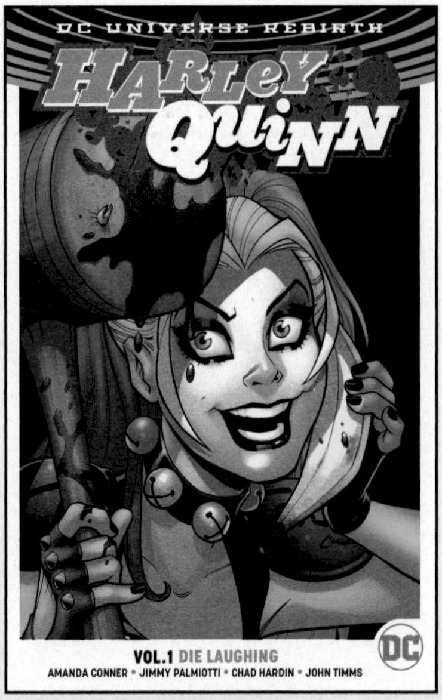
DC UNIVERSE REBIRTH
HARLEY QUINN
VOL.1 DIE LAUGHING
AMANDA CONNER • JIMMY PALMIOTTI • CHAD HARDIN • JOHN TIMMS

HARLEY QUINN VOL. 1: DIE LAUGHING

Get more DC graphic novels wherever comics and books are sold!

SUICIDE SQUAD

VOL. 1: KICKED IN THE TEETH

ADAM GLASS with FEDERICO DALLOCCHIO

SUICIDE SQUAD
VOL. 2: BASILISK RISING

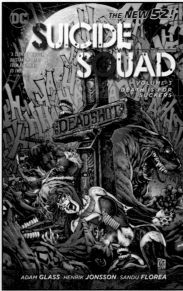

SUICIDE SQUAD
VOL. 3: DEATH IS FOR SUCKERS

READ THE ENTIRE EPIC

SUICIDE SQUAD VOL.
DISCIPLINE AND PUNIS

SUICIDE SQUAD VOL.
WALLED

"Chaotic and unabashedly fun."
– IGN

THE NEW YORK TIMES BESTSELLER
THE NEW 52!
HARLEY QUINN
VOLUME 1
HOT IN THE CITY
AMANDA CONNER JIMMY PALMIOTTI CHAD HARDIN
STEPHANE ROUX ALEX SINCLAIR PAUL MOUNTS

HARLEY QUINN

VOL. 1: HOT IN THE CITY

AMANDA CONNER
with JIMMY PALMIOTTI
& CHAD HARDIN

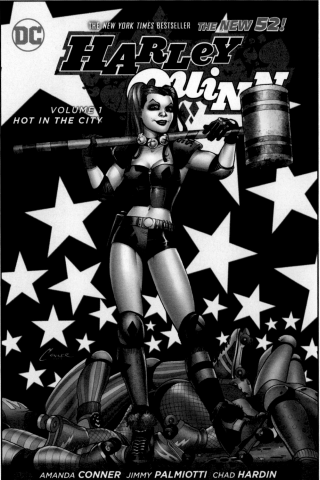

THE NEW YORK TIMES BEST-SELLING SERIES
HARLEY QUINN
VOLUME 2
POWER OUTAGE
AMANDA CONNER JIMMY PALMIOTTI
CHAD HARDIN JOHN TIMMS ALEX SINCLAIR

HARLEY QUINN
VOL. 2: POWER OUTAGE

THE #1 NEW YORK TIMES BEST-SELLING SERIES
HARLEY QUINN
VOLUME 3
KISS KISS
BANG STAB
AMANDA CONNER
JIMMY PALMIOTTI
CHAD HARDIN
JOHN TIMMS

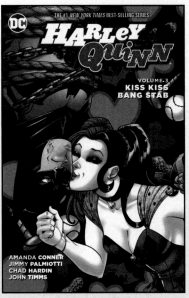

HARLEY QUINN
VOL. 3: KISS KISS BANG STAB

READ THE ENTIRE EPIC!

HARLEY QUINN VOL. 4:
A CALL TO ARMS

HARLEY QUINN VOL. 5:
THE JOKER'S LAST LAUGH

"I'm enjoying this a great deal;
it's silly, it's funny, it's irreverent."
– COMIC BOOK RESOURCES

Get more DC graphic novels wherever comics and books are sold!

"If you liked THE DARK KNIGHT, JOKER is a must-have for your bookshelf."
–MTV.com

"A deeply disturbing and completely unnerving work, a literary achievement that takes its place right alongside Alan Moore's THE KILLING JOKE."
–IGN

FROM THE EISNER AWARD-WINNING WRITER OF *100 BULLETS*

BRIAN AZZARELLO
with LEE BERMEJO

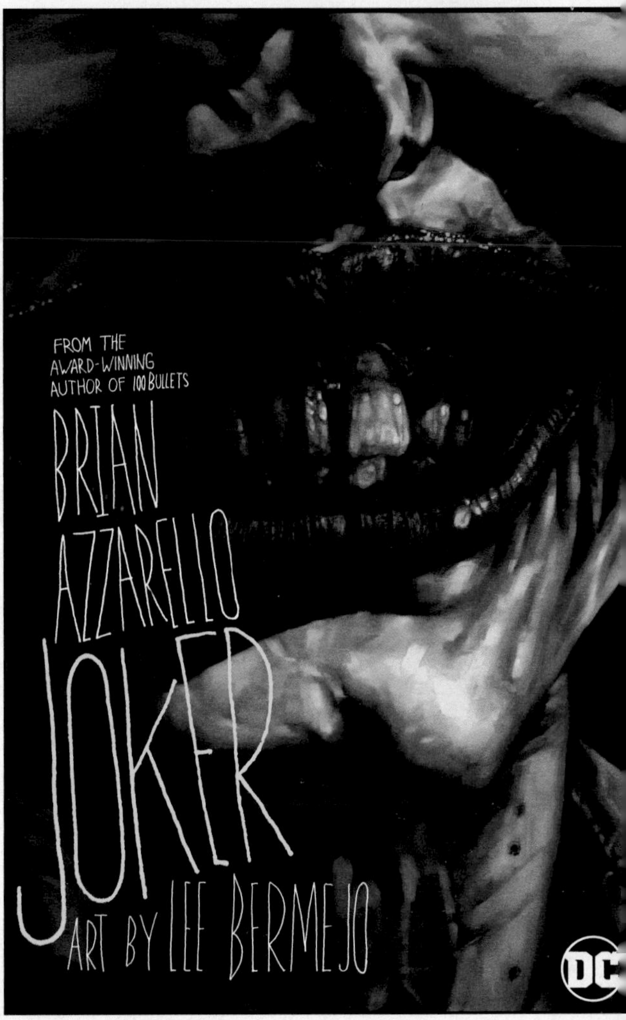

FROM THE AWARD-WINNING AUTHOR OF 100 BULLETS
BRIAN AZZARELLO
JOKER
ART BY LEE BERMEJO

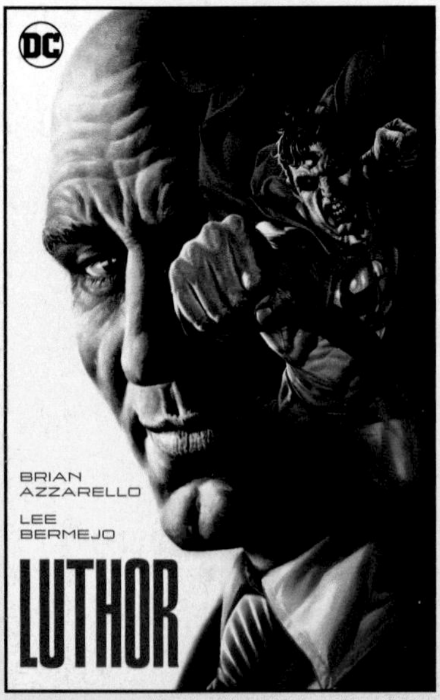

BRIAN AZZARELLO
LEE BERMEJO
LUTHOR

LUTHOR
with Lee Bermejo

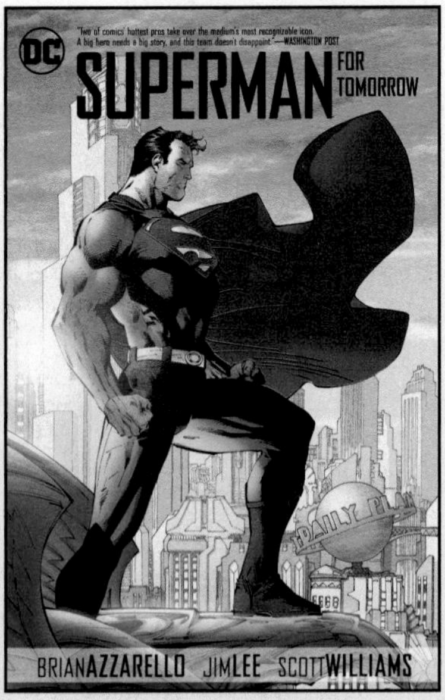

"Two of comics' hottest pros take over the medium's most recognizable icon. A big hero needs a big story, and this team doesn't disappoint." —WASHINGTON POST
SUPERMAN FOR TOMORROW
BRIAN AZZARELLO JIM LEE SCOTT WILLIAMS

SUPERMAN: FOR TOMORROW
with Jim Lee

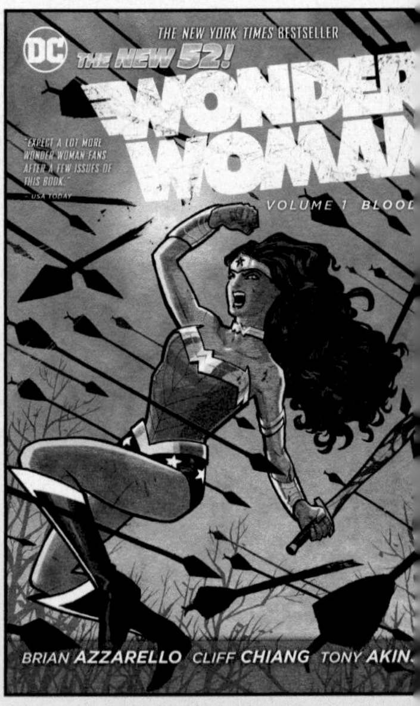

THE NEW YORK TIMES BESTSELLER
THE NEW 52!
"EXPECT A LOT MORE WONDER WOMAN FANS AFTER A FEW ISSUES OF THIS BOOK." —USA TODAY
BRIAN AZZARELLO CLIFF CHIANG TONY AKIN

WONDER WOMAN: BLOOD
with Cliff Chiang

Get more DC graphic novels wherever comics and books are sold!